Thinking Through The Test

A Study Guide for
The Florida College Basic Skills Exit Test

Reading

with Answer Key

Fourth Edition

Elizabeth Schmid Bellas and Peri Poland
Pasco-Hernando Community College

Longman

Boston   Columbus   Indianapolis   New York   San Francisco   Upper Saddle River
Amsterdam   Cape Town   Dubai   London   Madrid   Milan   Munich   Paris   Montreal   Toronto
Delhi   Mexico City   Sao Paulo   Sydney   Hong Kong   Seoul   Singapore   Taipei   Tokyo

Acquisitions Editor: Kate Edwards
Senior Supplements Editor: Donna Campion
Electronic Page Makeup: Grapevine Publishing Services, Inc.

Thinking Through the Test: A Study Guide for The Florida College Basic Skills Exit Test: Reading, with Answer Key, Fourth Edition

1 2 3 4 5 6 7 8 9 10–BIR–13 12 11 10

Longman
is an imprint of

www.pearsonhighered.com

ISBN 13: 978-0-205-77107-3
ISBN 10:   0-205-77107-6

Contents

PART THREE: TEST-TAKING STRATEGIES

PART FOUR: EXIT EXAMS

PART FIVE: CORRESPONDENCE CHARTS FOR TEST QUESTIONS

PART SIX: ANSWER KEYS

Introduction

"Chance favors the prepared mind."
—Louis Pasteur

For many of you, test taking is a most stressful and fearful task. Weeks and months of hard work and significant learning can seem to fly away in a single test session. You've been polishing your reading and writing skills, and you feel ready to enroll in college-level English classes, but now you have one more challenge ahead of you: to pass the Florida College Basic Skills Test in English. *Thinking Through the Test, Reading* will help you get ready.

At this moment, even the mere thought of having to pass a test as important as this one has probably raised your anxiety level! But don't worry: you're not alone. Many students have felt like you have about this test, and still thousands of students successfully pass it every year—you can too! The purpose of *Thinking Through the Test, Reading* is to help you prepare for the Florida College Basic Skills Exit Exam by lessening your anxiety and by strengthening your reading skills.

First of all, you should take comfort in the fact that those who write the state exit exam are community college teachers who are actively teaching reading and writing in classrooms throughout the state; therefore, the skills addressed on the exit exam and in this book are the **same skills** that you are already studying in your classrooms, textbooks, and learning centers. As a consequence, *Thinking Through the Test, Reading* not only helps you prepare for the exit exam, but it also helps you become a better reader and writer overall by supporting the instruction and learning that you need to be a more successful college student.

In order to support your classroom instruction and prepare you for the college classroom, passages for the items in this book have been taken from textbooks currently used in freshman college classes. These passages represent a variety of content courses such as biological sciences, social sciences, history, government, and education. Because these passages are taken from college-level textbooks that you could be reading in the near future, they may contain unfamiliar concepts and words and therefore may be more difficult than the passages on the actual state tests, so be sure to use the workbook as an opportunity to apply the new skills you are acquiring from your reading and writing classes.

You'll find *Thinking Through the Test, Reading* divided into six parts:

Part One: Pretest
Part Two: Reading Workbook
Part Three: Test-Taking Strategies
Part Four: Exit Exams
Part Five: Correspondence Charts for Test Questions and Tracking Sheets
Part Six: Answer Key

One of the benefits of this book is that all of the practice tests and exercises are very similar to the items you will face on the state tests. Therefore, some of the same passages appear in several different chapters because the state exam also uses a single passage to ask several types of questions. For example, there are ten passages in Chapter One of the Reading Workbook on main ideas; those same passages or portions of them are also in other chapters: the same passage, different questions. This repetition should help you see the connections between skills and questions as well as the benefit of re-reading for better understanding.

Remember to make connections whenever possible; for example, questions about the main idea and the author's purpose often have similar answers. Read the section "Test-Taking Strategies" for more helpful information.

New to the Fourth Edition

For the fourth edition of *Thinking Through the Test, Reading,* we have added several new features and enhanced the instructional content.

- **A revised Reading Pretest and 2 Brand-New Exit Exams** so you can test and re-test all the reading skills you will need to be successful
- **More Instruction, Examples, and Explanations** to illustrate each reading and writing skill presented in the various chapters
- **A Completely Revised Inferences Section** to distinguish between supporting details and true inferences and conclusions
- **A New Revised Test-Taking Strategies Section** located before the practice Exit Exams to provide helpful tips on what to study before the test, how to approach the test, and how to handle test anxiety

While these features are designed to help you make the most of your learning experience, remember: The more practice you have in *thinking through* your choices, the more likely you are to be successful on the state test and in future college courses.

In the meantime, as you study and practice for the test ahead, remember what baseball legend Ted Williams said: "Just keep going. Everybody gets better if they keep at it."

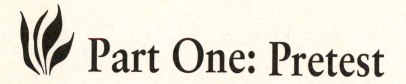# Part One: Pretest

Instructions: This Pretest has 36 questions. Read each passage below and answer the questions that follow.

Carnivorous plants trap their prey, which may vary from single-celled organisms, small crustaceans, mosquito larvae, and tiny water insects to small tadpoles, large insects, and small amphibians. Carnivorous plants fall into two groups: active and passive trappers.

Active trappers use rapid plant movements to open trap doors or to close traps. Two examples of active trappers are the Venus flytrap and the aquatic and semi-aquatic blad- 5 derworts. The Venus flytrap uses clam-shaped, hinged leaves. Around their unattached edges are many guard hairs and very small nectar glands that attract insects. On the surface of each half are three small trigger hairs and a covering of small digestive glands. An insect attracted to the brightly colored leaf touches the trigger hairs, causing the trap to close quickly. The bladderwort, as its name suggests, has small, elastic, flattened blad- 10 ders with the entrance sealed by a flap of cells. When prey touch the tactile cells on the flap, the trap door opens. The bladder walls spring apart, causing a sucking motion that sweeps a current of water into the bladder. Then the door closes, trapping the prey.

Passive trappers use pitfalls or sticky adhesive traps. Pitcher plants and sundews are ex- amples of passive trappers. Pitcher plants use pitfalls. The leaves are shaped into pitcher- 15 like or funnel-like traps that grow from underground stems. Bright coloration and secretions of nectar attract the insects. When they land and move down the leaf, the insects are unable to back up against the stiff, downward-directed hairs. They fall into watery fluid containing digestive enzymes produced by the leaf. The sundews attract insects to sticky leaves by color, scent, and glistening droplets of adhesive. Sundews have two types 20 of glands on the leaf surface that produce adhesive droplets. Long stalks on the edge of the leaf trap the insect. Shorter stalks slowly bend into the center of the leaf, holding the prey in the digestive area of the leaf. (Adapted from Robert Leo Smith and Thomas M. Smith, *Elements of Ecology*, 5th ed., San Francisco: Benjamin Cummings, 2003.)

1. Which sentence best states the main idea of the passage?
   A. Two examples of active trappers are the Venus flytrap and the aquatic and semi-aquatic bladderworts.
   B. Pitcher plants and sundews are examples of passive trappers.

C. Carnivorous plants fall into two groups: active and passive trappers.

D. Carnivorous plants trap their prey, which may vary from single-celled organisms, small crustaceans, mosquito larvae, and tiny water insects to small tadpoles, large insects, and small amphibians.

2. The overall pattern of organization for this passage is
   A. listing.
   B. classification.
   C. cause and effect.
   D. statement and clarification.

3. The authors' purpose is to
   A. describe Venus flytraps and Pitcher plants.
   B. define active trappers and give examples of each.
   C. explain how different types of carnivorous plants catch their prey.
   D. show the effects of prey landing upon carnivorous plants.

4. What is the relationship between the following sentences? "When prey touch the tactile cells on the flap, the trap door opens. The bladder walls spring apart, causing a sucking motion that sweeps a current of water into the bladder"?
   A. Compare and contrast
   B. Spatial order
   C. Statement and clarification
   D. Process

5. The authors' claim that "Carnivorous plants fall into two groups" is
   A. inadequately supported because it lacks evidence.
   B. adequately supported with relevant details.

6. What is the relationship within the sentence, "When prey touch the tactile cells on the flap, the trap door opens"?
   A. Example
   B. Listing
   C. Cause and effect
   D. Summary

7. The overall tone of the passage is
   A. objective.
   B. admiring.
   C. nostalgic.
   D. reverent.

8. The main idea of paragraph 2 is that
   A. carnivorous plants trap their prey in a complicated process.
   B. active trappers use rapid plant movements to open trap doors or to close traps.
   C. Venus flytraps use an active trapping process to catch their prey.
   D. all active trappers have nectar glands.

9. A conclusion that can be drawn from the passage is that
   A. Pitcher plants have a slower process for capturing their prey than bladderworts.
   B. Venus flytraps are not as common as bladderworts.
   C. bladderworts also use a sticky adhesive to trap their prey.
   D. all passive trappers have small trigger hairs to trap their prey.

Read the passage below and answer the questions that follow.

Karen Silkwood grew up in an unassuming middle-class family in Nederland, Texas, near the Gulf Coast. She baby-sat at her church nursery, earned straight A's through high school, and went to Lamar College on a full scholarship to study medical technology. Marriage, three children, and a divorce intervened, and in 1972 she began working as a laboratory analyst at Kerr-McGee's plutonium processing plant in Crescent, Oklahoma. There the highly poisonous radioactive material was made into fuel rods for nuclear power plants.   5

In the summer of 1974, at age 28, Silkwood was elected a local official of the union that represented many Kerr-McGee workers and began organizing for greater worker safety. She learned of numerous incidents of radioactive contamination at the plant. She also uncovered evidence of significant quantities of missing plutonium. On November 13, Silkwood set out for Oklahoma City to meet a national representative of her union and a *New York Times* reporter, intending to give them documents proving that Kerr-McGee was knowingly manufacturing defective nuclear products. She never made it. Her car was forced off the road, and she died instantly when it crashed into a concrete culvert.   10
                                                                                              15

Karen Silkwood challenged the power of one of the nation's largest energy corporations. Her brief career as a whistleblower brought together major issues of the 1970s: labor organizing, environmental damage, the safety record of nuclear energy, and the power of corporations over individual citizens. Her **dismissive** treatment by some fellow workers, her employers, and the media also suggested the lack of respect that women had long endured, especially when they moved out of the role of the traditional homemaker. (Jacqueline Jones et al., *Created Equal*, New York: Longman, 2003.)   20

10. Which statement best states the implied main idea of the passage?
    A. Karen Silkwood grew up in an unassuming middle-class family in Nederland, Texas, near the Gulf Coast.
    B. Karen Silkwood was murdered for trying to bring the energy company that she worked for to justice.
    C. Karen Silkwood was a union official and whistleblower who brought attention to many major issues of the 1970s.
    D. Karen Silkwood challenged the power of one of the nation's largest energy corporations.

11. A conclusion that can be drawn from the passage is that
    A. Karen Silkwood was unaware of the effects that radioactive material can have on humans.
    B. Karen Silkwood cared deeply about workers' rights.

C. most women in the 1970s were not traditional homemakers.

D. Kerr-McGee was sued for producing defective nuclear products.

12. According to the passage
    A. Karen Silkwood died on November 13, 1974.
    B. Kerr-McGee processed plutonium for nuclear weapons.
    C. Kerr-McGee was unaware that its nuclear products were defective.
    D. Karen Silkwood had a paying job working as a whistleblower.

13. The word **dismissive** in paragraph 3 means
    A. reverent.
    B. careless.
    C. disrespectful.
    D. supportive.

14. The following statement, "Her dismissive treatment by some fellow workers, her employers, and the media also suggested the lack of respect that women had long endured, especially when they moved out of the role of the traditional homemaker," is
    A. a fact.
    B. an opinion.

15. The author's claim that "Karen Silkwood challenged the power of one of the nation's largest energy corporations," is
    A. adequately supported by facts.
    B. inadequately supported by opinions or irrelevant facts.

16. The overall pattern of organization for the entire passage is
    A. compare and contrast.
    B. listing.
    C. spatial order.
    D. time order.

17. The relationship within the sentence, "Her car was forced off the road, and she died instantly when it crashed into a concrete culvert" is one of
    A. statement and clarification.
    B. spatial order.
    C. cause and effect.
    D. example.

18. The authors' purpose in writing the passage was
    A. to show how Karen Silkwood challenged one of the largest energy corporations.
    B. to illustrate how women who worked in careers were not respected in the 1970s.
    C. to warn readers of what could happen when someone challenges a powerful corporation.
    D. to caution readers about the harmful effects of radioactive material.

Read the passage below and answer the questions that follow.

Research in Japan on the personality of the "salarymen" males employed in the fast-paced corporate world, links male personality with the demands of the business world. Salarymen work long hours for the company. They leave home early in the morning and return late at night and thus are nicknamed "7–11 men."

Many Tokyo salarymen eat dinner with their family only a few times a year. After work, they typically spend many hours with fellow workers at expensive nightclubs. Groups of about five to ten men go out together after work. A few drinks and light snacks can result in a tab in the hundreds of dollars for one hour. The corporation picks up the bill. At the club, men relax and have fun after a long day of work. This is ensured by having a trained hostess sit at the table, keeping the conversation moving along in a lightly playful tone. Her job is to flatter and flirt with the men and to make them feel good.

While working as a hostess, one woman found that conversations are full of teasing and banter, with much of it directed at the hostess. This may be viewed as a reaction to their upbringing, with its total control by the mother. Club culture puts the man in control. The hostess can flirt with him but she will never control him.

Salarymen's nightclub behavior appears to be linked with their upbringing. Given the near total absence of the father from the home scene, children are raised mainly by the mother. The concentration of maternal attention is especially strong toward sons and their school achievements. The goal is that the boy will do well in school, get into a top university, and then gain employment with a large corporation. These corporations pay well, guarantee lifelong employment, and provide substantial benefits after retirement. Loyalty is required, work hours are long, and the pressure to perform is high. (Adapted from Barbara D. Miller, *Cultural Anthropology*, 2nd ed., Boston: Allyn and Bacon, 2002.)

19. What is the implied main idea of this passage?
   A. Salarymen's behavior is linked to their culture and the demands of their jobs.
   B. Club culture in Japan puts salarymen in control of any situation.
   C. In Japanese corporations, loyalty is required, work hours are long, and the pressure to perform is high.
   D. Salarymen's nightclub behavior appears to be linked with their upbringing.

20. Is the following statement one of fact or opinion? "This may be viewed as a reaction to their upbringing, with its total control by the mother."
   A. Fact
   B. Opinion

21. What is the relationship within the sentence, "Given the near total absence of the father from the home scene, children are raised mainly by the mother"?
   A. Compare and contrast
   B. Time order
   C. Example
   D. Cause and effect

22. The overall pattern of organization for this passage is
    A. listing.
    B. process.
    C. cause and effect.
    D. addition.

23. In this passage, the author is
    A. biased in favor of salarymen.
    B. biased in favor of Japanese mothers.
    C. biased against salarymen.
    D. unbiased.

24. The author's tone in this passage is
    A. critical.
    B. impassioned.
    C. humorous.
    D. straightforward.

25. Which of the following statements provides the best support for the author's claim, "Loyalty is required, work hours are long, and the pressure to perform is high"?
    A. The goal is that the boy will do well in school, get into a top university, and then gain employment with a large corporation.
    B. They leave home early in the morning and return late at night and thus are nicknamed "7–11 men."
    C. Groups of about five to ten men go out together after work.
    D. Given the near total absence of the father from the home scene, children are raised mainly by the mother.

26. What is the relationship between the following sentences? "Many Tokyo salarymen eat dinner with their family only a few times a year. After work, they typically spend many hours with fellow workers at expensive nightclubs."
    A. Addition
    B. Contrast
    C. Cause and effect
    D. Listing

27. Which of the following conclusions cannot be drawn from the passage?
    A. Japanese parents expect their sons to do well in school.
    B. A hostess at a nightclub often endures teasing from salarymen.
    C. Mothers in Japan do not work outside of the home.
    D. Japanese corporations have high expectations for their salarymen.

Read the passage below and answer the questions that follow.

Everywhere it occurred, industrialization drove society from an agricultural to an urban way of life. The old system, in which peasant families worked the fields during the summer and did their cottage industry work in the winter to their own standards and at their own pace, slowly disappeared. In its place came urban life tied to the factory system. The factory was a place where for long hours people did repetitive tasks using machines to process large amounts of raw materials. This was an efficient way to make a lot of high-quality goods cheaply. But the factories were often dangerous places, and the lifestyle connected to them had a terrible effect on the human condition.

In the factory system, the workers worked, and the owners made profits. The owners wanted to make the most they could from their investment and to get the most work they could from their employees. The workers, in turn, felt that they deserved more of the profits because their labor made production possible. This was a situation guaranteed to produce conflict, especially given the wretched conditions the workers faced in the first stages of industrialization.

The early factories were miserable places, featuring bad lighting, lack of ventilation, dangerous machines, and frequent breakdowns. Safety standards were practically nonexistent, and workers in various industries could expect to contract serious diseases; for example, laborers working with lead paint developed lung problems, pewter workers fell ill to palsy, miners suffered black lung disease, and operators of primitive machines lost fingers, hands, and even lives. Not until late in the nineteenth century did health and disability insurance come into effect. In some factories workers who suffered accidents were **deemed** to be at fault; and since there was little job security, a worker could be fired for almost any reason.

The demand for plentiful and cheap labor led to the widespread employment of women and children who worked long hours. Girls as young as 6 years old were used to haul carts of coal in Lancashire mines, and boys and girls of 5 years of age worked in textile mills, where their nimble little fingers could easily untangle jams in the machines. When they were not laboring, the working families lived in horrid conditions in Manchester, England. There were no sanitary, water, or medical services for the workers, and working families were crammed 12 and 15 individuals to a room in damp, dark cellars. Bad diet, alcoholism, cholera, and typhus reduced lifespans in the industrial cities. (Brummet, Palmira, et al., *Civilization: Past and Present*, New York: Longman, 2000.)

28. Which sentence best states the implied main idea of the passage?
    A. Industrialization changed society from an agricultural way of life to an urban life plagued by many problems.
    B. Early factories were miserable places that had numerous problems.
    C. Industrialization was an efficient way to make a lot of high-quality goods cheaply.
    D. Industrialization gave people the opportunity to work at jobs in factories.

29. What is the relationship within the sentence, "In the factory system, the workers worked, and the owners made profits"?
    A. Time order
    B. Addition
    C. Process
    D. Clarification

30. What is the overall pattern of organization?
    A. Listing
    B. Compare and contrast
    C. Example
    D. Cause and effect

31. In this passage, the authors
    A. are biased against the early factory system.
    B. are biased in favor of industrialization.
    C. are biased against agricultural societies.
    D. are unbiased.

32. As used in this sentence from paragraph three, "In some factories workers who suffered accidents were **deemed** to be at fault; and since there was little job security, a worker could be fired for almost any reason," the word **deemed** most nearly means
    A. used.
    B. injured.
    C. believed.
    D. controlled.

33. Which of the following conclusions cannot be drawn from the passage?
    A. Owners of factories exploited their workers.
    B. Industrialization had negative effects upon society.
    C. Industrialization caused a decrease in agriculture.
    D. There were no child labor laws during the beginning of industrialization.

34. What is the authors' tone in this passage?
    A. Optimistic
    B. Critical
    C. Nostalgic
    D. Ironic

35. Which of the following statements is an opinion?
    A. This was a situation guaranteed to produce conflict, especially given the wretched conditions the workers faced in the first stages of industrialization.
    B. The demand for plentiful and cheap labor led to the widespread employment of women and children who worked long hours.
    C. The factory was a place where for long hours people did repetitive tasks using machines to process large amounts of raw materials.
    D. In some factories workers who suffered accidents were deemed to be at fault; and since there was little job security, a worker could be fired for almost any reason.

36. What is the authors' purpose in this passage?
    A. To explain how industrialization replaced agriculture as the main source of employment in the early nineteenth century
    B. To compare industrialized society to agricultural society
    C. To show the early effects of industrialization on society
    D. To describe conditions in early factories

 # Part Two: Reading Workbook

Chapter 1: Concept Skills

Understanding the author's main point is the most important key to reading comprehension. To help you understand main ideas, you must understand the difference between a main idea, a thesis, and a topic sentence.

Main Idea: The author's most important point in a passage. There are three ways in which main ideas present themselves:

1. **Topic Sentence:** The main idea of a <u>paragraph</u>. Topic sentences are *generally* located at the beginning of a paragraph (first or second sentence).

2. **Thesis or Thesis Statement:** The main idea in a <u>multi-paragraph</u> passage. Thesis statements are generally located in one of four spots:

   • The last sentence of the first paragraph (most common)
   • The first sentence of the first paragraph (2nd most common)
   • The first sentence of the second paragraph (3rd most common)
   • The conclusion (most often seen in narratives, or passages that tell a story)

3. **Implied Main Idea:** If there is no one sentence in the passage that captures the author's main point, then the main idea is implied. Implied main ideas are the hardest to determine because they require the most thinking.

We can visualize main ideas and where they are located as follows:

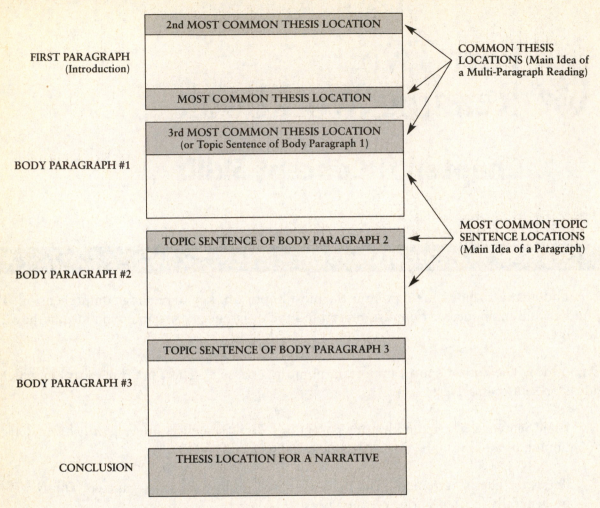

As you can see, each paragraph has a main idea (topic sentence). There is also a main idea for the whole reading selection (thesis statement). If you are unable to find a sentence that expresses a main idea, then the main idea is *implied* and you have to figure it out from the supporting details.

Keep in mind these two questions when looking for the main idea:

1. What is the topic (subject) of the passage?
2. What is the author's most important point about that topic, or what is he/she trying to say about the topic?

A good strategy is to begin reading every passage with these two questions in mind, and then to summarize the author's thesis or main idea in your own words before looking at the answer choices.

Read the following paragraph to find the answers to:

1. What is the topic (subject) of the passage?
2. What is the author's most important point about that topic?

> **Example #1**
> One of the most devastating problems facing children today can be found in every segment of society, among the rich or poor, the educated, or illiterate. The effects of child abuse are widespread and often irreversible, and can cause severe physical and psychological effects in children. Infants can suffer permanent brain damage when shaken violently. Abused children often suffer from emotional problems, such as schizophrenia or multiple personality disorders. They tend to become more withdrawn or more aggressive than children who are not abused. They also have a tendency for weaker social skills, as they withdraw from others and become more isolated than their non-abused peers. Such children may grow to be overly timid or to act out their anger and frustration with negative behaviors.

When seeking the topic, look for a key word which is most often repeated in the passage. In this case, "abused children" and "child abuse" appear frequently. But both are very general terms, and could include numerous subtopics such as the causes of child abuse, the solutions for child abuse, etc. On what subtopic of child abuse does this passage focus?

In this passage, there are several examples listed of the effects of child abuse. Therefore, the **topic** of this passage is *The effects of child abuse*.

When looking for a topic, be sure to select a topic that is not too broad and could include a wider scope of ideas than what is discussed in the passage, nor one that is too narrow and excludes information that *is* in the passage.

To find the main idea (or topic sentence, since this is a paragraph), ask yourself, "What is the author's point about the effects of child abuse?"

Look for the answer to the question stated in a general, broad statement that makes a strong point or summarizes the supporting details. In this passage, the broadest statement that summarizes the effects of child abuse is found in the second sentence, "The effects of child abuse are widespread and often irreversible, and can cause severe physical and psychological effects in children."

Remember, **the main idea is a broad and general statement**, and it is *not* a restatement of specific major details.

Check Your Work
When you think you have found the correct main idea, go back and look through the passage. Ask yourself: Do all of the other sentences tell more about this sentence? If they do, then your answer is correct.

Implied Main Ideas
Sometimes an author does not state the main idea in a topic sentence or a thesis statement. In these cases, the reader must infer the main idea by drawing a conclusion.

Think like a detective by looking for clues. Start by answering the two questions:

1. What is the topic? (Who or what is this about?)
2. What is the author's main point about the topic?

Pay close attention to the sentences that support the main idea, called **supporting details**.

The supporting details in the passage on the previous page are:

1. (Abused) infants can suffer permanent brain damage.
2. Abused children often suffer from emotional problems.
3. (Abused children) tend to become more withdrawn or more aggressive.
4. They also have a tendency for weaker social skills.

All of these sentences point out the effects of child abuse. If you had to write your own implied main idea of this passage, it may be something like:

Children who are abused may suffer many permanent and harmful effects.

This sentence would be broad enough to include all of the supporting details listed above.

> **Example #2**
> Although urban poverty is probably more familiar to most people, about one-fifth of poor people live in rural areas and another third in suburban areas. Rural poverty is not as visible as urban poverty. Separated from the mainstream of urban life, the rural poor are largely hidden on farms, on Indian reservations, in open country, and in small towns and villages. Unemployment rates in rural areas are far above the national average. Largely because of the technological revolution in agriculture and other occupations, poorly educated, unskilled rural workers have been left with no means of support. (Adapted from William Kornblum and Joseph Julian, *Social Problems*, 13th ed., Upper Saddle River, NJ: Pearson Prentice Hall, 2009.)
> **Topic:** Rural poverty

There is no topic sentence that expresses the main idea. The entire paragraph is composed of <u>supporting details</u> about rural poverty:

1. . . . about one-fifth of poor people live in rural areas and another third in suburban areas
2. . . . largely hidden on farms, on Indian reservations, in open country, and in small towns and villages.
3. Unemployment rates in rural areas are far above the national average.
4. Largely because of the technological revolution in agriculture and other occupations, poorly educated, unskilled rural workers have been left with no means of support.

All of the supporting details are giving features of rural poverty. A possible implied main idea that includes all of the ideas expressed in the supporting details might be:

Although it is less visible than urban poverty, rural poverty is common and has its own features and causes.

▶▶▌ *Secrets to Success*
  ────────────

- *When looking for the main idea, ask: What is the topic (subject) of the passage?*
- *What is the author's most important point about that topic?*
- *Most often, main ideas of multi-paragraph reading selections (thesis statements) are found in the first paragraph (last sentence or first sentence) or in the first sentence of the second paragraph.*

- *Look for a broad statement that sounds like an important point the author is making.*
- *Ask yourself: Do all of the other sentences tell more about this sentence?*
- *Sometimes an author does not state the main idea in a topic sentence or a thesis statement. In these cases, the reader must infer the main idea by drawing a conclusion.*

SECTION 1 ◆ DIAGNOSTIC: THE MAIN IDEA

Read the passages and apply the strategies described above for finding the main idea. When you are done, check your work with the answers immediately following the diagnostic. Even if you get a perfect score here, go ahead and complete the exercises in this section; they are designed to help build confidence and to give you practice for future test success.

Read the passage below and answer the questions that follow.

Evaluation research on drug education prevention programs done over the last thirty years indicates that these programs have not been effective. In fact, the findings state that these programs essentially had no effect on the drug problem. Although studies of the more recently developed programs are more optimistic, the findings still do not provide strong evidence of highly effective programs.   5

The goals of these programs have been to affect three basic areas: knowledge, attitudes, and behavior. The programs have had some success in increasing knowledge and, to a lesser extent, attitudes towards drugs; however, increases in knowledge and changed attitudes do not mean much if the actual drug behavior is not affected. In fact, those programs that only increase knowledge tend to reduce anxiety and fear of drugs and   10 may actually increase the likelihood of drug use. For example, one approach in the past was to provide students with complete information about all the possibilities of drug abuse, from the names of every street drug, to how the drugs are usually ingested, to detailed descriptions of possible effects of drugs and possible consequences of an overdose. Given the inquiring nature of children, such an approach could well amount   15 to a primer on how to take drugs, not how to avoid them.

The only effective approach to drug education is one in which children come to see that drug abuse constitutes unnecessary and self-abusive consequences. Too often, the real appeal of such drugs as marijuana or alcohol is dismissed by asking children to take up a sport or go bike riding or learn to play a musical instrument. Such suggestions   20 are fine as far as they go, but they often fail to take into account the personal problems that may tempt children into drug abuse.

Education programs that address social influence show the most promise in reducing or delaying onset of drug use. Psychological approaches in which social influences and skills are stressed are more effective than other approaches. The most effective pro-   25 grams in influencing both attitudes and behavior are peer programs that include either refusal skills—with more direct emphasis on behavior—or social and life skills, or both.

The use of scare tactics in any health education program, including drug abuse education programs, is counterproductive. Children soon learn to recognize the difference

between fact and possible fiction. Attempts to equate the dangers of marijuana with   30
those of heroin, suggestions that any drug can kill or permanently impair an individual,
and other dire warnings, no matter how true, are often disregarded as propaganda.
(David J. Anspaugh and Gene Ezell, *Teaching Today's Health*, 7th ed., San Francisco:
Benjamin Cummings, 2004.)

1. What is the topic of the passage?
    A. Drug abuse
    B. Drug education prevention programs
    C. Drug abusers
    D. The effects of drugs on children

2. Which sentence best states the main idea of the entire passage?
    A. The goals of these programs have been to affect three basic areas: knowledge, attitudes,
        and behavior.
    B. Although studies of the more recently developed programs are more optimistic, the findings
        still do not provide strong evidence of highly effective programs.
    C. Evaluation research on drug education programs done over the last thirty years indicates
        that these programs have not been effective.
    D. Education programs that address social influence show the most promise in reducing or
        delaying onset of drug abuse.

3. Which sentence best states the main idea of the second paragraph?
    A. The goals of these programs have been to affect three basic areas: knowledge, attitudes,
        and behavior.
    B. Programs that only increase knowledge tend to reduce anxiety and fear of drugs and may
        actually increase the likelihood of drug use.
    C. The programs have had some success in increasing knowledge and, to a lesser extent, at-
        titudes toward drugs; however, increases in knowledge and changed attitudes do not mean
        much if the actual drug behavior is not affected.
    D. Given the inquiring nature of children, such an approach could well amount to a primer
        on how to take drugs, not how to avoid them.

4. Which sentence best states the main idea of the third paragraph?
    A. Children who take up sports or learn a musical instrument will not abuse drugs.
    B. The most effective way to prevent drug abuse is to address personal problems that may
        tempt children into using drugs.
    C. The most effective approach to drug abuse prevention is successfully convincing children
        that drug use is unnecessary and harmful.
    D. The consequences of drug abuse are unnecessary and self-abusive.

5. Which sentence best states the main idea of the fourth paragraph?
    A. Psychological approaches in which social influences and skills are stressed are more effec-
        tive than other approaches.
    B. The most effective programs in influencing both attitudes and behavior are peer programs.
    C. Education programs that influence attitudes towards drugs are most effective.
    D. Education programs that address social influence show the most promise in reducing or
        delaying onset of drug use.

6. What is the topic of the fifth paragraph?
   A. Health education programs
   B. Scare tactics in drug prevention programs
   C. Propaganda
   D. The dangers of marijuana and heroin

7. Which sentence best states the main idea of the fifth paragraph?
   A. Using scare tactics in drug education programs is not effective.
   B. Children are not affected by drug education.
   C. The warnings about marijuana and heroin are not true.
   D. Drug abuse prevention programs use a lot of propaganda.

Answers to Diagnostic
1. B   2. C   3. B   4. C   5. D   6. B   7. A

SECTION 1 ◆ EXERCISES: THE MAIN IDEA

Use the following exercises to practice reading for the main idea.

PASSAGE #1
Read the passage and answer the questions that follow.

"Street gangs" are a more formal variety of youth gang. They generally have leaders and a hierarchy of membership roles and responsibilities. They are named, and their members mark their identity with tattoos or "colors." While many street gangs are involved in violence, not all are. An anthropologist who did research among nearly forty street gangs in New York, Los Angeles, and Boston learned much about why individuals join gangs, providing insights that contradict popular thinking on this subject.   5

One common stereotype is that young boys join gangs because they are from homes with no male authority figure with whom they could identify. This study showed that equal numbers of gang members were from intact nuclear households as from those with an absent father. Another common perception is that the gang replaces a missing   10 feeling of family as a motive. This study, again, showed that the same number of gang members reported having close family ties as those who did not.

Those who were gang members shared a personality type called a "defiant individualist." This type has five traits: intense competitiveness, mistrust or wariness, self-reliance, social isolation, and a strong survival instinct. Poverty, especially urban poverty, leads   15 to the development of this type of personality. Many of these youths want to be economically successful, but social conditions channel their interests and skills into illegal pursuits rather than into legal pathways of achievement. (Adapted from Barbara D. Miller, *Cultural Anthropology*, 2nd ed., Boston: Allyn and Bacon, 2002.)

1. Which of the following sentences is the best statement of the main idea in the entire passage?
   A. The reasons individuals join street gangs are not those commonly held.
   B. An anthropologist studied street gangs in New York, Los Angeles, and Boston.

C. Not all street gangs are involved in violence.

D. Street gangs are a type of youth gang that is organized and identifies itself with "colors."

2. The implied main idea of paragraph 3 is that
   A. street gang members are victims of society.
   B. street gang members would be successful if they weren't poor.
   C. street gang members are not competitive.
   D. individuals develop a "defiant individualist" personality type due to urban poverty.

3. The implied meaning of paragraph 2 is that
   A. many gang members have close family ties.
   B. most gang members have no male authority figures in the household.
   C. individuals do not join gangs for the reasons most people think.
   D. people think that the gang is a substitute for a missing family, but this is not true.

PASSAGE #2

Read the passage and answer the questions that follow.

Although many people think of First Ladies as well-dressed homemakers presiding over White House dinners, there is much more to the job. The First Lady has no official government position. Yet she is often at the center of national attention. The media chronicles every word she speaks and every hairstyle she adopts.

Abigail Adams (an early feminist) and Dolly Madison counseled and lobbied their husbands. Edith Galt Wilson was the most powerful First Lady, virtually running the government when her husband, Woodrow, suffered a paralyzing stroke in 1919. Eleanor Roosevelt wrote a nationally syndicated newspaper column and tirelessly traveled and advocated New Deal policies. She became her crippled husband's eyes and ears around the country and urged him to adopt liberal social welfare policies. Lady Bird Johnson chose to focus on one issue, beautification, and most of her successors followed this pattern. Rosalyn Carter chose mental health, Nancy Reagan selected drugs, and Barbara Bush picked literacy. 5 10

In what was perhaps a natural evolution in a society where women have moved into positions formerly held only by males, Hillary Rodham Clinton attained the most responsible and visible leadership position ever held by a First Lady. She had been an influential advisor to the President, playing an active role in the selection of nominees for cabinet and judicial posts, for example. Most publicly, she headed the planning for the President's massive health care reform plan in 1993 and became, along with her husband, its primary advocate. (Adapted from George C. Edwards, Martin P. Wattenberg, and Robert L. Lineberry, *Government in America*, 9th ed., New York: Longman, 2000.) 15 20

4. The implied idea of the entire passage is that
   A. the job of First Lady reflects the role of women in society at the time.
   B. the role of First Lady has become more important in the past 50 years.

    C. First Ladies have taken active roles during their husbands' presidencies.

    D. the media reports all of the First Lady's activities.

5. Which of the following sentences best states the main idea of paragraph 2?
    A. Some First Ladies focused on one issue while others were more involved in helping the President run the government.
    B. Edith Galt Wilson was the most powerful First Lady.
    C. Eleanor Roosevelt helped her husband run the government because he was disabled.
    D. First Ladies are champions of causes.

6. The implied idea of paragraph 3 is that
    A. Hillary Rodham Clinton was a model First Lady.
    B. Hillary Rodham Clinton planned the health care reform plan in 1993.
    C. Hillary Rodham Clinton was well educated.
    D. Hillary Rodham Clinton held the most responsible leadership position of all First Ladies.

PASSAGE #3

Read the passage and answer the questions that follow.

In the 1980s, a long-running TV public service advertisement showed a father confronting his son with what is obviously the boy's drug paraphernalia. The father asks his son incredulously, "Where did you learn to do this?" The son, half in tears, replies, "From you, okay? I learned it from watching you!" Observational learning, which results simply from watching others, clearly appears to be a factor in an adolescent's willingness to experiment with drugs and alcohol.   5

Andrews and her colleagues found that adolescents' relationships with their parents influence whether they will model the substance use patterns of the parents. Specifically, they found that adolescents who had a positive relationship with their mothers modeled her use (or nonuse) of cigarettes, and those who had a close relationship with their fathers modeled the father's marijuana use (or nonuse). Similarly, those who had a negative relationship with their parents were less likely to model their parents' use of drugs or alcohol. Although some of the more complex results of this study depended on the age and sex of the adolescent, the general findings can be understood by thinking about them from the three levels of analysis and their interactions.   10   15

At the level of the brain, observing someone engage in a behavior causes you to store new memories, which involves the hippocampus and related brain systems. These memories later can guide behavior, as they do in all types of imitation. At the level of the person, if you are motivated to observe someone, you are likely to be paying more attention to him or her and, therefore, increasing the likelihood of your learning from them and remembering what you learn. At the level of the group, you are more likely to be captivated by models who have certain attractive characteristics.   20

In this case, adolescents who had a positive relationship with their parents were more likely to do what their parents did; if their parents didn't smoke, the adolescents were less likely to do so. The events at these levels interact. Children who enjoy a positive   25 relationship with their parents may agree with their parents' higher status than do children who have a negative relationship with their parents. Thus, the former group of children probably increases the amount of attention they give to their parents' behavior. (Adapted from Stephen M. Kosslyn and Robin S. Rosenberg, *Psychology*, 2nd ed., Boston: Allyn and Bacon, 2004.)

7. Which of the following sentences is the best statement of the main idea of the entire passage?
    A. Your brain stores memories of observing someone's behavior.
    B. Children who have a positive relationship with their parents pay more attention to the way their parents act.
    C. A parent's use of drugs or alcohol will cause the child to use these substances.
    D. Watching people behaving a certain way on television becomes stored in your memory.

8. The implied main idea of paragraph 4 is that
    A. if a parent smokes, the adolescent will smoke.
    B. the parent-child relationship affects the child's behavior.
    C. children who have a negative relationship with their parents are likely to copy their parents' behavior.
    D. adolescents with positive relationships with their parents almost certainly pay closer attention to the way their parents act.

9. The implied main idea of paragraph 2 is that
    A. substance use or nonuse is dependent on an adolescent's relationship with his or her parents.
    B. adolescents who had negative relationships with their parents did not model the parents' use of alcohol or drugs.
    C. adolescents whose parents use drugs or alcohol may or may not copy their parents.
    D. adolescents who had negative relationships with parents who used drugs or alcohol are better off.

10. The implied main idea of paragraph 3 is that
    A. people are influenced by those who are attractive.
    B. behaviors you have observed become memories that will later influence your behavior.
    C. observational learning affects an individual on three levels.
    D. you will learn from someone you want to pay attention to.

SECTION 2 ◆ SUPPORTING DETAILS

Supporting details are sentences which give more specific information about the main idea. Quite often, main idea questions will include 2 or 3 supporting details as answer choices. Knowing the difference between main ideas and supporting details will help us answer the main idea questions correctly.

Long passages contain one main idea and may have one or several major supporting details. The number of major and minor details varies with each passage. Not every major detail has a minor detail to support it, while some major details may have several minor supporting details.

Major and Minor Details

Major details tell us more information about the main idea.
Minor details tell us more about the major details.

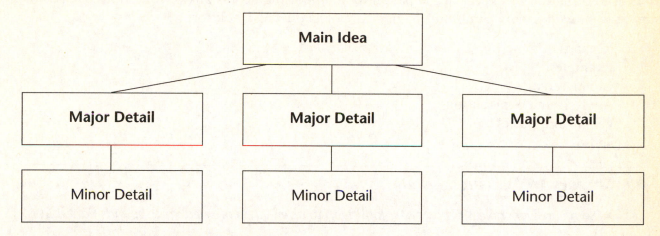

Read the following passage, and ask:
- What is the topic (subject) of the passage?
- What is the author's most important point about that topic?
- Which details support the main idea?

As portions of federal governmental debt become due, the government refinances the debt by selling new bonds. It uses the income from the sale of the new bonds to pay off the current debt, and the new bonds have a later maturity date, which allows them more time to pay off debt. Also, the federal government has the authority to raise taxes to generate funds to pay off its debt when necessary, something that private corporations and banks cannot do to avoid bankruptcy. Another way that the government can deal with its debt is by printing new money. Although printing new dollars may cause inflation, the government can use new dollars to pay off debt or to make interest payments.

Here is a concept map of the passage:

Topic: Governmental Debt

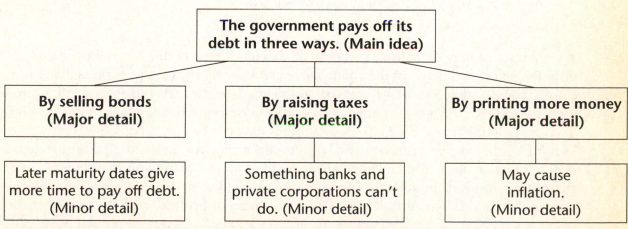

Notice that the three major details explain how (the three ways) the government pays off debt. The other (minor) details explain more about each of the three ways.

Identifying Supporting Details

To find supporting details, pay close attention to the <u>first sentence of each paragraph</u>. They often contain major details that support the main idea. They are also usually topic sentences that tell you what kind of information to expect in the paragraph. Supporting details answer questions such as, *who, what, when, where, why,* and *how.* To find supporting details, look for:

Reasons
Examples
Characteristics
Analysis and explanations
People and places
Senses

▶▶▎ *Secrets to Success*

- *Some answer choices distort the information to give you an answer which sounds right, but is, in fact, inaccurate.*
- *ALWAYS go back and reread the passage to check the facts; do not rely on your memory.*
- *Nearly all supporting detail questions ask about specific facts, and can be answered by finding the information as it is stated in the passage, not inferred or implied.*
- *Supporting detail questions often start out, "According to the passage . . ."*
- *Beware of answer choices that use words like "always," "never," "all," or "none." Unless it is directly stated in the passage, do not assume that these terms apply.*
- *Read questions carefully, looking for words like "except" and "not." Sometimes you are asked to look for the one answer that is not correct.*

SECTION 2 ◆ DIAGNOSTIC: SUPPORTING DETAILS

Read the passages and apply the strategies described above for finding supporting details. When you are done, check your work with the answers immediately following the diagnostic. Even if you get a perfect score here, go ahead and complete the exercises in this section; they are designed to help build confidence and to give you practice for future test success.

Read the passage below and answer the questions that follow.

A single parent may experience a variety of problems. First of all, it may be difficult to meet the emotional needs of the child. There are a variety of ways to express love for a child. Telling a child he or she is loved and demonstrating that love with quality time serve to express love; however, the demands of working and maintaining a home may be so overwhelming that a child's emotional needs may not be met adequately. It also may   5
be hard for the single parent to provide proper supervision for the child. Making arrangements for the child's care and supervision is difficult and costly and may take a large share of the budget. In addition, because women tend to make less money than men, households headed by women can experience financial difficulties. Finally, the single parent may experience unfulfilled emotional and sexual needs. Unmet emotional needs can   10
develop because of the lack of time to seek a relationship. Because most single parents wish to hide their sexual involvement from their child, finding a time and place can present problems. Nevertheless, being a single parent does not have to be a disaster. It is im-

portant that single parents have sufficient financial, material, and emotional support to
meet their own and their child's demands. (Adapted from David J. Anspaugh and Gene   15
Ezell, *Teaching Today's Health*, 7th ed., San Francisco: Benjamin Cummings, 2004.)

1. Which sentence best states the main idea of the passage? *(This question will also help you to
   determine the supporting details.)*
   A. Parents must have financial, material, and emotional support to meet their child's demands.
   B. Being a single parent does not have to be a disaster.
   C. A single parent may experience a variety of problems.
   D. Many children of single parents may have needs that are not being met.

2. The first major detail which the authors discuss is
   A. It may be hard for the single parent to provide proper supervision for the child.
   B. Women tend to make less money than men, and households headed by women can expe-
      rience financial difficulties.
   C. There are a variety of ways to express love for a child.
   D. It may be difficult for single parents to meet the emotional needs of the child.

3. According to the passage, which of the following statements is true?
   A. All single parents experience unfulfilled emotional and sexual needs.
   B. Women tend to make more money than men.
   C. Child care can be difficult and costly.
   D. Households headed by women always experience financial difficulties.

4. According to the passage, single parents
   A. may experience anger or frustration at having their own needs go unmet.
   B. can show their love for the child by telling a child he or she is loved.
   C. cannot maintain a home and a job, and still meet the child's emotional needs.
   D. find that the demands of working and maintaining a home are overwhelming.

5. In the passage, the authors
   A. give reasons why being a single parent is difficult.
   B. explain why single parents have more problems than two-parent families.
   C. tell the effects of single-parent families on children.
   D. tell single parents how to avoid common problems in raising children.

6. Which of the following is *not* one of the problems discussed in the passage?
   A. Children from single-parent families are often left unsupervised.
   B. It may be hard for the single parent to provide proper supervision for the child.
   C. Women tend to make less money than men, and households headed by women can expe-
      rience financial difficulties.
   D. Single parents may experience unfulfilled emotional and sexual needs.

7. The sentence, "Unmet emotional needs can develop because of lack of time to seek a relation-
   ship" (lines 10–11) is a
   A. topic.
   B. topic sentence.
   C. major detail.
   D. minor detail.

Answers to Diagnostic
1. C (The variety of problems described are the major supporting details.)
2. D   3. C   4. B   5. A   6. A   7. D

SECTION 2 ◆ EXERCISES: SUPPORTING DETAILS

Use the following exercises to practice reading for supporting details.

PASSAGE #1

Read the passage and answer the questions that follow.

Do you believe that your Zodiac sign matters? So many people apparently do that the home page for the *Yahoo!* site on the World Wide Web will automatically provide your daily horoscope. But astrology—along with palm reading and tea-leaf reading, and all their relatives—is not a branch of psychology; it is pseudopsychology. Pseudopsychology is superstition or unsupported opinion pretending to be science. Pseudopsychology is not just "bad psychology," which rests on poorly documented observations or badly designed studies and, therefore, has questionable foundations. Pseudopsychology is not psychology at all. It may look and sound like psychology, but it is not science.   5

Appearances can be misleading. Consider extrasensory perception (ESP). Is this pseudopsychology? ESP refers to a collection of mental abilities that do not rely on the ordinary senses or abilities. Telepathy, for instance, is the ability to read minds. This sounds not only wonderful but magical. No wonder people are fascinated by the possibility that they, too, may have latent, untapped, extraordinary abilities. The evidence that such abilities really exist is shaky. But the mere fact that many experiments on ESP have come up empty does not mean that the experiments themselves are bad or "unscientific." One can conduct a perfectly good experiment, guarding against bias and expectancy of effects, even on ESP. Such research is not necessarily pseudopsychology.   10   15

Let's say you wanted to study telepathy. You might arrange to test pairs of participants, with one member of each pair acting as "sender" and the other as "receiver." Both the sender and receiver would look at hands of playing cards that contained the same four cards. The sender would focus on one card (say, an ace), and would "send" the receiver a mental image of the chosen card. The receiver's job would be to guess which card the sender is seeing. By chance alone, with only four cards to choose from, the receiver would guess right about 25% of the time. So the question is, can the receiver do better than mere guesswork? In this study, you would measure the percentage of times the receiver picks the right card, and compare this to what you would expect from guessing alone.   20   25

However, what if the sender provided visible clues (accidentally or on purpose) that have nothing to do with ESP, perhaps smiling when "sending" an ace, grimacing when "sending" a two. A better experiment would have sender and receiver in different rooms, thus controlling for such possible problems. Furthermore, what if people have an unconscious bias to prefer red over black cards, which leads both sender and receiver to select them more often than would be dictated by chance? This difficulty can be countered by including a control condition, in which a receiver guesses cards when the   30

sender is not actually sending. Whether ESP can be considered a valid, reliable phe-   35
nomenon will depend on the results of such studies. If they conclusively show that there
is nothing to it, then people who claim to have ESP or to understand it will be trying
to sell a bill of goods—and will be engaging in pseudopsychology. But as long as proper
studies are under way, we cannot dismiss them as pseudopsychology. (Stephen M. Kosslyn and Robin S. Rosenberg, *Psychology,* 2nd ed., Boston: Allyn and Bacon, 2004.)   40

1. According to the passage, ESP
   A. is a pseudopsychology.
   B. has not as yet been proved or disproved.
   C. is related to astrology and palm reading.
   D. is an ability that everyone can learn to draw on.

2. According to paragraph 1, pseudopsychology is
   A. a branch of psychology.
   B. a science.
   C. a badly designed study.
   D. a superstition.

3. Research experiments on telepathy
   A. must guard against bias.
   B. are difficult to set up.
   C. have shown that telepathy is largely guesswork.
   D. are a waste of time.

4. According to paragraph 4, a better experiment would
   A. eliminate guesswork.
   B. eliminate problems of visible clues and unconscious bias.
   C. use playing cards.
   D. measure the percentage of times the receiver picks the right card.

PASSAGE # 2

Read the passage and answer the questions that follow.

North America has ten species of skunks. The one most people have seen—or at least
smelled—is the abundant and widespread striped skunk. Another species is the spotted
skunk, rarely seen but especially interesting because it illustrates some important concepts about biological species. This particular skunk belongs to a species called the western spotted skunk. The adult is only about the size of a house cat, but it has a potent   5
chemical arsenal that makes up for its small size. Before spraying her potent musk, a female guarding her young usually warns an intruder by raising her tail, stamping her
forefeet, raking the ground with her claws, or even doing a handstand. When all else
fails, she can spray her penetrating odor for three meters with considerable accuracy.

The western spotted skunk inhabits a variety of environments in the United States,   10
from the Pacific coast to the western Great Plains. It is closely related to the eastern
spotted skunk, which occurs throughout the southeastern and midwestern United
States. The ranges of these two species overlap, and the two species look so much alike

that even experts can have a difficult time telling them apart. Both are black with broken white stripes and spots. Individuals of the western species are, on average, slightly smaller, and some have a white tip on the tail, but these and other minor differences in body form are not always present.   15

For many years, biologists debated whether all spotted skunks belong to one species. But in the 1960s, studies of sexual reproduction in these animals showed that they are indeed two species. Reproduction in the eastern spotted skunk is a straightforward affair. Mating occurs in late winter, and young are born between April and July. In marked contrast, the western spotted skunk includes what is called delayed development in its reproductive cycle. Mating takes place in the later summer and early fall, and zygotes begin to develop in the uterus of the female. Further development, however, is temporarily stopped at an early point called the blastocyst stage. Blastocysts remain dormant in the female's uterus throughout the winter months and resume growth in the spring, with the young (usually 5–7) being born in May or June. Because mating occurs at different times of the year for the two species, there is no opportunity for gene flow between populations of eastern and western spotted skunks. Thus, they are separate species, despite the pronounced similarities in their body form and coloration.   20   25   30

Spotted skunks show us that looks can be deceiving. Without knowledge of the mating cycles, we could interpret the minor differences between the two species as insignificant and conclude that there is only one species of spotted skunk in North America. (Adapted from Neil A. Campbell, Lawrence G. Mitchell, and Jane B. Reece, *Biology*, 3rd ed., San Francisco: Benjamin Cummings, 2000.)

5. The western spotted skunk and the eastern spotted skunk
   A. are about the size of a house cat.
   B. are not difficult to tell apart.
   C. live in completely different parts of the United States.
   D. belong to the same species.

6. The female western spotted skunk guarding her young warns an intruder by
   A. hissing.
   B. running in circles.
   C. stamping her forefeet.
   D. swishing her tail.

7. Biologists discovered that the two skunks were different species by studying their
   A. migration patterns.
   B. range overlap.
   C. chemical composition of their potent musk sprays.
   D. mating habits.

8. The western spotted skunk's reproductive cycle
   A. occurs in late winter.
   B. occurs at the same time as the eastern spotted skunk.
   C. includes delayed development.
   D. takes longer than the eastern spotted skunk.

9. The eastern and western spotted skunks are interesting because
    A. they live in a variety of environments across the U.S.
    B. they illustrate some important concepts about biological species.
    C. they could become extinct.
    D. they have similar markings.

10. The most important discovery about the North American eastern and western spotted skunks is that
    A. their habitats overlap.
    B. there is more than one species of spotted skunk.
    C. they are difficult to tell apart.
    D. they defend their young similarly.

SECTION 3 ◆ AUTHOR'S PURPOSE

Now that you understand how to find the main idea and supporting details, you can use this knowledge to more easily find the author's purpose. This is because the author's purpose is VERY closely related to the main idea.

Every author has a purpose for writing and a main point that he or she is making about the topic. The three most common reasons for writing are:

- **To entertain** (examples: short stories, novels, poems, jokes, anecdotes)

- **To inform** (examples: newspaper articles, textbooks, reference materials, instruction manuals, legal documents)

- **To persuade** (examples: campaign speeches, advertising, music/art/literary criticism, sales pitches)

More specific purposes may include:

- To state a problem, then offer a solution
- To analyze or discuss an idea
- To explain something
- To criticize or praise something or someone
- To describe something in detail
- To illustrate something
- To define something

Sometimes an author may have more than one purpose when writing. For example, an author may combine a purpose to criticize with a purpose to persuade when trying to convince readers that a change needs to be made in the national health care system.

To find the author's purpose, ask: <u>Why did the author write this?</u> What was he or she trying to accomplish?

Look for Clues

Take a close look at the <u>main idea</u>. It often indicates the author's purpose.

Consider the <u>author's tone</u>. Is the author's "voice" serious or lighthearted? Does the author use emotional language with positive or negative connotations? Certain tones are related to specific purposes. For example, if the author is informing or instructing, the tone will usually be objective, straightforward, matter-of-fact, formal, or neutral. To entertain, authors often use tones that are lighthearted, humorous, amusing, or dramatic. Authors with persuasion in mind may use a tone that is critical, indignant, angry, impassioned, or insistent.

Does the author present mostly <u>facts or opinions</u>? Factual passages tend to be objective and informative, while passages with many opinions tend to be persuasive and biased.

Look for phrases that indicate the <u>author's intent</u>, such as "The goal of this essay . . ." or "It is my intent to show . . ."

Pay attention to the overall <u>pattern of organization</u> the author uses. For example, an author's purpose may be to compare two or more things, or to contrast them. Another may be to define or explain a term, or give the causes or effects of something.

What is the author's primary purpose in the following passages?

> **Example #1**
> Although physics and chemistry are considered separate fields of study, they have much in common. First, both are physical sciences and are concerned with studying and explaining physical occurrences. Second, to study and record these occurrences, each field has developed a precise set of signs and symbols. These might be considered a specialized language. Finally, both fields are closely tied to the field of mathematics and use mathematics in predicting and explaining physical occurrences. (Hewitt, *Conceptual Physics*, 8th ed.)

The primary purpose in the passage above is
- A. to explain the fields of chemistry and physics.
- B. to persuade the reader that physics and chemistry are closely tied to mathematics.
- C. to compare the similarities between chemistry and physics.
- D. to give the reasons why mathematics is related to chemistry and physics.

How to Find the Author's Purpose
First, determine the topic and main idea:

Topic: Physics and Chemistry

Main Idea: Although physics and chemistry are considered separate fields of study, they have much in common.

Then look for the author's **pattern of organization:** The author is comparing the similarities between physics and chemistry.

Consider the **author's tone:** Serious and objective, containing mostly facts.

The correct answer is C, which restates the main idea and the overall pattern of organization.

Example #2

Hate sites began on the Internet in the mid-1990s, and their number expanded rapidly. Now hate groups in general across the nation are on the rise because of the Internet. Hate sites advocate violence toward immigrants, Jews, Arabs, gays, abortion providers, and others. Through the Internet, disturbed minds effectively fuel hatred, violence, sexism, racism, and terrorism. Never before has there been such an intensive way for depraved people to gather to reinforce their prejudices and hatred. (Adapted from Shedletsky and Aitknen, *Human Communication on the Internet*, Boston: Allyn and Bacon, 2004.)

The primary purpose in the passage above is

    A. to show how the number of hate sites on the Internet has increased rapidly.
    B. to show how the Internet has caused the increase of hate groups in general.
    C. to criticize hate groups.
    D. to persuade the reader to not visit hate sites on the Internet.

Topic: Hate sites on the Internet

Main Idea: Hate groups in general across the nation are on the rise because of the Internet.

Pattern of Organization: (Cause and effect) The Internet is the cause of the (effect) increase in the number of hate groups.

The correct answer is B, *To show how the Internet has caused the increase of hate groups in general.*

▶▶ Secrets to Success

- *Begin by stating the topic and main idea in your own words, and try to find a topic sentence in the passage.*
- *Ask: Why did the author write this?*
- *Look at the overall pattern of organization.*
- *Pay close attention to the author's tone.*
- *Look at the language used: is it biased?*
- *Look for facts and opinions.*

SECTION 3 ◆ DIAGNOSTIC: AUTHOR'S PURPOSE

Read the passages and apply the strategies described above for finding the author's purpose. When you are done, check your work with the answers immediately following the diagnostic. Even if you get a perfect score here, go ahead and complete the exercises in this section; they are designed to help build confidence and to give you practice for future test success.

Read the passages below and answer the questions that follow.

PASSAGE #1

Inside those (television) networks, a growing number of people with Ph.D.'s are injecting the latest in child development theory into new programs. That's the good news.

The bad news is that working these shows into kids' lives in a healthy way remains a challenge. Much of what kids watch remains banal or harmful. Many kids watch too much. There are also troubling socioeconomic factors at work. In lower income homes, for instance, kids watch more and are more likely to have TV in their bedrooms, a practice pediatricians discourage. (Daniel McGinn, *Newsweek*, November 11, 2002.)

5

1. The primary purpose of this passage is to
   A. list the reasons why television is harmful to children.
   B. explain why children in lower income homes watch more television than children in higher income homes.
   C. persuade the reader that making television healthy for children is still a challenge.
   D. inform the reader that child development theory in television is harmful.

PASSAGE #2

Think of your speech as beginning as soon as the audience focuses on you. Similarly, think of it ending not after you have spoken the last sentences, but only after the audience directs its focus away from you. Here are a few suggestions for before and after you give your speech. (DeVito, *Essentials of Human Communication*, 3rd ed., Boston: Allyn and Bacon, 1999.)

2. The author's purpose will probably be to
   A. convince the reader that a speech lasts longer than the spoken part.
   B. instruct the reader on what to do before and after a speech.
   C. explain when a speech really begins.
   D. compare what happens before a speech to what happens afterward.

PASSAGE #3

Public opinion polling sounds scientific with its talk of random samples and sampling error; it is easy to take results for solid fact. But being an informed consumer of polls requires more than just a nuts and bolts knowledge of how they are conducted; you should think about whether the questions are fair and unbiased before making too much of the results. The good—or the harm—that polls do depends on how well the data are collected and how thoughtfully the data are interpreted. (Edwards, Wattenberg, and Lineberry, *Government in America*, 9th ed., New York: Longman, 2000.)

5

3. The main purpose of the passage above is to
   A. narrate a story about public opinion polling.
   B. criticize the use of public opinion polls.
   C. inform the reader about how public opinion polls are conducted.
   D. convince the reader to be an informed consumer of public opinion polls.

PASSAGE #4

During the 1950s, the Cleavers on the television show "Leave It to Beaver" epitomized the American family. In 1960, over 70% of all American households were like the

Cleavers: made up of a breadwinner father, a homemaker mother, and their kids. Today, "traditional" families with a working husband, an unemployed wife, and one or more children make up less than 15% of the nation's households. (Alexander, Lombardi, et al., *Joining a Community of Readers*, New York: Longman, 1998.)   5

4. The authors' primary purpose is
   A. to persuade the reader that American families are not as stable as they used to be.
   B. to contrast the differences between American families of the 1950s and families of today.
   C. to contrast the differences between television show families and real American families.
   D. to inform the readers about the television show families of the 1950s.

PASSAGE #5

Articulation refers to movements of the speech organs as they modify and interrupt the air stream being sent from the lungs. Different movements of the tongue, lips, teeth, palate, or vocal cords produce different sounds. Pronunciation refers to the production of the syllables or words according to some accepted standard, such as the dictionary. (DeVito, *Essentials of Human Communication*, 3rd ed., Boston: Allyn and Bacon, 1999.)

5. The author's primary purpose is
   A. to define the terms *articulation* and *pronunciation*.
   B. to compare the differences between articulation and pronunciation.
   C. to inform the reader about how articulation occurs.
   D. to give examples of articulation.

Answers to Diagnostic
   1. C   2. B   3. D   4. B   5. A

SECTION 3 ◆ EXERCISES: AUTHOR'S PURPOSE

Use the following exercises to practice reading for the author's purpose.

PASSAGE #1

Read the passage and answer the question that follows.

Fungi have a number of practical uses for humans. Most of us have eaten mushrooms although we may not have realized that we were ingesting the fruiting bodies of subterranean fungi. In addition, mushrooms are not the only fungi we eat. The distinctive flavors of certain kinds of cheeses, including Roquefort and blue cheese, come from the fungi used to ripen them. Highly prized by gourmets are truffles, the fruiting bodies of certain mycorrhizal fungi associated with tree roots. The unicellular fungi, the yeasts, are important   5
in food production. Yeasts are used in baking, brewing, and winemaking. Fungi are medically valuable as well. Some fungi produce antibiotics that are used to treat bacterial diseases. In fact, the first antibiotic discovered was penicillin, which is made by the common mold called *Penicillium*. (Adapted from Neil A. Campbell, Lawrence G. Mitchell, and   10
Jane B. Reece, *Biology*, 3rd ed., San Francisco: Benjamin Cummings, 2000.)

1. The primary purpose of the above passage is to
   A. describe foods that are fungi.
   B. explain how fungi are used to ripen cheeses.
   C. give examples of the uses of fungi.
   D. analyze the medical and nutritional benefits of fungi.

PASSAGE #2

Read the passage and answer the question that follows.

John Castle's lifestyle gives us a glimpse into how the super-rich live. After earning a degree in physics at MIT and an MBA at Harvard, John went into banking and securities, where he made more than $100 million. Wanting to be close to someone famous, John bought President John F. Kennedy's "Winter White House," an oceanfront estate in Palm Beach, Florida. John spent $11 million to remodel the 13,000-square-foot house so it would be more to his liking. Among those changes: adding bathrooms numbers 14 and 15. He likes to show off John F. Kennedy's bed and also the dresser that has the drawer labeled "black underwear," carefully hand-lettered by Rose Kennedy.

If John gets bored at his beachfront estate—or tired of swimming in the Olympic-size pool where JFK swam the weekend before his assassination—he entertains himself by riding one of his thoroughbred horses at his nearby 10-acre ranch. If this fails to ease his boredom, he can relax aboard his custom-built, 45-foot Hinckley yacht. The yacht is a real source of diversion. He once boarded it for an around-the-world trip.

He didn't stay on board, though—just joined the cruise from time to time. A captain and crew kept the vessel sailing in the right direction, and whenever John felt like it, he would fly in and stay a few days. Then he would fly back to the States to direct his business. He did this about a dozen times, flying perhaps 150,000 miles, an interesting way to get around the world.

How much does a custom-built Hinckley yacht cost? John can't tell you. As he says, "I don't want to know what anything costs. When you've got enough money, price doesn't make a difference. That's part of the freedom of being rich." (Adapted from James M. Henslin, *Sociology*, 6th ed., Boston: Allyn and Bacon, 2003.)

2. The primary purpose of the above passage is to
   A. persuade the reader that John Castle's lifestyle should be envied.
   B. describe John Castle's lifestyle as an example of how the super-rich live.
   C. criticize John Castle's squandering his money.
   D. inspire the reader to become wealthy.

PASSAGE #3

Read the passage and answer the question that follows.

The National Child Abuse Prevention and Treatment Act of 1974 defines child abuse and neglect as "physical or mental injury, sexual abuse or exploitation, negligent treatment, or maltreatment of a child under the age of eighteen or the age specified under the child protection law of the state in question, by a person who is responsible for the

child's welfare, under circumstances which indicate that the child's health or welfare   5
is harmed or threatened thereby."

The laws of every state require teachers to report suspected cases of child abuse and
neglect. Every state grants teachers who make such reports immunity from civil and
criminal suits. State laws vary in their requirements, and teachers should become familiar with the laws where they teach. Most states require an oral report to an admin-   10
istrator followed by a written statement. The law will protect teachers who act in good
faith. Teachers should not hesitate to file a report if they believe a student is a victim
of abuse or neglect. In most states teachers can be fined or imprisoned if they do *not*
make the report, and in some states they can be sued for neglect.

A teacher who sees a student exhibit indicators of child abuse and neglect over a period   15
of time should think seriously about why the indicators are present. As in other areas
of the law, the *reasonable person* standard applies: Under similar circumstances, would
a reasonable person suspect abuse or neglect? If your answer is yes, you should make
a report. Remember, the law will protect you if you act in good faith. Do not be blind
to the problem. (Adapted from Joseph W. Newman, *America's Teachers*, 4th ed.,   20
Boston: Allyn and Bacon, 2002.)

3. The author's primary purpose in the above passage is to
    A. define child abuse to teachers.
    B. explain state laws regarding child abuse to teachers.
    C. inform teachers about child abuse indicators.
    D. convince teachers that it is their duty to report child abuse.

PASSAGE #4

Read the passage and answer the question that follows.

There are vast cultural differences in what is considered proper when it comes to criticism. In some cultures, being kind to the person is more important than telling the ab-
solute truth, and so members may say things that are complimentary, but untrue, in a
logical sense. Those who come from cultures that are highly individual and competitive,
such as the United States, Germany, and Sweden, may find public criticism a normal   5
part of the learning process. Those who come from cultures that are more collectivist
and that emphasize the group rather than the individual, such as Japan, Mexico, and
Korea, are likely to find giving and receiving public criticism uncomfortable. Thus,
people from individual cultures may readily criticize others and are likely to expect the
same "courtesy" from other listeners. After all, this person might reason, "If I'm going   10
to criticize your skills to help you improve, I expect you to help me in the same way."
Persons from collectivist cultures, on the other hand, may feel that it's more important
to be polite and courteous than to help someone learn a skill. Cultural rules to maintain
peaceful relations among the Japanese and politeness among many Asian cultures may
conflict with the Western classroom cultural norm to voice criticism.   15

The difficulties are compounded when you interpret unexpected behavior through your
own cultural filters. For example, if a speaker who expects comments and criticism
gets none, he or she may interpret the silence to mean that the audience didn't care or

wasn't listening. But they may have been listening very intently. They may simply be
operating with a different cultural rule—a rule that says it's impolite to criticize or eval-   20
uate another person's work, especially in public. (Adapted from Joseph A. DeVito, *Essentials of Human Communication*, 3rd ed., New York: Longman, 1999.)

4. The main purpose of the above passage is to
    A. contrast cultural differences in public criticism.
    B. explain how to criticize effectively.
    C. persuade the reader to respect cultural differences.
    D. describe the effects of cultural miscommunications.

PASSAGE #5

Read the passage and answer the question that follows.

Although many people think of First Ladies as well-dressed homemakers presiding over
White House dinners, there is much more to the job. The First Lady has no official
government position. Yet she is often at the center of national attention. The media
chronicles every word she speaks and every hairstyle she adopts.

Abigail Adams (an early feminist) and Dolly Madison counseled and lobbied their hus-   5
bands. Edith Galt Wilson was the most powerful First Lady, virtually running the government when her husband, Woodrow, suffered a paralyzing stroke in 1919. Eleanor
Roosevelt wrote a nationally syndicated newspaper column and tirelessly traveled and
advocated New Deal policies. She became her crippled husband's eyes and ears around
the country and urged him to adopt liberal social welfare policies. Lady Bird Johnson   10
chose to focus on one issue, beautification, and most of her successors followed this
pattern. Rosalyn Carter chose mental health, Nancy Reagan selected drugs, and Barbara Bush picked literacy.

In what was perhaps a natural evolution in a society where women have moved into
positions formerly held only by males, Hillary Rodham Clinton attained the most re-   15
sponsible and visible leadership position ever held by a First Lady. She had been an
influential advisor to the President, playing an active role in the selection of nominees
for cabinet and judicial posts, for example. Most publicly, she headed the planning
for the President's massive health care reform plan in 1993 and became, along with
her husband, its primary advocate. (Adapted from George C. Edwards, Martin P.   20
Wattenberg, and Robert L. Lineberry, *Government in America*, 9th ed., New York:
Longman, 2000.)

5. The main purpose of the above passage is to
    A. contrast the activities of the First Ladies.
    B. explain the way the First Lady does her job.
    C. convince the reader that First Ladies are feminists.
    D. illustrate the public roles of the First Ladies.

PASSAGE #6

Read the passage and answer the question that follows.

President Truman's decision to order the atomic bombings on the Japanese cities of Hiroshima and Nagasaki has been the subject of intense historical debate. Truman's defenders argue that the bombs ended the war quickly, avoiding the necessity of a costly invasion and the probable loss of tens of thousands of Americans' lives and hundreds of Japanese lives. According to some intelligence estimates, an invasion might have cost 268,000 American casualties, with Japanese costs several times that figure. 5

Truman's defenders also argue that Hiroshima and Nagasaki were legitimate targets with both military bases and war industry, and their civilian populations had been showered with leaflets warning them to evacuate. Finally, they argue that two bombs were ultimately necessary to end the war. They note that even after the atomic bomb had fallen on Hiroshima, the Japanese war minister implored the nation's Supreme Council "for one last great battle on Japanese soil—as demanded by the national honor. . . . Would it not be wondrous for this whole nation to be destroyed like a beautiful flower." 10

Truman's critics argue that the war might have ended even without the atomic bombings. They maintain that the Japanese economy would have been strangled by a continued naval blockade and forced to surrender by conventional firebombing. The revisionists also contend that the President had options apart from using the bombs. They believe that it might have been possible to induce a Japanese surrender by a demonstration of the atomic bomb's power or by providing a more specific warning of the damage it could produce or by guaranteeing the emperor's position in postwar Japan. 15

20

The revisionists also believe that estimates of potential American casualties were grossly inflated after the war to justify the bombing. Finally, they argue that the bomb might have been dropped mainly to justify its cost or to scare the Soviet Union. The Soviet Union entered the Japanese war August 8, and some revisionists charge that the bombings were designed to end the war before the Red army could occupy northern China. (Adapted from James Kirby Martin et al., *America and Its Peoples*, 5th ed., New York: Longman, 2004.) 25

6. The authors' purpose in the above passage is to
    A. describe the effects of the U.S. dropping the atomic bombs on the Japanese.
    B. inform the reader of the reasons for dropping the atomic bombs on Hiroshima and Nagasaki.
    C. persuade the reader that the dropping of atomic bombs on Hiroshima and Nagasaki was wrong.
    D. present the two sides of the debate over the dropping of the atomic bombs on Hiroshima and Nagasaki.

PASSAGE #7

Read the passage and answer the question that follows.

A single parent may experience a variety of problems. First of all, it may be difficult to
meet the emotional needs of the child. There are a variety of ways to express love for a
child. Telling a child he or she is loved and demonstrating that love with quality time
serve to express love; however, the demands of working and maintaining a home may be
so overwhelming that a child's emotional needs may not be met adequately. It also may
be hard for the single parent to provide proper supervision for the child. Making arrangements for the child's care and supervision is difficult and costly and may take a large
share of the budget. In addition, because women tend to make less money than men,
households headed by women can experience financial difficulties. Finally, the single parent may experience unfulfilled emotional and sexual needs. Unmet emotional needs can
develop because of the lack of time to seek a relationship. Because most single parents
wish to hide their sexual involvement from their child, finding a time and place can present problems. Nevertheless, being a single parent does not have to be a disaster. It is important that single parents have sufficient financial, material, and emotional support to
meet their own and their child's demands. (Adapted from David J. Anspaugh and Gene
Ezell, *Teaching Today's Health*, 7th ed., San Francisco: Benjamin Cummings, 2004.)

7. The authors' purpose in the above passage is to
   A. argue the disadvantages of single parenthood.
   B. explain the types of problems single parents have.
   C. convince the reader that children in single parent homes suffer.
   D. give the effects of divorce on children.

PASSAGE #8

Read the passage and answer the question that follows.

Many overweight and obese individuals are trying to lose weight. Although it took several months and years to put on the extra weight, many of them are looking for a quick
way to lose that weight. This attitude results in choosing quick-weight-loss diets that
are not effective and may be harmful.

Some choose metabolic products, such as herbs or caffeine, to lose weight. Herbs have not
been shown to speed the loss of fat, and caffeine shows little promise as a weight-loss aid.

Others go on very-low-calorie diets, which severely restrict nutrients and can result in
serious metabolic imbalances. Weight can be lost on this type of diet; much of the
weight lost will be lean protein tissue and/or water, not fat. This results in harm to the
muscles (including the heart), loss of essential vitamins and minerals through the water
loss, and dizziness and fatigue. Further, if one cuts calories, this slows the metabolism;
once this person goes off the diet, the metabolism remains slow and the body continues
to use few calories—and the pounds come back.

Liquid protein diets operate on the theory that insulin is controlled and therefore more
fat is burned. With this type of diet, ketosis will result. Ketosis will increase blood levels
of uric acid, a risk factor for gout and kidney stones. There is new research evidence

that carbohydrates lead to fat storage and weight; further, the excessive protein in this diet can damage the kidneys and cause osteoporosis.

Prescription drugs, such as Redux and Pondimin (fen-phen), curb hunger by increasing the level of serotonin in the brain. These were intended for the obese, but they were banned in 1997 after the FDA found strong evidence that they could seriously damage the heart.

Some people try crash diets to lose a moderate amount of weight in a very short period. These types of diets can damage several body systems and have been proven not to work because most of these individuals regain their weight. This yo-yo dieting causes many health problems and shortens lifespan. The best way to lose weight is to lose weight slowly (no more than one-half to one pound a week), eat properly and in moderation, and exercise. (Adapted from David J. Anspaugh and Gene Ezell, *Teaching Today's Health*, 7th ed., San Francisco: Benjamin Cummings, 2004.)

8. The main purpose of the above passage is to
   A. describe the various types of quick diets that are ineffective and harmful.
   B. persuade the reader that crash diets are harmful.
   C. describe fad diets.
   D. explain the best way to lose weight.

PASSAGE #9

Read the passage and answer the question that follows.

The dramatic difference between the social status of the Egyptian nobility and that of the common people is reflected in their respective burial rites. The keen Egyptian interest in the afterlife, combined with strikingly materialistic criteria for happiness, made lavish tombs for the pharaohs (Egyptian rulers) seem particularly important. Elaborate goods were buried with the pharaoh to assure him a gracious existence in the world beyond, and a processional causeway linked each pyramid to a temple constructed for the worship of the pharaoh; adjacent to the pyramid was a building to house the special cedar boat that would carry him on his voyage to the land of the dead. The pyramid served as the core of an entire necropolis, or city of the dead, which included small pyramids for the wives and daughters of the pharaoh and mastabas for the nobility. Even a minor royal official spent a considerable portion of his time preparing an elaborate tomb for his afterlife, and he would want his corpse to be mummified because of the Egyptian belief that the *ka*, the spirit of life in each person, periodically returned to the body. The corpse of an average farmer, however, was typically wrapped in a piece of linen and deposited in a cave or pit with only a staff and a pair of sandals to facilitate the journey to the next world; some bodies were even left in the open sand of the desert. (Adapted from Richard L. Greaves, Robert Zaller, and Jennifer Tolbert Roberts, *Civilizations of the West*, 2nd ed., New York: Longman, 1997.)

9. The authors' main purpose in the above passage is to
   A. explain the Egyptian belief in the afterlife.
   B. give reasons for building pyramids for the pharaohs.
   C. show the difference in burial rites according to social status.
   D. describe the lavish tombs of the pharaohs.

PASSAGE #10

Read the passage and answer the question that follows.

"Street gangs" are a more formal variety of youth gang. They generally have leaders and a hierarchy of membership roles and responsibilities. They are named, and their members mark their identity with tattoos or "colors." While many street gangs are involved in violence, not all are. An anthropologist who did research among nearly forty street gangs in New York, Los Angeles, and Boston learned much about why individuals join gangs, providing insights that contradict popular thinking on this subject.

One common stereotype is that young boys join gangs because they are from homes with no male authority figure with whom they could identify. This study showed that equal numbers of gang members were from intact nuclear households as from those with an absent father. Another common perception is that the gang replaces a missing feeling of family as a motive. This study, again, showed that the same number of gang members reported having close family ties as those who did not.

Those who were gang members shared a personality type called a "defiant individualist." This type has five traits: intense competitiveness, mistrust or wariness, self-reliance, social isolation, and a strong survival instinct. Poverty, especially urban poverty, leads to the development of this type of personality. Many of these youths want to be economically successful, but social conditions channel their interests and skills into illegal pursuits rather than into legal pathways of achievement. (Adapted from Barbara D. Miller, *Cultural Anthropology*, 2nd ed., Boston: Allyn and Bacon, 2002.)

10. The main purpose of the above passage is to
    A. discourage youths from joining a gang.
    B. argue that street gang members come from homes with no authority figure.
    C. give reasons why youths join street gangs.
    D. define the typical gang personality type.

KEEP IN MIND ◆ SUMMARY OF CHAPTER 1

Understanding the author's main point is the most important key to comprehension. Keep in mind these two questions when looking for the main idea:

1. What is the topic (subject) of the passage?
2. What is the author's most important point about that topic?

- Most often, main ideas are found in the first paragraph. A second place to look is in the last paragraph. Then check the sentences in the middle.
- Look for a broad statement that sounds like an important point the author is making.
- When you think you have found the correct main idea, go back and look through the passage. Ask yourself: Do all of the other sentences tell more about this sentence? If they do, then your answer is correct.

Sometimes an author does not state the main idea in a topic sentence or a thesis statement. In these cases, the reader must infer the main idea by drawing a conclusion.

Supporting Details

Supporting details are sentences which give more specific information about the main idea. Long passages contain one main idea and may have one or several major supporting details. The number of major and minor details varies with each passage. Not every major detail has a minor detail to support it, while some major details may have several minor supporting details.

Major details tell us more information about the main idea.

Minor details tell us more about the major details.

To find supporting details,

- pay close attention to the <u>first sentence of each paragraph</u>. They often contain major details that support the main idea. They are also usually topic sentences that tell you what kind of information to expect in the paragraph.
- Supporting details answer questions such as *who, what, when, where, why,* and *how.* To find supporting details, look for:

> Reasons
> Examples
> Characteristics
> Analysis and explanations
> People and places
> Senses

Author's Purpose

Every author has a purpose for writing, and a main point that he or she is making about the topic.

- Begin by stating the topic and main idea in your own words, and try to find a topic sentence in the passage.
- Ask: Why did the author write this? Look at the overall pattern of organization.
- Pay close attention to the author's tone.
- Look at the language used: is it biased?
- Look for facts and opinions which may reveal the author's purpose.

All three components—the main idea, supporting details, and author's purpose—work together to convey the author's intended meaning. Knowing these skills will help readers to understand the structural skills covered in the next section.

Chapter 2: Structural Skills

There are more questions concerning organizational patterns than any other skill on the Exit Exam, so understanding this concept is absolutely vital to success on the test. There are actually three different questions on the Exit Exam that concern patterns of organization: overall pattern of organization, relationship between two sentences, and relationship within a sentence. This first section concerns the overall pattern of organization, which is the arrangement of the details in a reading into a clear structure.

The other two Exit Exam questions that concern patterns of organization are covered in the next two sections, but the three question types are closely related. Each pattern of organization has a set of "clue words" or *transitional words* related to its meaning. These transitional words found in and between sentences convey the organizational pattern.

Some Common Patterns of Organization

Chronological Order (Time Order): Arranges information in the order in which the events occurred. (Example: A story about what happened on the day that John F. Kennedy was assassinated.)

Steps In a Process: Arranges information in the order in which the steps occur in a process, much the same as chronological order. The only difference is that instead of discussing events that occurred over a period of time, the author is explaining a process that takes place in a certain order. (Example: The directions for installing computer software.)

Cause and Effect: Shows how one or more events caused another (or several others). (Example: A textbook section on the causes of World War II and its effects on the economy of Europe.)

Compare and Contrast: Shows the way(s) that two or more things are alike (compare) or different (contrast). (Example: A biology report comparing and contrasting how plants and animals convert food to energy.)

Simple Listing (also known as Listing or Addition): Arranges information in a list in no particular order. The key words for this pattern are very similar to those for Time Order and Process. However, the big difference is that with Time Order and Process, you cannot mix up the items or steps. With Simple Listing, you can. (Example: An article showing the various ways that computers are used in engineering and manufacturing is LISTING. An article showing how to install a software patch for your computer is PROCESS.)

Generalization and Example: States a main idea and then gives one or more examples to explain it. (Example: "Plagiarism is a serious infraction in most settings. For instance, students can be suspended or expelled from school.")

Definition and Example: The author uses a term and then explains it with an example. (Example: A term that is defined in a biology textbook: "An **organ** consists of several tissues adapted to perform specific functions as a group. The heart, for example, while mostly muscle, also has epithelial, connective, and nervous tissue." —Campbell et al., *Biology: Concepts & Connections*, 3rd ed., 2000.)

Statement and Clarification: States a broad, general idea and then explains in further detail, without using a specific example. (Example: An ecology text that states a point and follows it with more information: "Forest decline is not a new phenomenon. During the past two centuries, our forests have experienced several declines, with different species affected." —Smith and Smith, *Elements of Ecology*, 5th ed., 2003.)

Spatial Order: Arranges details according to their location in space. (Example: A travel brochure which describes the geography of an island according to location, beginning in the north and ending in the south.)

Classification: Sorts ideas into categories according to similar characteristics. (Example: A health textbook chapter describing the different types of drugs by their function and effects.)

Transitional Words (Key Words)—knowing these makes it much easier to identify the pattern of organization.

- **Chronological Order (Time Order) and Steps in a Process:** first, second, third, etc., finally, and, also, next, then, meanwhile, during, afterward, another. Dates are also clue words for time order.
- **Cause and Effect:** result, effect, cause, consequently, thus, then, if, since, because, therefore, accordingly, results in, leads to, so.
- **Compare and Contrast:** different, whereas, while, although, even though, despite, despite the fact that, opposite, in spite of, but, contrast, instead of, however, nevertheless, yet, unlike, like, alike, similar, both, compare, also.
- **Simple Listing (also known as Listing or Addition):** and, first, second, third, etc., finally, also, next, then, another, moreover, furthermore, in addition.
- **Generalization and Example:** for example, to illustrate, to show, in general, for instance, such as, generally.
- **Statement and Clarification:** to clarify, to explain, to understand, namely, specifically, thus.
- **Spatial Order:** next to, beside, under, over, around, between, outside of, inside of, within, front, side, back, interior, exterior, north, south, east, west.
- **Classification:** types, classifies, classifications, groups, categories, styles.

How to Determine the Overall Pattern of Organization

To determine the correct overall pattern of organization, you must:

- Identify the topic and main idea, and note any transitional words
- For multi-paragraph readings, compare the thesis statement (main idea of the whole reading) to the topic sentences (main idea of each paragraph). See how these main ideas relate, and note any transitional expressions that are common to all of them.
- Think about the author's purpose
- Look for relationships between ideas
- **Learn the transitional phrases associated with each pattern**

Example #1
While mainland Europe suffered through the Thirty Years' War, England faced serious domestic stress under the first two Stuart kings. Conflict between the first, James I, and his English subjects began immediately after he came to the throne in 1603, but the wily monarch avoided any real constitutional crisis. This fate fell to his son, Charles I, who succeeded his father in 1635. During the next 15 years, misguided royal policies produced steadily mounting opposition, until the country stood at the brink of war. (Brummett et al., *Civilizations Past and Present*, 9th ed., 2000.)

Topic: England's first two Stuart kings

Main Idea: While mainland Europe suffered through the Thirty Years' War, England faced serious domestic stress under the first two Stuart kings.

How are the supporting details arranged?
  A. Listing
  B. Chronological order
  C. Cause and effect
  D. Compare and contrast

Look for transitional phrases to help you decide. (Another clue in this passage is the use of dates in chronological order.)

The correct answer is B. Chronological order.

Example #2
The heavily populated coastline in the south is the center for business and manufacturing. In the central region, the land grows into rolling hills and pastures for dairy farming and sheep herding. The northern part of the state boasts of its majestic snow-covered mountains and dramatic waterfalls from granite precipices. To the west are the broad plains and rich farmland that are the heart and soul of its people.

Topic: A state's geography

Main Idea (implied): The state has a variety of geographical regions.

What is the overall pattern of organization?
  A. Classification
  B. Cause and effect
  C. Generalization and example
  D. Spatial order

Look at the transitional phrases the author uses (south, central, northern, west).

The correct answer is D. Spatial order.

> ▶▶▌ *Secrets to Success*

- *Learn the transitional phrases associated with each pattern.*
- *Identify the topic and main idea.*
- *Focus on the supporting details.*
- *Think about the author's purpose.*
- *Be aware that authors may combine two or more patterns.*
- *When looking for an overall pattern, think about the author's main idea and purpose.*

SECTION 1 ◆ DIAGNOSTIC: PATTERNS OF ORGANIZATION

Read the passages and apply the strategies described above for finding the patterns of organization. When you are done, check your work with the answers immediately following the diagnostic. Even if you get a perfect score here, go ahead and complete the exercises in this section; they are designed to help build confidence and to give you practice for future test success.

Read the following passages to determine the author's overall pattern of organization.

PASSAGE #1

One of the most important results of the Civil War was the freedom gained by southern slaves. In the decade following the defeat of the Confederacy, hundreds of thousands of men and women migrated throughout the South, searching for land, work, and relatives lost through prewar sale. Some former slaves, however, took an even bolder step, leaving the South altogether and traveling west in search of cheap farmland or north seeking industrial employment. While most faced difficult years adjusting to the world of free labor and white prejudice, none would have exchanged their life of freedom for the days of bondage. (Nash and Schultz, *Retracing the Past: Readings in the History of the American People*, 4th ed., New York: Longman, 2000.)

1. The author's overall pattern of organization
   A. contrasts the differences between the southern slaves.
   B. lists the changes in the South after the Civil War.
   C. summarizes the changes in slavery.
   D. shows the effects of Civil War upon southern slaves.

PASSAGE #2

Walt Whitman, whose *Leaves of Grass* (1855) was the last of the great literary works of his brief outpouring of genius, was the most romantic and by far the most distinctly American writer of his age. He was born on Long Island, outside of New York City, in 1819. At 13, he left school and became a printer's devil; thereafter he held a succession of newspaper jobs in the metropolitan area. He was an ardent Jacksonian and later a

Free Soiler, which got him into hot water with a number of the publishers for whom he worked. (Garraty and Carnes, *The American Nation: A History of the United States*, 10th ed., New York: Longman, 2000.)

2. The author's overall pattern of organization
    A. is a presentation of Walt Whitman's life in chronological order.
    B. explains the reasons why Walt Whitman was not published much.
    C. shows the effects of Whitman's political views.
    D. shows the cause of Whitman's creative genius.

PASSAGE #3

Active listening serves several important functions. First, it helps you, as a listener, check your understanding of what the speaker said and, more important, what he or she meant. Reflecting back on your understanding of what you think the speaker means gives the speaker an opportunity to offer clarification. In this way, future messages will have a better chance of being relevant. Second, through active listening, you let the speaker know that you acknowledge and accept his or her feelings. (Rigolosi and Campion, eds., *The Longman Electronic Test Bank for Developmental Reading*, 2001.)

5

3. The passage is organized by
    A. clarifying an explanation of active listening.
    B. listing the important functions of active listening.
    C. classifying the different functions of active listening.
    D. showing the effects of active listening.

PASSAGE #4

Self-disclosure is a type of communication in which you reveal information about yourself, in which you move information from the hidden self into the open self. Overt statements about the self as well as slips of the tongue, unconscious nonverbal movements, and public confessions would all be considered forms of self-disclosure.

Self-disclosure is information previously unknown by the receiver. This may vary from the relatively commonplace ("I'm really afraid of that French exam") to the extremely significant (I'm so depressed, I feel like committing suicide"). (DeVito, *Essentials of Human Communication*, 3rd ed., Boston: Allyn and Bacon, 1999.)

5

4. The author's overall pattern of organization
    A. lists the types of self-disclosure.
    B. contrasts self-disclosure with other forms of communication.
    C. discusses the importance of self-disclosure in communication.
    D. defines self-disclosure and provides examples.

PASSAGE #5

Presidents and prime ministers govern quite differently. Prime ministers never face divided government, for example. Since they represent the majority party or coalition, they can almost always depend on winning on votes. In addition, party discipline is better in parliamentary systems than in the United States. Prime ministers generally differ from presidents in background as well. They must be party leaders, as we have seen, and they are usually very effective communicators, their skills honed in the rough and tumble of parliamentary debate. In addition, they have had substantial experience dealing with national issues, unlike American governors who may move directly into presidency. Cabinet members, who are usually senior members of parliament, have similar advantages. (Edwards, Wattenberg, and Lineberry, *Government in America*, 9th ed., New York: Longman, 2000.)

5. The author's overall pattern of organization
    A. contrasts the roles of the president and the prime minister.
    B. compares the roles of the president and the prime minister.
    C. lists additional information about the roles of the president and the prime minister.
    D. analyzes which form of government has the most advantages.

PASSAGE #6

Deprived of access to Middle Eastern oil, the American economy sputtered. The price of oil rose to $12 a barrel, up from $3. This sent prices soaring for nearly everything else. Homes were heated with oil, factories were powered with it and utility plants used it to generate electricity. Nylon and other synthetic fibers as well as paints, insecticides, fertilizers, and many plastic products were based on petrochemicals. Above all else, oil was refined into gasoline. By the time of the Yom Kippur War, American car owners were driving more than a trillion miles a year, the major reason why the United States, formerly a major oil exporter, imported one third of its oil. The Arab oil embargo pushed up gas prices; service stations intermittently ran out of gasoline and long lines formed at those that remained open. (Garraty and Carnes, *The American Nation: A History of the United States*, 10th ed., New York: Longman, 2000.)

6. The author's overall pattern of organization
    A. lists examples of products and services dependent upon oil.
    B. shows the effects of the oil embargo on the American economy.
    C. explains why Americans use so much oil.
    D. illustrates ways that oil is used in the United States.

PASSAGE #7

Communicate your information with varying levels of abstraction. For example, in talking about the freedom of the press, you can talk in high-level abstractions about the importance of getting information to the public, by referring to the Bill of Rights, and by relating a free press to the preservation of democracy. You can also talk in low-level abstractions, for example, by citing how a local newspaper was prevented from running a story critical of the town council or about how Lucy Rinaldo was fired from the *Accord Sentinel* after she wrote a story critical of the Mayor. Combining high and low abstractions seems to work best. (DeVito, *Essentials of Human Communication*, 3rd ed., 1999.)

7. The author's overall pattern of organization
   A. shows the effects of high and low level abstractions.
   B. makes a general statement and follows it with specific examples.
   C. compares high level and low level abstractions.
   D. gives a definition of high level and low level abstractions.

Answers to Diagnostic
   1. D   2. A   3. B   4. D   5. A   6. B   7. B

SECTION 1 ◆ EXERCISES: PATTERNS OF ORGANIZATION

Use the following exercises to practice reading for patterns of organization.

PASSAGE #1

Read the passage and answer the question that follows.

Regardless of the type of job you have, you have to divide your time between work and school. The following suggestions will help you balance these two segments of your life. First of all, make sure that your supervisor knows you are attending college and that your job helps pay for it. He or she may be more understanding and helpful if he or she knows you are a serious student. In addition, try to find a coworker who   5
may be willing to switch work hours or take your hours if you need extra time to study. Next, if possible, try to build a work schedule around your class schedule. For example, if you have an eight o'clock class on Tuesday mornings, try not to work until midnight on Monday night. Finally, allow study time for each class. Make sure you have time between class sessions to do homework and complete assigned readings. For example,   10
if you have a Tuesday/Thursday class, make sure you have some study time between the two sessions. (Adapted from Kathleen T. McWhorter, *Study and Critical Thinking Skills in College*, 5th ed., New York: Longman, 2003.)

1. For this passage, the author uses an organizational pattern that
   A. summarizes the problems of a working student.
   B. gives reasons for attending school full-time instead of working and studying at the same time.
   C. discusses how to get along with your supervisor and coworkers.
   D. gives instructions on how to balance work and school time.

PASSAGE #2

Read the passage and answer the question that follows.

Contrary to popular assumption, slavery was not usually based on racism, but on one of three other factors. The first was debt. In some cultures, an individual who could not pay a debt could be enslaved by the creditor. The second was crime. Instead of being killed, a murderer or thief might be enslaved by the family of the victim as compensation for their loss. The third was war and conquest. When one group of people   5 conquered another, they often enslaved some of the vanquished. Historian Gerda Lerner notes that the first people enslaved through warfare were women. When premodern men raided a village or camp, they killed the men, raped the women, and then brought the women back as slaves. The women were valued for sexual purposes, for reproduction, and for their labor. (James M. Henslin, *Sociology*, 6th ed., Boston: Allyn and Bacon, 2003.)   10

2. For this passage, the author uses an organizational pattern that
   A. describes what happened to women after warfare in premodern times.
   B. explains the reasons for slavery.
   C. contrasts premodern and modern forms of slavery.
   D. defines slavery.

PASSAGE #3

Read the passage and answer the question that follows.

Cyberliteracy is not purely a print literacy, nor is Internet literacy purely an oral literacy. Cyberliteracy is an electronic literacy—newly emerging in a new medium—that combines features of both print and the spoken word, and the medium does so in ways that change how we read, speak, think, and interact with others. Once we see that on-line texts are not exactly written or spoken, we begin to understand that cyberliteracy   5
requires a special form of critical thinking. Communication in the online world is not quite like anything else. Written messages, such as letters (even when written on a computer), are usually created slowly and with reflection, allowing the writer to think and revise even as the document is chugging away at the printer. But electronic *discourse*—talking, conversing, interacting—encourages us to reply quickly, often in a more oral   10
style. In discourse, we blur the normally accepted distinctions, such as writing versus speaking, and conventions, such as punctuation and spelling. Normal rules about writing, editing, and revising a document do not make much sense in this environment. (Adapted from Leonard J. Shedletsky and Joan E. Aitken, *Human Communication on the Internet*, Boston: Allyn and Bacon, 2004.)

3. For this passage, the authors use an organizational pattern that
   A. defines cyberliteracy.
   B. shows similarities between online and written communication.
   C. describes critical thinking.
   D. explains how to become cyberliterate.

PASSAGE #4

Read the passage and answer the questions that follow.

The most boisterous forms of entertainment in the Roman Empire involved the excitement of a roaring crowd. The huge seating capacity of the Circus Maximus, which could probably accommodate a quarter of a million spectators, made chariot races an extremely popular diversion in the city of Rome. Bets were placed both on and off the track, and the seating regulations of the Colosseum, which separated the sexes, did not   5 operate in the Circus, where men and women sat together, heightening the tension and festivity of the atmosphere. An element of danger also contributed to the air of excitement, as ancient chariot races afforded the same kinds of entertaining and often fatal crashes that are common to automobile competitions today. But the tumult of the races was tame in comparison to the spectacles offered in the amphitheaters of the empire, where emperors, local officials, and public-minded citizens vied with one another to give the most memorable shows.   10

Sadism and voyeurism were key elements in Roman entertainment. Savage gladiatorial combats to the death and the feeding of humans to wild beasts are not inventions of Hollywood; they were a staple of Roman entertainment. Most residents of the empire   15 who lived anywhere near a city saw a number of people killed in the arena over their lifetimes. Nearly all would have been mystified by the anxieties people feel today about the make-believe violence in the movies and on television, and the ghoulish curiosity about witnessing bloody deaths that people try to suppress and deny in our own society seems to have caused the Romans no embarrassment. Uninhibitedly, they flocked in   20 great numbers to the arenas of doom. (Adapted from Richard L. Greaves, Robert Zaller, and Jennifer Tolbert Roberts, *Civilizations of the West*, New York: Longman, 1997.)

4. For this passage, the authors use an overall organizational pattern that
    A. gives the effects of violent entertainment on the Roman people.
    B. explains how gladiators fought in the arena.
    C. gives examples of the forms of entertainment that excited the Romans.
    D. analyzes the reasons Romans enjoyed sadism and voyeurism.

5. The second paragraph is organized by
    A. contrasting the Romans' acceptance of violence to our anxiety about seeing violence in movies and television.
    B. defining sadism.
    C. explaining the key elements of Roman entertainment: sadism and voyeurism.
    D. describing Hollywood gladiator movies.

PASSAGE #5

Read the passage and answer the question that follows.

Nonflowing bodies of water such as lakes become contaminated in stages. First, pollutants such as animal fertilizer, detergents, industrial waste, and sewage are dumped into the water supply. As a result, an accelerated growth of algae occurs. As algae growth skyrockets on a diet of inorganic pollutants, especially nitrogen and phosphorus, a blanket of slime covers the water. Eventual death of the algae results in   5 bacterial decomposition that consumes the oxygen present. This oxygen deficit kills fish and other lake inhabitants, many of which are valuable as food resources, and as recently suggested, disrupts freshwater animals' endocrine systems. Eventually, the body of water becomes contaminated beyond use. (Adapted from David J. Anspaugh and Gene Ezell, *Teaching Today's Health*, 7th ed., San Francisco: Benjamin Cummings, 2004.)

6. This paragraph is organized by
   A. listing the types of chemicals that pollute our water.
   B. describing the growth of algae.
   C. defining water pollution.
   D. explaining the process of water contamination.

PASSAGE #6

Read the passage and answer the questions that follow.

One type of anxiety disorder is the panic disorder. The hallmark of panic disorder is the experience of panic attacks, episodes of intense fear or discomfort accompanied by symptoms such as palpitations, breathing difficulties, chest pain, nausea, sweating, dizziness, fear of going crazy or doing something uncontrollable, fear of impending doom, and a sense of unreality. Symptoms reach their peak within a few minutes of the beginning of an attack, which can last from minutes to hours. Often these attacks are not associated with a specific situation or object and may even seem to occur randomly. One study of college students found that 12% of the participants experienced spontaneous panic attacks during their lifetimes. Some people may have episodes of panic attacks, with years of remission; others may have more persistent symptoms.

People with panic disorder worry constantly about having more attacks, and in their attempts to avoid or minimize panic attacks, they may change their behavior. People may go to great lengths to try to avoid panic attacks, quitting their jobs, avoiding places (such as hot, crowded rooms or events) or activities that increase their heart rate (such as exercise or watching suspenseful movies or sporting events). Some people fear or avoid places that might be difficult to leave should a panic attack occur, for example, a plane or car. They may avoid leaving home or do so only with a close friend or relative. Such fear and avoidance can lead to agoraphobia, a condition in which the avoidance of places or activities restricts daily life. In some cases, people have agoraphobia without panic attacks, avoiding many places because either they fear losing control of themselves in some way (such as losing bladder control) or they fear the occurrence of less severe but still distressing panic symptoms. (Stephen M. Kosslyn and Robin S. Rosenberg, *Psychology*, 2nd ed., Boston: Allyn and Bacon, 2004.)

7. For this passage, the authors use the overall organizational pattern that
   A. contrasts panic attacks with agoraphobia.
   B. explains one type of disorder, panic disorder.
   C. explains recommended strategies for dealing with panic attacks.
   D. classifies the causes of panic attacks.

8. The second paragraph is organized by
   A. giving examples of things people do to avoid or minimize panic attacks.
   B. defining panic disorder.
   C. giving the steps for treatment.
   D. comparing types of panic avoidance behavior.

PASSAGE #7

Read the passage and answer the questions that follow.

Plagiarism is using someone else's words and ideas without giving that person proper credit. Even when your use of information may be perfectly legal, you may still be violating ethical standards if you do not give credit to the information source.

Assume, for example, that you are writing a class report on genetically modified foods. In your research, you discover a very good paper on the Web. You decide that parts of this paper would complement your report quite nicely. Under copyright and fair use guidelines, you can reproduce portions of this paper without permission. But does this legal standard mean that you can use someone else's material freely, without giving that person credit? Even though it might be legal under fair use guidelines to reprint the material without notifying the copyright holder, using someone else's material or ideas without giving them credit is plagiarism.

Plagiarism is a serious infraction in most settings. Students can be suspended or expelled from school. Researchers can lose their jobs and their standing in the academic community. Most importantly, plagiarism is serious because it violates several of the reasonable criteria for ethical decision making. Plagiarism violates your obligation to yourself to be truthful, and it violates your obligation to society to produce fair and accurate information. It also violates your obligation to other students and researchers. (Adapted from Laura J. Gurak and John M. Lannon, *A Concise Guide to Technical Communication*, New York: Longman, 2001.)

9. For this passage, the authors use the overall organizational pattern that
   A. analyzes a situation in which plagiarism occurs.
   B. lists types of plagiarism.
   C. defines plagiarism.
   D. tells how to use information from the Web.

10. The third paragraph is organized by
   A. describing the effects of plagiarism on students.
   B. defining ethical decision making.
   C. contrasting plagiarism at college and at work.
   D. giving reasons why plagiarism is a serious infraction.

PASSAGE #8

Read the passage and answer the questions that follow.

During the seventeenth and eighteenth centuries, the process of childbirth in colonial America was conducted by women. The typical woman gave birth to her children at home, while female relatives and neighbors clustered at her bedside to offer support and encouragement.

Most women were assisted in childbirth not by a doctor but by a midwife. Most midwives were older women who relied on practical experience in delivering children. One midwife, Martha Ballard, who practiced in Augusta, Maine, delivered 996 babies with only 4 recorded fatalities. Skilled midwives were highly valued. Communities tried to attract experienced midwives by offering a salary or a rent-free house. In addition to assisting in childbirth, midwives helped deliver the offspring of animals, attended the baptisms and burials of infants, and testified in court cases of illegitimate babies.   10

During labor, midwives administered no painkillers, except for alcohol. Pain in child-birth was considered God's punishment for Eve's sin of eating the forbidden fruit in the Garden of Eden. Women were merely advised to have patience, to pray, and during labor, to restrain their groans and cries which upset the people near them.   15

After delivery, new mothers were often treated to a banquet. At one such event, visitors feasted on boiled pork, beef, poultry, roast beef, turkey pie, and tarts. Women from well-to-do families were then expected to spend three to four weeks in bed convalescing. Their attendants kept the fireplace burning and wrapped them in a heavy blanket in order to help them sweat out "poisons." Women from poorer families were generally   20 back at work in one or two days. (Adapted from James Kirby Martin et al., *America and Its Peoples*, New York: Longman, 2004.)

11. For this passage, the authors use the overall organizational pattern that
     A. gives religious reasons for pain in childbirth.
     B. illustrates the ways in which women assisted childbirth.
     C. explains the differences between childbirth for rich and poor women.
     D. describes the dangers of childbirth.

12. The second paragraph is organized by
     A. describing midwives.
     B. arguing the advantages of midwives over doctors.
     C. listing the achievements of Martha Ballard.
     D. explaining how the midwife assists in childbirth.

PASSAGE #9

Read the passage and answer the questions that follow.

Deborah Tannen, sociologist and author, explains the differences in the listening be-havior of men and women. Women seek to build rapport and establish a closer rela-tionship and so they use listening to achieve these ends. For example, women use more listening cues that let the other person know they are paying attention and are interested. On the other hand, men not only use fewer listening cues but interrupt   5 more and will often change the topic to one they know more about or one that is less relational or people-oriented to one that is more factual, for example, sports, statistics, economic developments, or political problems. Men, research shows, play up their expertise, emphasize it, and use it to dominate the conversation. Women play down their expertise.   10

Research shows that men communicate with women in the same way they do with other men. Men are not showing disrespect for their female conversational partners, but are simply communicating as they normally do. Women, too, communicate as they do not only with men but also with other women.

Tannen argues that the goal of a man in conversation is to be accorded respect, and so he seeks to display his knowledge and expertise even if he has to change the topic from one he knows little about to one he knows a great deal about. A woman, on the other hand, seeks to be liked, and so she expresses agreement and less frequently interrupts to take her turn as speaker.   15

Men and women also show that they are listening in different ways. A woman is more apt to give lots of listening cues, such as interjecting "yeah, uh-uh," nodding in agreement, and smiling. A man is more likely to listen quietly, without giving lots of listening cues as feedback. Tannen also argues, however, that men do listen less to women than women listen to men. The reason is that listening places the person in an inferior position whereas speaking places the person in a superior position.   20

There is no evidence to show that these differences represent any negative motives on the part of men to prove themselves superior or of women to ingratiate themselves. Rather, these differences in listening are largely the result of the way in which men and women have been socialized. (Adapted from Joseph A. DeVito, *Essentials of Human Communication*, 3rd ed., New York: Longman, 1999.)   25

13. For this passage, the author uses the overall organizational pattern that
    A. illustrates conversational behaviors of men and women.
    B. argues that men need to prove themselves superior when in conversation.
    C. contrasts the listening behaviors of men and women.
    D. discusses the negative effects of male listening behavior on women.

14. The first paragraph is organized by
    A. offering examples of how men do not listen to women.
    B. contrasting the listening cues used by men and women.
    C. explaining how women use listening to get close to a person.
    D. developing the theory that men do not disrespect female conversational patterns.

Study Hint

The following section of exercises includes some passages that you have already seen in one or more of the previous sections. The purpose of presenting you with the same passages in different sections is two-fold. First, the repetition imitates the state exit exam, which presents you with a passage and then asks you several different types of questions based on that one passage. These sets of questions address different skills. For example, one passage may have the questions about the following skills: main idea, relevance of supporting details, author's purpose, types of organization, word meaning in context.

The state exit test's use of one passage for several questions is the second reason for working with the same passages throughout the workbook. Many of these skills are connected to each other. For example, the author's purpose is closely connected to the pattern of organization and reinforced by tone. So it is important for you to see how one passage uses each of these skills for an overall effect. Study smart; compare these questions to the other sections where the passages also appear, and think about the relationship between the skills.

PASSAGE #10

Read the passage and answer the question that follows.

On April 20, 1999, a school shooting of such immense proportions occurred which radically, if not permanently, altered public thinking and debate about student safety and security. After months of planning and preparation, 18-year-old Eric Harris and 17-year-old Dylan Klebold armed themselves with guns and explosives and headed off to Columbine High School in Littleton, Colorado, to celebrate Adolph Hitler's birthday in a manner fitting their hero. By the time the assault ended with self-inflicted fatal gunshots, a dozen students and one teacher lay dead. 5

In understanding the horrific actions of schoolyard snipers, it is as important to examine friendships as it is to delve into family background. At Columbine, Harris and Klebold were generally seen as geeks or nerds, from the point of view of any of the large student cliques—the jocks, the punks, etc. Though excluded from mainstream student culture, they banded together and bonded together with several of their fellow outcasts in what they came to call the "Trench Coat Mafia." The image they attempted to create was clearly one of power and dominance—the barbaric incivility, the forces of darkness, the preoccupation with Hitler, the celebration of evil and villainy. Harris and Klebold desperately wanted to feel important; and in the preparations they made to murder their classmates, the two shooters got their wish. For more than a year, they plotted and planned, colluded and conspired to put one over on their schoolmates, teachers, and parents. They amassed an arsenal of weapons, strategized about logistics, and made final preparations—yet, until it was too late, not a single adult got wind of what Harris and Klebold intended to do. 10 15 20

Birds of a feather may kill together. Harris, the leader, would likely have enjoyed the respect and admiration from Klebold, who in turn would have felt uplifted by the praise he received from his revered buddy. In their relationship, the two boys got from one another what was otherwise missing from their lives—they felt special, they gained a sense of belonging, they were united against the world. As Harris remarked, as he and his friend made last-minute preparations to commit mass murder: "This is just a two-man war against everything else." (Adapted from James Alan Fox and Jack Levin, *The Will to Kill*, Boston: Allyn and Bacon, 2001.) 25

15. For this passage, the authors use the overall organizational pattern that
    A. describes the Columbine High School massacre.
    B. lists the effects of the Columbine High School massacre.
    C. tells the process Harris and Klebold used to prepare for the shootings.
    D. analyzes Harris and Klebold's friendship to understand their crime.

PASSAGE #11

Read the passage and answer the question that follows.

Each of the 2000 or so species of firefly has its own way to signal a mate. When a female sees flashes of light from a male of her species, she reacts with flashes of her own. If the male sees her flashes, he automatically gives another display and flies in the female's di-

rection. Members of both sexes are responding to particular patterns of light flashes
characteristic of their species. Some flash more often than others or during different   5
hours, while other species give fewer but longer flashes. Many species produce light of
a characteristic color: yellow, bluish-green, or reddish. Mating occurs when the female's
display leads a male to her, and most females stop flashing after they mate. But in a few
species, a mated female will continue to flash, using a pattern that attracts males of other
firefly species. A veritable *femme fatale*, she waits until an alien male gets close, then   10
grabs and eats him. (Adapted from Neil A. Campbell, Lawrence G. Mitchell, and Jane
B. Reece, *Biology*, 3rd ed., San Francisco: Benjamin Cummings, 2000.)

16. This paragraph is organized by
    A. explaining the flashing patterns of fireflies.
    B. illustrating the cannablistic female firefly behavior.
    C. describing the process fireflies use to signal mates.
    D. giving examples of the length and color of fireflies' flashes.

PASSAGE #12

Read the passage and answer the questions that follow.

Many overweight and obese individuals are trying to lose weight. Although it took several months and years to put on the extra weight, many of them are looking for a quick
way to lose that weight. This attitude results in choosing quick-weight-loss diets that
are not effective and may be harmful.

Some choose metabolic products, such as herbs or caffeine, to lose weight. Herbs have   5
not been shown to speed the loss of fat, and caffeine shows little promise as a weight-
loss aid.

Others go on very-low-calorie diets, which severely restrict nutrients and can result in
serious metabolic imbalances. Weight can be lost on this type of diet; much of the
weight lost will be lean protein tissue and/or water, not fat. This results in harm to the   10
muscles (including the heart), loss of essential vitamins and minerals through the water
loss, and dizziness and fatigue. Further, if one cuts calories, the metabolism slows; once
this person goes off the diet, the metabolism remains slow and the body continues to
use few calories—and the pounds come back.

Liquid protein diets operate on the theory that insulin is controlled and therefore more   15
fat is burned. With this type of diet, ketosis will result. Ketosis will increase blood levels
of uric acid, a risk factor for gout and kidney stones. There is new research evidence
that carbohydrates lead to fat storage and weight; further, the excessive protein in this
diet can damage the kidneys and cause osteoporosis. Prescription drugs, such as Redux
and Pondimin (fen-phen), curb hunger by increasing the level of serotonin in the brain.   20
These were intended for the obese, but they were banned in 1997 after the FDA found
strong evidence that they could seriously damage the heart.

Some people try crash diets to lose a moderate amount of weight in a very short period.
These types of diets can damage several body systems and have been proven not to
work because most of these individuals regain their weight. This yo-yo dieting causes   25

many health problems and shortens lifespan. The best way to lose weight is to lose weight slowly (no more than one-half to one pound a week), eat properly and in moderation, and exercise. (Adapted from David J. Anspaugh and Gene Ezell, *Teaching Today's Health*, 7th ed., San Francisco: Benjamin Cummings, 2004.)

17. For this passage, the authors use the overall organizational pattern that
    A. explains the effects of many quick-weight-loss diets.
    B. describes the types of quick-weight-loss-diets.
    C. gives the effects of the prescription drugs Redux and Pondimin (fen-phen).
    D. contrasts liquid protein diets with very-low-calorie diets.

18. The third paragraph is organized by
    A. explaining how weight is lost on very-low-calorie diets.
    B. describing the effects of very-low-calorie diets.
    C. defining very-low-calorie diets.
    D. arguing against using a very-low-calorie diet for weight loss.

PASSAGE #13

Read the passage and answer the question that follows.

President Truman's decision to order the atomic bombings on the Japanese cities of Hiroshima and Nagasaki has been the subject of intense historical debate. Truman's defenders argue that the bombs ended the war quickly, avoiding the necessity of a costly invasion and the probable loss of tens of thousands of Americans' lives and hundreds of Japanese lives. According to some intelligence estimates, an invasion might have cost   5
268,000 American casualties, with Japanese costs several times that figure.

Truman's defenders also argue that Hiroshima and Nagasaki were legitimate targets with both military bases and war industry, and their civilian populations had been showered with leaflets warning them to evacuate. Finally, they argue that two bombs were ultimately necessary to end the war. They note that even after the atomic bomb   10
had fallen on Hiroshima, the Japanese war minister implored the nation's Supreme Council "for one last great battle on Japanese soil—as demanded by the national honor. . . . Would it not be wondrous for this whole nation to be destroyed like a beautiful flower."

Truman's critics argue that the war might have ended even without the atomic bomb-   15
ings. They maintain that the Japanese economy would have been strangled by a continued naval blockade and forced to surrender by conventional firebombing. The revisionists also contend that the President had options apart from using the bombs. They believe that it might have been possible to induce a Japanese surrender by a demonstration of the atomic bomb's power or by providing a more specific warning of the   20
damage it could produce or by guaranteeing the emperor's position in postwar Japan.

The revisionists also believe that estimates of potential American casualties were grossly inflated after the war to justify the bombing. Finally, they argue that the bomb might have been dropped mainly to justify its cost or to scare the Soviet Union. The Soviet Union entered the Japanese war August 8, and some revisionists charge that the bomb-   25

ings were designed to end the war before the Red army could occupy northern China. ⁵
(Adapted from James Kirby Martin et al., *America and Its Peoples*, 5th ed., New York:
Longman, 2004.)

19. For this passage, the authors use the overall organizational pattern that
    A. gives reasons that the bombing of Hiroshima and Nagasaki ended the war.
    B. presents the arguments for and against Truman's decision to bomb Hiroshima ¹⁰
       and Nagasaki.
    C. gives the sequence of events that led to the dropping of the bombs.
    D. explains causes for dropping atomic bombs on Hiroshima and Nagasaki.

PASSAGE #14

¹⁵

Read the passage and answer the question that follows.

Fungi have a number of practical uses for humans. Most of us have eaten mushrooms
although we may not have realized that we were ingesting the fruiting bodies of subterranean fungi. In addition, mushrooms are not the only fungi we eat. The distinctive ²⁰
flavors of certain kinds of cheeses, including Roquefort and blue cheese, come from
the fungi used to ripen them. Highly prized by gourmets are truffles, the fruiting bodies
of certain mycorrhizal fungi associated with tree roots. The unicellular fungi, the yeasts,
are important in food production. Yeasts are used in baking, brewing, and winemaking.
Fungi are medically valuable as well. Some fungi produce antibiotics that are used to
treat bacterial diseases. In fact, the first antibiotic discovered was penicillin, which is ²⁵
made by the common mold called *Penicillium.* (Adapted from Neil A. Campbell,
Lawrence G. Mitchell, and Jane B. Reece, *Biology*, 3rd ed., San Francisco: Benjamin
Cummings, 2000.)

20. This paragraph is organized by
    A. describing how fungi ripens cheeses.
    B. defining fungi.
    C. classifying the types of fungi.
    D. giving examples of how people use fungi.

SECTION 2 ◆ RELATIONSHIPS *WITHIN* A SENTENCE

This is the second type of question that concerns patterns of organization. With this question, you
are expected to understand *how the parts of a sentence relate to one another.* Once again, knowing
the transitional words (key words) that go with each pattern is vital for understanding how the parts
of a sentence relate so that you can answer these questions correctly. (See the section in this book on
Patterns of Organization for a list of patterns and common transitions.)
When you are asked to find the relationship within a sentence, use the following process:

1. **Identify the <u>parts</u> of the sentence, or where the sentence breaks.**
   Many times, although not always, the parts of the sentence are joined by a piece of punctuation: a comma, a colon, dashes, a semicolon, etc.

2. **Look for transitional words (key words) at the beginning of one of the parts.**
   The transitional word will often clarify the relationship between the parts of the sentence.

3. **If there are no key words, try to analyze how the two parts relate.**
   Is one part an example of the other? Does one part contrast with the other? Does one part cause another?

> **Example #1**
> While mainland Europe suffered through the Thirty Years' War, England faced serious domestic stress under the first two Stuart kings.

Using the process outlined above, you can find the parts of the sentence by noting that there is a comma that separates the sentence into two parts: "While mainland Europe suffered through the Thirty Years' War" and "England faced serious domestic stress under the first two Stuart Kings." Next, if you look for transitional words at the beginning of one of the parts, you'll notice the word "while" at the beginning of the first part. That word is a transitional word for the "compare and contrast" pattern. Therefore, the relationship within the sentence is one of contrast, or compare and contrast. The author is showing how the situation of mainland Europe was different from that of the country of England.

Important: **The relationship within a sentence has nothing to do with the overall pattern of organization.**

> **Example #2 – What is the relationship within the LAST sentence of this paragraph?**
> All college students experience stress, which is *caused* by many factors. For example, a new student who is unfamiliar with the campus may become stressful just trying to find his or her way around on campus to arrive at class on time. *Another* cause of stress in university students is being away from family and friends, an important emotional support system. *Although* both male and female students feel stress, female students are *more likely to* display their feelings *than* male students.

The overall pattern of organization is <u>cause and effect</u> because the passage points out the causes and effects of stress experienced by college students. However, in the last sentence, there is a relationship of compare and contrast <u>within</u> the sentence. The sentence breaks into two parts at the comma, and the word "although" appears at the beginning of the first part. "Although" is a transitional word for compare and contrast. Thus, the author is contrasting the differences between male and female students:

> *Although* both male and female students feel stress, female students are *more likely to* display their feelings *than* male students.

> **Example #3**
> Plagiarism violates your obligation to yourself to be truthful, and it violates your obligation to society to produce fair and accurate information. (Gurak and Lannon, *A Concise Guide to Technical Communication*, New York: Longman, 2001.)

The sentence breaks into two parts at the comma, and the transitional word "and" appears at the beginning of the second part. "And" is a clue word for the addition pattern. Therefore, the relationship within this sentence is one of addition because the author is adding one more detail about the subject.

Example #4
Children who enjoy a positive relationship with their parents may agree more with their parents' higher status than do children who have a negative relationship with their parents. (Adapted from Stephen M. Kosslyn and Robin S. Rosenberg, *Psychology,* 2nd ed., Boston: Allyn and Bacon, 2004.)

In this sentence, there is no punctuation to indicate where the sentence breaks into parts. Therefore, you must find the parts without that aid. Logically, you'll notice "Children who enjoy a positive relationship with their parents" and "children who have a negative relationship with their parents." Even though there is no transitional word to indicate the relationship within the sentence, logic shows that it is one of compare and contrast because the author is comparing children who have a positive relationship with their parents to children who have a negative relationship.

Example #5
Although the rainforest is lush, its soils are poor because torrential rains cause soil erosion and intense heat leaches the soil of nutrients and burns off humus or organic matter that is essential for soil fertility. (Brummet, Palmira, et al., *Civilization,* 9th ed., New York: Longman, 2000.)

This final example illustrates another difficulty with identifying relationships within a sentence: sometimes, more than one pattern can be seen because the sentence breaks into more than two parts. When that happens, you must identify the two MAIN parts of the sentence and select the pattern that corresponds to that relationship.

In this sentence, there is a break after the comma, and there is the transitional word "although" at the beginning of the first part. Therefore, you might conclude that the sentence is contrasting the lushness of the rainforest with the poorness of its soils. However, that is not the real point of the sentence. Instead, most of the sentence shows WHY the soil is so poor. Therefore, the MAIN relationship within the sentence is one of cause and effect. The transitional word "because" helps clarify this relationship. When you have to decide upon two patterns, consider the author's purpose: why did he or she write the sentence? Here, the author's purpose is to show what causes the rainforest soil to be poor even though the vegetation (implied) is lush.

▶▶| *Secrets to Success*

- *Find where the sentence breaks into parts (usually at a piece of punctuation).*
- *Look for transitional words (clue words for the pattern) at the beginning of one of the parts.*
- *Ask yourself,* What is the relationship between the ideas? *Are they showing an example of something? Making a comparison? Showing an effect or cause of something? Or perhaps using some other type of relationship?*
- *Be aware that not all sentences have transitional phrases, and some phrases used may not match the relationship that is being shown. For this reason, always ask,* What is the relationship between the ideas?
- *When it looks like there are two patterns within a sentence, try to identify the MAIN relationship by asking yourself why the author wrote the sentence. What is he or she trying to tell you?*

SECTION 2 ◆ DIAGNOSTIC: RELATIONSHIPS *WITHIN* A SENTENCE

Read the passages and apply the strategies described above for finding relationships within sentences. When you are done, check your work with the answers immediately following the diagnostic. Even if you get a perfect score here, go ahead and complete the exercises in this section; they are designed to help build confidence and to give you practice for future test success.

Read the passages below and answer the questions that follow.

PASSAGE #1

One of the most important results of the Civil War was the freedom gained by southern slaves. In the decade following the defeat of the Confederacy, hundreds of thousands of men and women migrated throughout the South searching for land, work, and relatives lost through prewar sale. Some former slaves, however, took an even bolder step, leaving the South altogether and traveling west in search of cheap farmland or north   5
seeking industrial employment. While most faced difficult years adjusting to the world of free labor and white prejudice, none would have exchanged their life of freedom for the days of bondage. (Nash and Schultz, *Retracing the Past: Readings in the History of the American People*, 4th ed., New York: Longman, 2000.)

1. What is the relationship within the sentence, "While most faced difficult years adjusting to the world of free labor and white prejudice, none would have exchanged their life of freedom for the days of bondage"?
   A. Cause and effect
   B. Summary
   C. Contrast
   D. Comparison

2. What is the relationship within the sentence, "In the decade following the defeat of the Confederacy, hundreds of thousands of men and women migrated throughout the South searching for land, work, and relatives lost through prewar sale"?
   A. Cause and effect
   B. Time order
   C. Example
   D. Contrast

PASSAGE #2

Walt Whitman, whose *Leaves of Grass* (1855) was the last of the great literary works of his brief outpouring of genius, was the most romantic and by far the most distinctly American writer of his age. He was born on Long Island, outside of New York City, in 1819. At 13, he left school and became a printer's devil; thereafter he held a succession of newspaper jobs in the metropolitan area. He was an ardent Jacksonian and later a   5
Free Soiler, which got him into hot water with a number of the publishers for whom he worked. (Garraty and Carnes, *The American Nation: A History of the United States*, 10th ed., New York: Longman, 2000.)

3. What is the relationship within the sentence, "He was an ardent Jacksonian and later a Free Soiler, which got him into hot water with a number of the publishers for whom he worked"?
    A. Cause and effect
    B. Addition
    C. Process
    D. Comparison

PASSAGE #3

Self-disclosure is a type of communication in which you reveal information about your-self, in which you move information from the hidden self into the open self. Overt statements about the self as well as slips of the tongue, unconscious nonverbal move-ments, and public confessions would all be considered forms of self-disclosure.

Self-disclosure is information previously unknown by the receiver. This may vary from   5
the relatively commonplace ("I'm really afraid of that French exam") to the extremely
significant ("I'm so depressed, I feel like committing suicide"). (DeVito, *Essentials of
Human Communication*, 3rd ed., Boston: Allyn and Bacon, 1999.)

4. What is the relationship within the sentence, "Overt statements about the self as well as slips of the tongue, unconscious nonverbal movements, and public confessions would all be con-sidered forms of self-disclosure"?
    A. Addition
    B. Summary
    C. Example
    D. Definition

5. What is the relationship within the sentence, "This may vary from the relatively commonplace ('I'm really afraid of that French exam') to the extremely significant ('I'm so depressed, I feel like committing suicide')"?
    A. Contrast
    B. Comparison
    C. Example
    D. Definition

PASSAGE #4

Presidents and prime ministers govern quite differently. Prime ministers never face di-vided government, for example. Since they represent the majority party or coalition, they can almost always depend on winning on votes. In addition, party discipline is better in parliamentary systems than in the United States. Prime ministers generally dif-fer from presidents in background as well. They must be party leaders, as we have seen,   5
and they are usually very effective communicators, their skills honed in the rough and tumble of parliamentary debate. In addition, they have had substantial experience deal-ing with national issues, unlike American governors who may move directly into pres-idency. Cabinet members, who are usually senior members of parliament, have similar

advantages. (Edwards, Wattenberg, and Lineberry, *Government in America*, 9th ed.,   10
New York: Longman, 2000.)

6. What is the relationship within the sentence, "Since they represent the majority party or coalition, they can almost always depend on winning on votes"?
    A. Statement and clarification
    B. Addition
    C. Compare and contrast
    D. Cause and effect

7. What is the relationship within the sentence, "In addition, they have had substantial experience dealing with national issues, unlike American governors who may move directly into presidency"?
    A. Addition
    B. Comparison
    C. Contrast
    D. Definition

Answers to Diagnostic

1. C
2. A (This sentence shows time order at the beginning, but the MAIN point of the sentence is to show WHY they were migrating, which is cause and effect.)
3. A
4. C
5. A (This sentence shows examples in the parentheses, but the MAIN point of the sentence is to contrast the two extremes of "commonplace" and "significant.")
6. D
7. C (This sentence shows addition at the beginning, but the MAIN point of the sentence is to contrast prime ministers and presidents.)

📚 *Study Hint*

Just as before, the following section of exercises pulls passages that you have already seen in one or more of the previous sections. Remember, the purpose of presenting you with the same passages in different sections is to imitate the state exit exam, which presents you with a passage and then asks you several different types of questions based on that one passage. Also, many of these skills are connected to each other.

For example, the author's purpose is closely connected to the pattern of organization and reinforced by tone, so it is important for you to see how one passage uses each of these skills for an overall effect. For example, the preceding section, Patterns of Organization, and this section, Relationships Within a Sentence, and the next section, Relationships Between Sentences, are all so closely related that you will benefit from seeing how they tie into each other.

So, study smart. Compare these questions to each of the sections where the passages also appear, and think about the relationships between the skills.

SECTION 2 ◆ EXERCISES: RELATIONSHIPS *WITHIN* A SENTENCE

Use the following exercises to practice reading for relationships within a sentence.

PASSAGE #1

Read the passage and answer the questions that follow.

Contrary to popular assumption, slavery was not usually based on racism, but on one of three other factors. The first was debt. In some cultures, an individual who could not pay a debt could be enslaved by the creditor. The second was crime. Instead of being killed, a murderer or thief might be enslaved by the family of the victim as compensation for their loss. The third was war and conquest. When one group of people conquered another, they often enslaved some of the vanquished. Historian Gerda Lerner notes that the first people enslaved through warfare were women. When premodern men raided a village or camp, they killed the men, raped the women, and then brought the women back as slaves. The women were valued for sexual purposes, for reproduction, and for their labor. (James M. Henslin, *Sociology*, 6th ed., Boston: Allyn and Bacon, 2003.)

5

10

1. "When one group of people conquered another, they often enslaved some of the vanquished." (lines 5–6)

   The relationship of parts within the sentence above is

   A. contrast.
   B. cause and effect.
   C. process.
   D. summary.

2. "The women were valued for sexual purposes, for reproduction, and for their labor." (lines 9–10)

   The relationship of parts within the sentence above is

   A. summary.
   B. example.
   C. clarification.
   D. listing.

PASSAGE #2

Read the passage and answer the question that follows.

Nonflowing bodies of water such as lakes become contaminated in stages. First, pollutants such as animal fertilizer, detergents, industrial waste, and sewage are dumped into the water supply. As a result, an accelerated growth of algae occurs. As algae growth skyrockets on a diet of inorganic pollutants, especially nitrogen and phosphorus, a blanket of slime covers the water. Eventual death of the algae results in bacterial decomposition that consumes the oxygen present. This oxygen deficit kills fish and other lake inhabitants, many of which are valuable as food resources, and, as recently suggested, disrupts freshwater animals' endocrine systems. Eventually, the body of

5

water becomes contaminated beyond use. (Adapted from David J. Anspaugh and Gene Ezell, *Teaching Today's Health*, 7th ed., San Francisco: Benjamin Cummings, 2004.)

3. "As algae growth skyrockets on a diet of inorganic pollutants, especially nitrogen and phosphorus, a blanket of slime covers the water." (lines 3–5)

The relationship of parts within the sentence above is

A. spatial order.
B. example.
C. addition.
D. cause and effect.

PASSAGE #3

Read the passage and answer the question that follows.

Cyberliteracy is not purely a print literacy, nor is Internet literacy purely an oral literacy. Cyberliteracy is an electronic literacy—newly emerging in a new medium—that combines features of both print and the spoken word, and the medium does so in ways that change how we read, speak, think, and interact with others. Once we see that online texts are not exactly written or spoken, we begin to understand that cyberliteracy requires a special form 5
of critical thinking. Communication in the online world is not quite like anything else. Written messages, such as letters (even when written on a computer), are usually created slowly and with reflection, allowing the writer to think and revise even as the document is chugging away at the printer. But electronic *discourse*—talking, conversing, interacting—encourages us to reply quickly, often in a more oral style. In discourse, we blur the 10
normally accepted distinctions, such as writing versus speaking, and conventions, such as punctuation and spelling. Normal rules about writing, editing, and revising a document do not make much sense in this environment. (Adapted from Leonard J. Shedletsky and Joan E. Aitken, *Human Communication on the Internet*, Boston: Allyn and Bacon, 2004.)

4. "Cyberliteracy is an electronic literacy—newly emerging in a new medium—that combines features of both print and the spoken word, and the medium does so in ways that change how we read, speak, think, and interact with others." (lines 2–4)

The relationship of parts within the sentence above is

A. definition.
B. addition.
C. cause and effect.
D. summary.

PASSAGE #4

Read the passage and answer the question that follows.

Research shows that men communicate with women in the same way they do with other men. Men are not showing disrespect for their female conversational partners, but are simply communicating as they normally do. Women, too, communicate as they do not only with men but also with other women. (Adapted from Joseph A. DeVito, *Essentials of Human Communication*, 3rd ed., New York: Longman, 1999.)

5. "Research shows that men communicate with women in the same way they do with other men." (lines 1–2)

The relationship of parts within the sentence above is

A. example.
B. cause and effect.
C. comparison.
D. clarification.

PASSAGE #5

Read the passage and answer the questions that follow.

Most women were assisted in childbirth not by a doctor but by a midwife. Most midwives were older women who relied on practical experience in delivering children. One midwife, Martha Ballard, who practiced in Augusta, Maine, delivered 996 babies with only 4 recorded fatalities. Skilled midwives were highly valued. Communities tried to attract experienced midwives by offering a salary or a rent-free house. In addition to   5
assisting in childbirth, midwives helped deliver the offspring of animals, attended the baptisms and burials of infants, and testified in court cases of illegitimate babies.

During labor, midwives administered no painkillers, except for alcohol. Pain in childbirth was considered God's punishment for Eve's sin of eating the forbidden fruit in the Garden of Eden. Women were merely advised to have patience, to pray, and during   10
labor, to restrain their groans and cries, which upset the people near them.

After delivery, new mothers were often treated to a banquet. At one such event, visitors feasted on boiled pork, beef, poultry, roast beef, turkey pie, and tarts. Women from well-to-do families were then expected to spend three to four weeks in bed convalescing. Their attendants kept the fireplace burning and wrapped them in a heavy blanket in   15
order to help them sweat out "poisons." Women from poorer families were generally back at work in one or two days. (Adapted from James Kirby Martin et al., *America and Its Peoples*, New York: Longman, 2004.)

6. What is the relationship between parts of the following sentence?

"In addition to assisting in childbirth, midwives helped deliver the offspring of animals, attended the baptisms and burials of infants, and testified in court cases of illegitimate babies." (lines 6–8)

A. Addition
B. Time
C. Process
D. Summary

7. What is the relationship between parts of the following sentence?

"After delivery, new mothers were often treated to a banquet." (line 13)

A. Cause and effect
B. Summary
C. Addition
D. Time

PASSAGE #6

Read the passage and answer the question that follows.

Birds of a feather may kill together. Harris, the leader, would likely have enjoyed the respect and admiration from Klebold, who in turn would have felt uplifted by the praise he received from his revered buddy. In their relationship, the two boys got from one another what was otherwise missing from their lives—they felt special, they gained a sense of belonging, they were united against the world. As Harris remarked, as he and his friend made last-minute preparations to commit mass murder: "This is just a two-man war against everything else." (Adapted from James Alan Fox and Jack Levin, *The Will to Kill*, Boston: Allyn and Bacon, 2001.)

5

8. What is the relationship between parts of the following sentence?

"In their relationship, the two boys got from one another what was otherwise missing from their lives—they felt special, they gained a sense of belonging, they were united against the world." (lines 3–5)

A. Comparison
B. Statement and clarification
C. Contrast
D. Time

PASSAGE #7

Read the passage and answer the question that follows.

Each of the 2000 or so species of firefly has its own way to signal a mate. When a female sees flashes of light from a male of her species, she reacts with flashes of her own. If the male sees her flashes, he automatically gives another display and flies in the female's direction. Members of both sexes are responding to particular patterns of light flashes characteristic of their species. Some flash more often than others or during different hours, while other species give fewer but longer flashes. Many species produce light of a characteristic color: yellow, bluish-green, or reddish. Mating occurs when the female's display leads a male to her, and most females stop flashing after they mate. But in a few species, a mated female will continue to flash, using a pattern that attracts males of other firefly species. A veritable *femme fatale*, she waits until an alien male gets close, then grabs and eats him. (Adapted from Neil A. Campbell, Lawrence G. Mitchell, and Jane B. Reece, *Biology*, 3rd ed., San Francisco: Benjamin Cummings, 2000.)

5

10

9. What is the relationship between parts of the following sentence?

"Some flash more often than others or during different hours, while other species give fewer but longer flashes." (lines 5–6)

A. Comparison
B. Addition
C. Contrast
D. Process

PASSAGE #8

Read the passage and answer the question that follows.

The dramatic difference between the social status of the Egyptian nobility and that of the common people is reflected in their respective burial rites. The keen Egyptian interest in the afterlife, combined with strikingly materialistic criteria for happiness, made lavish tombs for the pharaohs (Egyptian rulers) seem particularly important. Elaborate goods were buried with the pharaoh to assure him a gracious existence in the world beyond, and a processional causeway linked each pyramid to a temple constructed for the worship of the pharaoh; adjacent to the pyramid was a building to house the special cedar boat that would carry him on his voyage to the land of the dead. The pyramid served as the core of an entire necropolis, or city of the dead, which included small pyramids for the wives and daughters of the pharaoh and mastabas for the nobility. Even a minor royal official spent a considerable portion of his time preparing an elaborate tomb for his afterlife, and he would want his corpse to be mummified because of the Egyptian belief that the *ka*, the spirit of life in each person, periodically returned to the body. The corpse of an average farmer, however, was typically wrapped in a piece of linen and deposited in a cave or pit with only a staff and a pair of sandals to facilitate the journey to the next world; some bodies were even left in the open sand of the desert. (Adapted from Richard L. Greaves, Robert Zaller, and Jennifer Tolbert Roberts, *Civilizations of the West*, 2nd ed., New York: Longman, 1997.)

10. What is the relationship between parts of the following sentence?

"Elaborate goods were buried with the pharaoh to assure him a gracious existence in the world beyond, and a processional causeway linked each pyramid to a temple constructed for the worship of the pharaoh; adjacent to the pyramid was a building to house the special cedar boat that would carry him on his voyage to the land of the dead." (lines 4–8)

A. Listing
B. Time
C. Spatial order
D. Addition

SECTION 3 ◆ RELATIONSHIPS *BETWEEN* SENTENCES

As described above in the section *Relationships Within a Sentence*, the same patterns of organization and transitional phrases are used to show the relationship between ideas in two different sentences.

How to Find the Relationship Between Sentences
- Ask: What is the author trying to tell me about the relationship between these two ideas?
- Look at the beginning of the second sentence. Are there any transitional phrases?
- **Be very careful NOT be distracted by the overall pattern or by the pattern *within* one (or both) of the sentences.** The relationship between the two sentences has nothing to do with those.

Example #1
In the paragraph below, the overall pattern is cause and effect, but the relationship between the first and second sentences is the pattern of generalization and example. The author begins with a broad, general statement (the main idea) and follows it with a specific example:

All college students experience stress, which is *caused* by many factors. For example, a new student who is unfamiliar with the campus may become stressful just trying to find his or her way around on campus to arrive at class on time. *Another* cause of stress in university students is being away from family and friends, an important emotional support system. *Although* both male and female students feel stress, female students are *more likely to* display their feelings *than* male students.

Example #2
What is the relationship between these two sentences?

> "For example, a new student who is unfamiliar with the campus may become stressful just trying to find his or her way around on campus to arrive at class on time. *Another* cause of stress in university students is being away from family and friends, an important emotional support system."

The relationship is addition (or simple listing) because the second sentence adds more information to the sentences before it.

Example #3
Tannen argues that the goal of a man in conversation is to be accorded respect, and so he seeks to display his knowledge and expertise even if he has to change the topic from one he knows little about to one he knows a great deal about. A woman, on the other hand, seeks to be liked, so she expresses agreement and less frequently interrupts to take her turn as a speaker. (DeVito, *Essentials of Human Communication,* 3rd ed., Boston: Allyn and Bacon, 1999.)

The second sentence shows a contrasting idea from the first one. Note the transitional phrase, *on the other hand.*

Example #4
Most of us have eaten mushrooms, although we may not have realized that we are ingesting the fruiting bodies of subterranean fungi. In addition, mushrooms are not the only fungi we eat. (Campbell, Mitchell, and Reece, *Biology,* 3rd ed., 2000.)

Here, in the second sentence, the author is adding more details about the subject of the first sentence, so the pattern between the sentences is one of addition.

Example #5
Federal courts ordered registration (for the draft) suspended while several young men filed suit. These men argued that the registration requirement was a gender-based discrimination that violated the due process clause of the Fifth Amendment. (Edwards, Wattenberg, and Lineberry, *Government in America,* 9th ed., New York: Longman, 2000.)

In the absence of any helpful transitions, the reader must try to determine why the author wrote the second sentence. Is it to explain the first one? To add more detailed information to the first one? To show a contrast or similarity to the ideas in the first one?

The author states that the registration for the draft was suspended. In the second sentence, the author tells why registration was suspended. The relationship between these two sentences is one of cause and effect.

▶▶ **Secrets to Success**

- *Learn the common patterns of organization and their transitions (refer to the first section of this chapter).*
- *Read both sentences carefully and paraphrase the ideas in each one.*
- *Look for a relationship that matches one of the common patterns.*
- *Look closely at the beginning of the second sentence for transitional phrases.*
- *Ask: Why did the author write the second sentence? (To add more details? To show an effect or cause? To compare or contrast with something in the first sentence?)*

Study Hint

If the relevant transition word is implied, not provided by being explicitly stated, then insert between the given sentences the word(s) for the choices of relationships listed in the questions option. For example, if option A gives "Cause and effect" as a possible answer, then insert a cause and effect word like "therefore," and then reread the two sentences to see if the word makes sense. If not, go to the next option and insert a word related to its pattern of organization.

Just remember to try a variety of words from any one pattern, for each word expresses a definite relationship.

SECTION 3 ◆ DIAGNOSTIC: RELATIONSHIPS *BETWEEN* SENTENCES

Read the passages and apply the strategies described above for distinguishing relationships between sentences. When you are done, check your work with the answers immediately following the diagnostic. Even if you get a perfect score here, go ahead and complete the exercises in this section; they are designed to help build confidence and to give you practice for future test success.

Read the passages below and answer the questions that follow.

PASSAGE #1

One of the most important results of the Civil War was the freedom gained by southern slaves. In the decade following the defeat of the Confederacy, hundreds of thousands of men and women migrated throughout the South, searching for land, work, and relatives lost through prewar sale. Some former slaves, however, took an even bolder step, leaving the South altogether and traveling west in search of cheap farmland or north seeking industrial employment. While most faced difficult years adjusting to the world of free labor and white prejudice, none would have exchanged their life of freedom for the days of bondage. (Nash and Schultz, *Retracing the Past: Readings in the History of the American People*, 4th ed., New York: Longman, 2000.)

5

1. What is the relationship between the sentences, "In the decade following the defeat of the Confederacy, hundreds of thousands of men and women migrated throughout the South, searching for land, work, and relatives lost through prewar sale. Some former slaves, however, took an

even bolder step, leaving the South altogether and traveling west in search of cheap farmland or north seeking industrial employment"?

A. Comparison
B. Example
C. Definition
D. Contrast

PASSAGE #2

Walt Whitman, whose *Leaves of Grass* (1855) was the last of the great literary works of his brief outpouring of genius, was the most romantic and by far the most distinctly American writer of his age. He was born on Long Island, outside of New York City, in 1819. At 13, he left school and became a printer's devil; thereafter he held a succession of newspaper jobs in the metropolitan area. He was an ardent Jacksonian and later a Free Soiler, which got him into hot water with a number of the publishers for whom he worked. (Garraty and Carnes, *The American Nation: A History of the United States*, 10th ed., New York: Longman, 2000.)   5

2. What is the relationship between the sentences, "He was born on Long Island, outside of New York City, in 1819. At 13, he left school and became a printer's devil; thereafter he held a succession of newspaper jobs in the metropolitan area"?

A. Addition
B. Spatial order
C. Time order
D. Statement and clarification

PASSAGE #3

Active listening serves several important functions. First, it helps you, as a listener, check your understanding of what the speaker said and, more important, what he or she meant. Reflecting back on your understanding of what you think the speaker means gives the speaker an opportunity to offer clarification. In this way, future messages will have a better chance of being relevant. Second, through active listening, you let the speaker know that you acknowledge and accept his or her feelings. (Rigolosi and Campion, eds., *The Longman Electronic Test Bank for Developmental Reading*, 2001.)   5

3. What is the relationship between the sentences, "In this way, future messages will have a better chance of being relevant. Second, through active listening, you let the speaker know that you acknowledge and accept his or her feelings"?

A. Listing
B. Chronological order
C. Process
D. Example

PASSAGE #4

Self-disclosure is a type of communication in which you reveal information about yourself, in which you move information from the hidden self into the open self. Overt statements about the self as well as slips of the tongue, unconscious nonverbal movements, and public confessions would all be considered forms of self-disclosure.

Self-disclosure is information previously unknown by the receiver. This may vary from   5
the relatively commonplace ("I'm really afraid of that French exam") to the extremely significant ("I'm so depressed, I feel like committing suicide"). (DeVito, *Essentials of Human Communication,* 3rd ed., Boston: Allyn and Bacon, 1999.)

4. What is the relationship between the sentences, "Self-disclosure is information previously unknown by the receiver. This may vary from the relatively commonplace ('I'm really afraid of that French exam') to the extremely significant ('I'm so depressed, I feel like committing suicide')"?
   A. Compare and contrast
   B. Definition and example
   C. Spatial order
   D. Process

5. What is the relationship between the sentences, "Self-disclosure is a type of communication in which you reveal information about yourself, in which you move information from the hidden self into the open self. Overt statements about the self as well as slips of the tongue, unconscious nonverbal movements, and public confessions would all be considered forms of self-disclosure"?
   A. Example
   B. Statement and clarification
   C. Spatial order
   D. Process

PASSAGE #5

Presidents and prime ministers govern quite differently. Prime ministers never face divided government, for example. Since they represent the majority party or coalition, they can almost always depend on winning on votes. In addition, party discipline is better in parliamentary systems than in the United States. Prime ministers generally differ from presidents in background as well. They must be party leaders, as we have seen, and they are   5
usually very effective communicators, their skills honed in the rough and tumble of parliamentary debate. In addition, they have had substantial experience dealing with national issues, unlike American governors who may move directly into presidency. Cabinet members, who are usually senior members of parliament, have similar advantages. (Edwards, Wattenberg, and Lineberry, *Government in America,* 9th ed., New York: Longman, 2000.)

6. What is the relationship between the sentences, "In addition, they have had substantial experience dealing with national issues, unlike American governors who may move directly into presidency. Cabinet members, who are usually senior members of parliament, have similar advantages"?
   A. Summary
   B. Generalization and example
   C. Comparison
   D. Contrast

7. What is the relationship between the sentences, "Presidents and prime ministers govern quite differently. Prime ministers never face divided government, for example"?
    A. Summary
    B. Generalization and example
    C. Comparison
    D. Contrast

Answers to Diagnostic
1. D   2. C   3. A   4. B   5. A   6. C   7. B

SECTION 3 ◆ EXERCISES: RELATIONSHIPS *BETWEEN* SENTENCES

Use the following exercises to practice reading for the relationships between sentences.

PASSAGE #1
Read the passage and answer the questions that follow.

One factor that affects the formation of friendship in prisons is the duration of the sentence. Three stages of short-term (one or two years) inmate adaptation are typical. First, inmates experience uncertainty and fear, based on their images of what life is like in prison. Therefore, they avoid contact with other prisoners and guards as much as possible. The next stage involves the creation of a survival niche. The prisoner has   5
selective interactions with other inmates and may develop a "partnership" with another inmate. Partners hang around together and watch out for each other. Maintaining a close tie with another inmate is difficult. In the third phase, the prisoner anticipates his eventual release, transfers to a minimum security area, increases contact with outside visitors, and begins the transition to the outside. In this stage, partners   10
begin to detach from each other as one of the pair moves toward the outside world. (Adapted from Barbara D. Miller, *Cultural Anthropology*, 2nd ed., Boston: Allyn and Bacon, 2002.)

1. What is the relationship between the sentences, "First, inmates experience uncertainty and fear, based on their images of what life is like in prison. Therefore, they avoid contact with other prisoners and guards as much as possible"? (lines 3–5)
    A. Summary
    B. Comparison
    C. Process
    D. Cause and effect

2. What is the implied relationship between the sentences, "The prisoner has selective interactions with other inmates and may develop a 'partnership' with another inmate. Partners hang around together and watch out for each other"? (lines 5–7)
    A. Comparison
    B. Cause and effect
    C. Statement and clarification
    D. Restatement

PASSAGE #2

Read the passage and answer the question that follows.

As a result of Robert Fulton's construction of the North River Steamboat in 1907, the day of the steamboat had dawned. In the 1820s its major effects were clear. The great Mississippi Valley, in the full tide of its development, was immensely enriched. Produce poured down to New Orleans, which soon ranked with New York and Liverpool among the world's great ports. Only 80,000 tons of freight reached New Orleans from the in- 5 terior in 1816 and 1817. Later, in 1840 and 1841, more than 542,000 tons of freight were transported. Upriver traffic was affected even more spectacularly. Freight charges plummeted, in some cases to a tenth of what they had been after the War of 1812. Around 1818, coffee cost 16 cents a pound more in Cincinnati than in New Orleans, a decade later less than 3 cents more. The Northwest emerged from self-sufficiency with 10 a rush and became part of the national market. (Adapted from John A. Garraty and Mark C. Carnes, *The American Nation*, 10th ed., New York: Longman, 2000.)

3. What is the implied relationship between the sentences, "Only 80,000 tons of freight reached New Orleans from the interior in 1816 and 1817. Later, in 1840 and 1841, more than 542,000 tons of freight were transported"? (lines 5–7)
    A. Contrast
    B. Example
    C. Time order
    D. Addition

PASSAGE #3

Read the passage and answer the questions that follow.

Different things motivate different people: A monk is not motivated to make money; an entrepreneur is not motivated to give away all earthly possessions and seek enlightenment on a mountaintop. Moreover, you are not motivated by the same forces day in and day out; rather, motivation comes to the fore when you have a *need* or a *want*. A **need** is a condition that arises from the lack of a requirement. Needs give rise to drives, which 5 push you to reach a particular goal that will reduce the need. For example, lacking nu-trients creates a need; hunger is a drive that will lead you to fill that need. In contrast, a **want** is a condition that arises when you have an unmet goal that will not fill a require-ment. A want causes the goal to act as an incentive. You might *need* to eat, but you don't *need* a fancier car, although you might desperately *want* one—and the promise of a new 10 car for working hard over the summer would be an incentive for you to put in long hours on the job. You are not necessarily aware of your needs or wants; **implicit motives** are needs and wants that direct your behavior unconsciously. (Adapted from Stephen M. Kosslyn and Robin S. Rosenberg, *Psychology*, 2nd ed., Boston: Allyn and Bacon, 2004.)

4. Identify the relationship between these two sentences from the above paragraph.

    "Different things motivate different people: A monk is not motivated to make money: an en-trepreneur is not motivated to give away all earthly possessions and seek enlightenment on a mountaintop. Moreover, you are not motivated by the same forces day in and day out; rather, motivation comes to the fore when you have a *need* or a *want*." (lines 1–4)

The second sentence

A. exemplifies (is an example of) the first.
B. adds to the first.
C. shows the effect of the first.
D. contrasts with the first.

5. Identify the relationship between these two sentences from the above paragraph.

"Needs give rise to drives, which push you to reach a particular goal that will reduce the need. Lacking nutrients creates a need; hunger is a drive that will lead you to fill that need." (lines 5–7)

The second sentence

A. exemplifies (is an example of) the first.
B. summarizes the first.
C. defines the first.
D. compares with the first.

PASSAGE #4

Read the passage and answer the questions that follow.

North America has ten species of skunks. The one most people have seen—or at least smelled—is the abundant and widespread striped skunk. Another species is the spotted skunk, rarely seen but especially interesting because it illustrates some important concepts about biological species. This particular skunk belongs to a species called the western spotted skunk. The adult is only about the size of a house cat, but it has a potent   5
chemical arsenal that makes up for its small size. Before spraying her potent musk, a female guarding her young usually warns an intruder by raising her tail, stamping her forefeet, raking the ground with her claws, or even doing a handstand. When all else fails, she can spray her penetrating odor for three meters with considerable accuracy.

The western spotted skunk inhabits a variety of environments in the United States,   10
from the Pacific coast to the western Great Plains. It is closely related to the eastern spotted skunk, which occurs throughout the southeastern and midwestern United States. The ranges of these two species overlap, and the two species look so much alike that even experts can have a difficult time telling them apart. Both are black with broken white stripes and spots. Individuals of the western species are, on average, slightly   15
smaller, and some have a white tip on the tail, but these and other minor differences in body form are not always present.

For many years, biologists debated whether all spotted skunks belong to one species. But in the 1960s, studies of sexual reproduction in these animals showed that they are indeed two species. Reproduction in the eastern spotted skunk is a straightforward af-   20
fair. Mating occurs in late winter, and young are born between April and July. In marked contrast, the western spotted skunk includes what is called delayed development in its reproductive cycle. Mating takes place in the later summer and early fall, and zygotes begin to develop in the uterus of the female. Further development, however, is temporarily stopped at an early point called the blastocyst stage. Blastocysts remain   25
dormant in the female's uterus throughout the winter months and resume growth in

the spring, with the young (usually 5–7) being born in May or June. Because mating occurs at different times of the year for the two species, there is no opportunity for gene flow between populations of eastern and western spotted skunks. Thus, they are separate species, despite the pronounced similarities in their body form and coloration.   30

Spotted skunks show us that looks can be deceiving. Without knowledge of the mating cycles, we could interpret the minor differences between the two species as insignificant and conclude that there is only one species of spotted skunk in North America. (Adapted from Neil A. Campbell, Lawrence G. Mitchell, and Jane B. Reece, *Biology*, 3rd ed., San Francisco: Benjamin Cummings, 2000.)

6. Identify the relationship between these two sentences from the first paragraph.

"Before spraying her potent musk, a female guarding her young usually warns an intruder by raising her tail, stamping her forefeet, raking the ground with her claws, or even doing a handstand. When all else fails, she can spray her penetrating odor for three meters with considerable accuracy." (lines 6–9)

A. Contrast
B. Cause and effect
C. Example
D. Addition

7. Identify the relationship between these two sentences from the second paragraph.

"The ranges of these two species overlap, and the two species look so much alike that even experts can have a difficult time telling them apart. Both are black with broken white stripes and spots." (lines 14–16)

A. Addition
B. Example
C. Summary
D. Comparison

8. Identify the relationship between these two sentences from the third paragraph.

"Further development, however, is temporarily stopped at an early point called the blastocyst stage. Blastocysts remain dormant in the female's uterus throughout the winter months and resume growth in the spring, with the young (usually 5–7) being born in May or June." (lines 25–28)

A. Addition
B. Restatement
C. Cause and effect
D. Time order

PASSAGE #5

Read the passage and answer the questions that follow.

In the 1980s, a long-running TV public service advertisement showed a father confronting his son with what is obviously the boy's drug paraphernalia. The father asks his son incredulously, "Where did you learn to do this?" The son, half in tears, replies, "From you, okay? I learned it from watching you!" Observational learning, which re-

sults simply from watching others, clearly appears to be a factor in an adolescent's will- 5
ingness to experiment with drugs and alcohol.

Andrews and her colleagues found that adolescents' relationships with their parents influence whether they will model the substance use patterns of the parents. Specifically, they found that adolescents who had a positive relationship with their mothers modeled her use (or nonuse) of cigarettes, and those who had a close relationship with their fa- 10 thers modeled the father's marijuana use (or nonuse). Similarly, those who had a negative relationship with their parents were less likely to model their parents' use of drugs or alcohol. Although some of the more complex results of this study depended on the age and sex of the adolescent, the general findings can be understood by thinking about them from the three levels of analysis and their interactions. 15

At the level of the brain, observing someone engage in a behavior causes you to store new memories, which involves the hippocampus and related brain systems. These memories later can guide behavior, as they do in all types of imitation. At the level of the person, if you are motivated to observe someone, you are likely to be paying more attention to him or her and, therefore, increasing the likelihood of your learning from 20 them and remembering what you learn. At the level of the group, you are more likely to be captivated by models who have certain attractive characteristics.

In this case, adolescents who had a positive relationship with their parents were more likely to do what their parents did; if their parents didn't smoke, the adolescents were less likely to do so. The events at these levels interact. Children who enjoy a positive relationship with 25 their parents may agree with their parents' higher status than do children who have a negative relationship with their parents. Thus, the former group of children probably increases the amount of attention they give to their parents' behavior. (Adapted from Stephen M. Kosslyn and Robin S. Rosenberg, *Psychology*, 2nd ed., Boston: Allyn and Bacon, 2004.)

9. Identify the relationship between these two sentences from the second paragraph.

   "Andrews and her colleagues found that adolescents' relationships with their parents influence whether they will model the substance use patterns of the parents. Specifically, they found that adolescents who had a positive relationship with their mothers modeled her use (or nonuse) of cigarettes, and those who had a close relationship with their fathers modeled the father's marijuana use (or nonuse)." (lines 7–11)

   A. Addition
   B. Cause and effect
   C. Generalization and example
   D. Statement and clarification

10. Identify the relationship between these two sentences from the third paragraph.

    "The events at these levels interact. Children who enjoy a positive relationship with their parents may agree with their parents' higher status than do children who have a negative relationship with their parents." (lines 26–28)

    A. Clarification
    B. Contrast
    C. Cause and effect
    D. Summary

KEEP IN MIND ◆ SUMMARY OF CHAPTER 2

The Overall Pattern of Organization

The organizational pattern is the arrangement of the details into a clear structure. You must be able to recognize organizational patterns to understand the author's main point and how the details are related to one another. Knowing the main idea and the author's purpose can help you to identify the overall organizational pattern. To find the overall pattern of organization:

- First identify the topic and main idea, focusing on the supporting details.
- Think about the author's purpose, asking why did the author write this? Learn the transitional phrases associated with each pattern. Be aware that authors may combine two or more patterns.

Relationships Within a Sentence

It is important to identify the MAIN parts of the sentence in order to see how they relate. The possible relationships within a sentence are the same as those for overall pattern of organization. (See the section on Patterns of Organization for a list of patterns and common transitions.)

The relationship within a sentence <u>may not be the same as the overall pattern of organization.</u> To find the relationship within a sentence,

- Find where the sentence breaks into parts (usually at a piece of punctuation).
- Look for transitional words (clue words for the pattern) at the beginning of one of the parts.
- Ask yourself, "What is the relationship between the ideas? Are they showing an example of something? Making a comparison? Showing an effect or cause of something? Or perhaps using some other type of relationship?"
- Be aware that not all sentences have transitional phrases, and some phrases used may not match the relationship that is being shown. For this reason, always ask, "What is the relationship between the ideas?"
- When it looks like there are two patterns within a sentence, try to identify the MAIN relationship by asking yourself why the author wrote the sentence. What is he or she trying to tell you?

Relationships Between Sentences

The same patterns of organization and transitional phrases are used to show the relationship between ideas in two different sentences.

- Learn the common patterns of organization and their transitions.
- Read both sentences carefully and paraphrase the ideas in each one.
- Look for a relationship that matches one of the common patterns.
- Look closely at the beginning of the second sentence for transitional phrases.
- Ask: Why did the author write the second sentence? (To add more details? To show an effect or cause? To compare or contrast with something in the first sentence?)

Chapter 3: Language Skills

SECTION 1 ◆ WORD CHOICE: CONTEXT CLUES

Using context clues correctly can help you to determine the meaning of an unfamiliar word. Context is the language that surrounds a word that helps to determine its meaning. Thus, many vocabulary in context questions may offer more than one correct definition of the word in the answer choices. However, the question is really asking you for <u>the meaning of the word as it is used in the context of the reading passage</u>.

In these types of questions, a good strategy is to read the question first, then go back and reread the sentence that contains the word. If necessary, read the sentences before and after, and even the entire paragraph to help determine the answer which is the closest in meaning to the word.

Example
What is the meaning of the underlined word?

A common <u>lament</u> of many instructors is that students do not spend enough time studying or doing assignments.

lament means:

a. to grieve
b. to mourn
c. complaint
d. compliment

To answer this question, we should consider several factors:

First of all, dictionary definitions for *lament* include both choices *a* and *b*. So simply knowing a word's meaning may not be able to help you, especially when that word can be used in several different senses. **Always** go back to the sentence to determine which sense is the closest for the context of that sentence. The answer may not be a perfect definition of the word, but one that is the *closest* in meaning.

Also, consider what part of speech *lament* is. Is it a noun? A verb? An adjective? Knowing the part of speech will help you determine the correct meaning.

Lament is used as a noun (a thing) in the sentence above. That eliminates choices *a* and *b*, which begin with "to," indicating an action (a verb).

Substitute a blank in place of the word *lament* and ask which answer choice seems to make most sense.

A common _____ of many instructors is that students do not spend enough time studying or doing assignments.

Which would instructors be most likely to do: complain about students not spending enough time studying or doing assignments, or compliment them? Obviously, instructors are more likely to complain about students not spending enough time on studying or doing assignments.

Another technique is to use other information in the sentence as clues to what the word means. Look for:

1. **Definition:** Often authors will give a definition of the word and set it off using commas, dashes, or parentheses:

Example: The definition of *cosmos* follows in parentheses:

The scientific revolution had reordered Western people's views of the **cosmos** (the universe, which is considered in harmony and well-ordered) and themselves.

Example: The definition of *nobility* follows, set off by dashes:

The **nobility**—kings and their courts—was still predominant.

Example: The definition of *milled* is set off by commas:

The crowd **milled**, moving confused and aimlessly, in the streets.

2. **Synonyms:** Often an author provides another word of similar meaning. Synonyms use the same kinds of punctuation and clue words as definitions. Also look for transitions that indicate the author is comparing two things (see Patterns of Organization for a list of transitions).

Example: A substantial British tax was **levied** (charged) on tea as well as the three-penny Townsend Duty tax. (**Levied** means *charged*.)

Example: Crowds milled in the streets, **harangued**—scolded and criticized—by Adams and his friends. (**Harangued** means *scolded and criticized*.)

Example: For a generation, all of Europe was caught up in the **convulsive**—shuddering—changes. (**Convulsive** means something similar to *shuddering*.)

3. **Antonyms** (words that mean the opposite): Sometimes an author will provide another word of opposite meaning to help you understand the full meaning through contrast. Look for transitions that indicate a contrast (see Patterns of Organization for a list of transitions).

Example: Your essays reveal a good deal about your level of mastery of the course content as well as your ability to organize and **synthesize**; instead of *isolating* skills, you apply them. (The word **synthesize** means the opposite of *isolating*. Notice the transition *instead of*.)

4. **Examples** of the unfamiliar word: Authors often include examples or illustrations of the word to help you understand its meaning. Look for transitions that indicate examples (see Patterns of Organization for a list of transitions).

Example: America could hardly hold a national **referendum**, such as *a direct public vote*, on every policy issue on the government agenda. (A direct public vote is one example of a referendum.)

5. **General sense of the passage:** Many times you must rely on your ability to use the details of the entire passage to reason out the logical meaning of an unknown word.

Example: If Parliament could grant the East India Company a monopoly of the tea trade, it could **parcel** out all or any part of American commerce to whomever it pleased. More important, the act appeared utterly **diabolical** and **dastardly**.

> **parcel** means to distribute
> **diabolical** means evil
> **dastardly** means mean and cowardly

The general sense of the passage tells you that Parliament's act was something negative.

Use Word Structure

Knowing the meanings of prefixes, roots, and suffixes can help determine the meaning of an unknown word. Look for smaller words within bigger words. For example:

> **inaccessible** = in (not) + access (root word) + ible (able to)
> Means: not able to have access to, as in "the building was **inaccessible** to anyone in a wheelchair."

> **intertropical** = inter (between) + tropic (root word) + al (referring to)
> Means: referring to an area between the tropics, as in "Many of the **intertropical** islands suffered extreme damage from the hurricane."

Most good readers use a combination of <u>all</u> of the strategies listed above to determine the meaning of unfamiliar words.

More Examples

1. Although her house was somewhat orderly, it was far from <u>impeccable</u>. In fact, there was often dirt on the floors and in the sinks.

Note the transitional word "Although" at the beginning of the sentence. It leads you to expect a contrast.

Also, try to substitute your choice in the sentence to see if it makes sense:

> **impeccable** means:
> a. messy
> b. to clean
> c. spotless
> d. sanitation

2. Orlando was a city that had an abundance of theme parks but a <u>dearth</u> of good restaurants.

> **dearth** means:
> a. great amount
> b. shortage
> c. to consider
> d. inspection

This sentence makes a comparison between the number of theme parks and the number of good restaurants. Notice the word "but," which indicates an opposite (an antonym).

An <u>abundance</u> of theme parks means a great many. What is the antonym of abundance?

See if your choice makes sense in the sentence:

> Orlando was a city that had an abundance of theme parks but a _____ of good restaurants.

3. Members of Congress may spend so much of their time servicing their <u>constituencies</u> such as the tobacco industry that they have little time to be involved in the policy making process.

Note the example given, *such as the tobacco industry*, and try to think of a meaning that would match this example.

> **constituencies** means:
> a. offices
> b. contracts
> c. groups of supporters
> d. consultants

Answers to Examples
    1. C   2. B   3. C

▶▶ *Secrets to Success*

- *The answer choices sometimes include more than one correct definition of the word. <u>ALWAYS</u> go back and reread the sentence containing the word in the question to determine which meaning is the closest for the context of that sentence. If necessary, reread the entire paragraph.*
- *Knowing the part of speech will help determine the correct meaning.*
- *Substitute a blank in place of the word, and ask which answer choice seems to make most sense when put into the blank.*
- *Use other information in the sentence as clues to what the word means. Look for synonyms, antonyms, examples, and definitions, and consider the general sense of the passage.*
- *Look for smaller words within bigger words. Use word structure (prefixes, roots, and suffixes) to determine the meaning of a word.*
- *Remember that the correct answer may not be the word's exact meaning, but is the <u>closest</u> of the four choices offered.*
- *Use a combination of <u>all</u> of the strategies listed above to determine the meaning of unfamiliar words.*

SECTION 1 ◆ DIAGNOSTIC: VOCABULARY IN CONTEXT

Read the passages and apply the strategies described above for finding the vocabulary in context. When you are done, check your work with the answers immediately following the diagnostic. Even if you get a perfect score here, go ahead and complete the exercises in this section; they are designed to help build confidence and to give you practice for future test success.

Read the passages and answer the questions that follow.

PASSAGE #1

Prime ministers generally differ from presidents in background as well. They must be party leaders, as we have seen, and they are usually very effective communicators, their skills **honed** in the rough and tumble of parliamentary debate. In addition, they have had substantial experience dealing with national issues, unlike American governors who may move directly into presidency. Cabinet members, who are usually senior members of parliament, have similar advantages. (Edwards, Wattenberg, and Lineberry, *Government in America*, 9th ed., New York: Longman, 2000.)

5

1. As used in the sentence, "They must be party leaders, as we have seen, and they are usually very effective communicators, their skills **honed** in the rough and tumble of parliamentary debate," the word *honed* means
   A. a grindstone.
   B. sharpened.
   C. excited.
   D. argument.

PASSAGE #2

Inside those (television) networks, a growing number of people with Ph.D.'s are injecting the latest in child development theory into new programs. That's the good news. The bad news is that working these shows into kids' lives in a healthy way remains a challenge. Much of what kids watch remains **banal** or harmful. (Daniel McGinn, *Newsweek*, November 11, 2002.)

2. As used in the sentence, "Much of what kids watch remains **banal** or harmful," the word *banal* means
   A. commonplace.
   B. hurtful.
   C. beneficial.
   D. irrelevant.

PASSAGE #3

Emigration to the New World in the seventeenth century was an **arduous** undertaking. The journey required two to six months at sea, with passengers huddled in cramped quarters with little provision for privacy. During the long voyage one could expect minimal—and at times rotten—**provisions**. (Nash and Schultz, *Retracing the Past: Readings in the History of the American People*, 4th ed., New York: Longman, 2000.)

3. As used in the sentence, "Emigration to the New World in the seventeenth century was an **arduous** undertaking," the word *arduous* means
   A. brief.
   B. businesslike.
   C. profitable.
   D. difficult.

4. As used in the sentence, "During the long voyage one could expect minimal—and at times rotten—**provisions**," the word *provisions* means
    A. beds.
    B. money.
    C. food.
    D. social life.

PASSAGE #4

There were two black regiments in the regular army and a number of black national guard units when the war began, and once these outfits were brought up to combat strength, more volunteers were accepted. Indeed, at first, no blacks were **conscripted**; Southerners in particular found the thought of giving large numbers of guns to blacks and teaching them how to use them most disturbing. However, blacks were soon drafted, and once they were, a larger proportion of them than whites were taken. (Garraty and Carnes, *The American Nation: A History of the United States*, 10th ed., New York: Longman, 2000.)

5

5. In the sentence, "Indeed, at first, no blacks were **conscripted**," the word *conscripted* means
    A. successful.
    B. drafted.
    C. freed.
    D. excused.

PASSAGE #5

The last decade of the nineteenth century was a time of upheaval in a century marked by **unprecedented** change. In the Northeast, mammoth factories and the immigrants who labored in them dominated the cities of America's industrial heartland. Throughout the country, an ever-growing network of railroads connected even outlying regions to the **burgeoning** metropolises of the nation. And in these metropolises, financial and industrial cartels, monopolies, and holding companies exercised an economic and political influence unparalleled in American life. (Nash and Schultz, *Retracing the Past: Readings in the History of the American People*, 4th ed., New York: Longman, 2000.)

5

6. In the sentence, "The last decade of the nineteenth century was a time of upheaval in a century marked by **unprecedented** change," the word *unprecedented* means
    A. predictable.
    B. not beneficial.
    C. inside of.
    D. never before matched.

7. In the sentence, "Throughout the country, an ever-growing network of railroads connected even outlying regions to the **burgeoning** metropolises of the nation," the word *burgeoning* means
    A. ordinary.
    B. rich.
    C. growing.
    D. connecting.

Answers to Diagnostic

    1. B   2. A   3. D   4. C   5. B   6. D   7. C

Study Hint

Have you noticed how difficult many of the passages in this workbook are? That is because these passages have been taken from the very textbooks you may use in your college classrooms, and the language is advanced. This is a very important skill for you to master.

As you read these passages, take the time to work with the words you don't know. Imitate the examples above and make up context clue cards for the words that get in the way of your understanding. Use your dictionary and thesaurus and write out definitions, synonyms, examples, antonyms. Or reword the sentences around the unfamiliar word using your own words to see if you can guess the meaning of the word that you don't know.

The key to understanding begins with words—one word at a time. Invest the time in your own success and develop a strong vocabulary!

SECTION 1 ◆ EXERCISES: CONTEXT CLUES

Use the following exercises to practice reading for vocabulary with context clues.

PASSAGE #1

Read the passage and answer the questions that follow.

Future teachers not only need to consider the kinds of students they will be working with; they also need to think seriously about the kind of work they will be doing. Some prospective teachers, not particularly fond of any academic subject, may <u>gravitate</u> toward elementary, early childhood, or special education, where they believe the emphasis will be on "getting along with the kids." They think much of the school day will be   5 filled with games and activities. The human side of teaching will be fun and rewarding. As for the academic side, surely they will know more than their students. Besides, a number of people—including some teachers and administrators—have told them you don't have to be very smart to be a teacher. They may even have heard that being too bright can hurt.   10

Let me <u>dispel</u> several myths about teaching. In spite of all the publicity about teacher burnout, some people cling to the belief that teaching is a fun job. It is not. Getting through to students can certainly be rewarding, but reaching them takes hour after hour of effort. Fun is not the right word. Listen to the counsel of a Florida teacher: "Teaching is work. It is the hardest job there is. Learning is work. We try to make it   15 enjoyable, interesting, exciting, motivating, relevant, palatable, etc. But any way you slice it, it's work."

Notwithstanding the public outcry over academically <u>incompetent</u> teachers, some people believe another myth. Rudimentary literacy is the only academic qualification teachers of the youngest or least able students must have. It is not. This myth, another   20 holdover from the past, finds no support in the research on teacher effectiveness.

(Joseph W. Newman, *America's Teachers: An Introduction to Education*, 4th ed., Boston: Allyn and Bacon, 2002.)

1. As used in line 3, the word <u>gravitate</u> means
   A. be sympathetic.
   B. be attracted.
   C. be agreeable.
   D. be prejudiced.

2. The word <u>dispel</u> (line 11) means
   A. describe.
   B. explain.
   C. remove.
   D. expose.

3. As used in line 17, <u>incompetent</u> most nearly means
   A. weak.
   B. irresponsible.
   C. unproductive.
   D. inadequate.

PASSAGE #2

Read the passage and answer the questions that follow.

Today television is the most <u>prevalent</u> means used by candidates to reach voters. Thomas Patterson stresses that "today's presidential campaign is essentially a mass media campaign. . . . It is not exaggeration to say that, for the majority of voters, the campaign has little reality apart from its media version."

The most important goal of any media campaign is simply to get attention. Media coverage is determined by two factors: (1) how candidates use their advertising budget, and (2) the "free" attention they get as newsmakers. The first, obviously, is relatively easy to control; the second is more difficult but not impossible. Almost every logistical decision in a campaign—where to eat breakfast, whom to include on the rostrum, when to announce a major policy proposal—is calculated according to its intended media impact. About half the total budget for a presidential or senatorial campaign will be used for television advertising.

Candidates attempt to <u>manipulate</u> their images through advertising and image building, but they have less control over the other aspect of the media news coverage. To be sure, most campaigns have press aides who feed "canned" news releases to reporters. Still, the media largely determine for themselves what is happening in a campaign. Campaign coverage seems to be a constant <u>interplay</u> between hard news about what candidates say and do and the human interest angle, which most journalists think sells newspapers or interests television viewers. (Adapted from George C. Edwards, Martin P. Wattenberg, and Robert L. Lineberry, *Government in America*, 9th ed., New York: Longman, 2000.)

4. As used in line 1, <u>prevalent</u> most nearly means
   A. modern.
   B. common.
   C. ordinary.
   D. powerful.

5. The word <u>manipulate</u> (line 13) most nearly means
   A. control.
   B. use.
   C. apply.
   D. plan.

6. As used in line 17, <u>interplay</u> means
   A. competition.
   B. relationship.
   C. link.
   D. interaction.

PASSAGE #3

Read the passage and answer the questions that follow.

Ignorance of African geography and environment has contributed greatly to the prevailing misconceptions about African culture and history. Many Americans, for instance, have thought of the continent as an immense "jungle." In reality, more than half of the area south of the Sahara consists of grassy plains known as *savanna*, whereas "jungle" or tropical rain forest takes up just seven percent of the land surface.   5

The most <u>habitable</u> areas have been the savannas, their grasslands and trees favoring both human settlement and long-distance trade and agriculture. The northern savanna stretches across the continent just south of the central desert, the Sahara. Other patches of savanna are <u>interspersed</u> among the mountains and lakes of East Africa and another belt of grassland that runs east and west across southern Africa, north and east of the   10
Kalahari Desert.

Between the northern and southern savannas, in the region of the equator, is dense rain forest. Although the rain forest is lush, its soils are poor because torrential rains cause soil <u>erosion</u> and intense heat leaches the soil of nutrients and burns off <u>humus</u> (organic matter) that is essential for soil fertility. The rain forests also harbor insects that carry   15
deadly diseases. Mosquitoes transmit malaria and yellow fever, and the tsetse fly is a carrier of sleeping sickness to which both humans and animals, such as horses and cattle, are susceptible. (Brummet, Palmira, et al., *Civilization*, 9th ed., New York: Longman, 2000.)

7. As used in line 6, <u>habitable</u> most nearly means
   A. livable.
   B. convenient.
   C. spacious.
   D. fertile.

8. The word <u>interspersed</u> in line 9 most nearly means
   A. located.
   B. planted.
   C. scattered.
   D. hidden.

9. As used in line 14, <u>humus</u> means
   A. sewage.
   B. organic matter.
   C. nutrients.
   D. chemicals.

10. The word <u>erosion</u> (line 14) most nearly means
    A. destruction.
    B. pollution.
    C. washing away.
    D. contamination.

SECTION 2 ◆ BIASED LANGUAGE

Authors often choose words that reveal their attitudes toward their subjects. A bias is an attitude that is for or against the subject, and sometimes this bias toward or against something can be very subtle. Being able to recognize the author's use of positive or negative language will help you to determine the author's bias for or against the topic.

When an author uses more opinion than fact or a great deal of positive or negative language to present his or her argument, it is easy to spot bias. However, sometimes bias is not so obvious. One way to recognize subtle bias is to ask yourself if the author considers anything in the text to be <u>inherently</u> good or bad. In other words, is there anything that the author considers to be *positive* or *negative by its very nature*? For example, an author who writes about how wonderfully adapted cockroaches are to a multitude of environments may be showing bias in favor of creatures that are able to adapt to many environments. That characteristic may seem like an obviously positive feature, but in fact, it is only positive if the author sees it that way. Others may be horrified at the thought that one particular creature could take over after a nuclear disaster. They might consider that feature to be disastrous. Thus, subtle bias can be hard to spot, especially if the bias is one that you share with the author.

If the author does not seem to have either a positive or a negative attitude, then the writing is considered unbiased or neutral. In unbiased writing, the author attempts to balance opposing views without appearing to be for or against the topic.

Bias is very closely related to *tone*. If an author seems to present only the facts with very little opinion or judgment, then the tone is neutral, objective, straightforward, or matter-of-fact. If an author is extremely biased in favor or against something, then the tone will also be extremely positive or negative.

Consider the following when determining the author's bias:

- Is the author's language mostly positive toward the subject?
- Is the author's language mostly negative toward the subject?
- Does the author balance both negative and positive aspects of the topic?
- Does the author present mostly facts or opinions?
- Does the author consider anything in the text to be inherently good or bad?

> **Example #1**
> Hate sites began on the Internet in the mid-1990s, and their number expanded rapidly. Now hate groups in general across the nation are on the rise because of the Internet. Hate sites advocate violence toward immigrants, Jews, Arabs, gays, abortion providers, and others. Through the Internet, disturbed minds effectively fuel hatred, violence, sexism, racism, and terrorism. Never before has there been such an intensive way for depraved people to gather to reinforce their prejudices and hatred. (Adapted from Shedletsky and Aitknen, *Human Communication on the Internet*, Boston: Allyn and Bacon, 2004.)

Begin with stating the topic and main idea:

Topic: Hate sites on the Internet

Main Idea: Increases in hate sites on the Internet have enabled depraved people to express their hatred and prejudice.

Notice the adjectives the author has chosen: *disturbed* minds, *fuel* hatred, *depraved* people.

Ask: Is the author sounding positive or negative toward the subject?

This author clearly shows a negative attitude, or bias, against Internet hate sites.

> **Example #2**
> Efficiency brings dependability. You can expect your burger and fries to taste the same whether you buy them in Los Angles or Beijing. Efficiency also lowers prices. But efficiency does come at a cost. Predictability washes away spontaneity, changing the quality of our lives. It produces a sameness, a bland version of what used to be unique experiences. For good or bad, our lives are being McDonaldized, and the predictability of packaged settings seems to be our social destiny. (Henslin, *Sociology*, 6th ed., Boston: Allyn and Bacon, 2003.)

Topic: Efficiency

Main Idea: Efficiency is changing the quality of our lives to a bland version of what used to be unique experiences.

Ask: Is the author more positive about efficiency or more negative about it? Look at the sentence, "It produces a sameness, a *bland* version of what used to be unique experiences."

This author is biased against efficiency because it produces a "*bland* version of what used to be unique experiences."

> **Example #3**
> Harriet Tubman was born a slave in Maryland in 1820 and escaped to Philadelphia in 1849. Her own escape presumably required tremendous courage, but that was just the beginning. Through her work on the Underground Railroad, Harriet Tubman led more than 300 slaves to freedom. During the Civil War, Tubman continued her efforts toward the abolition of slavery by working as a nurse and a spy for the Union forces. Today, Americans of all races consider Harriet Tubman one of the most heroic figures in our country's history. (From K. McWhorter, *Reading Across the Disciplines*, New York: Longman, 2005.)

Topic: Harriet Tubman

Main Idea: Harriet Tubman is considered a heroic figure because of her efforts to abolish slavery.

Does the author use positive or negative language? Notice the phrases: "Her own escape presumably required *tremendous courage*" and "one of the most *heroic* figures . . ."

The author is biased in favor of Harriet Tubman.

▶▶┃ *Secrets to Success*

- *Begin by stating the author's topic and main idea. They may give you a clue to the author's bias.*
- *Look for biased language with positive or negative connotations.*
- *Ask: Is the author sounding positive or negative toward the subject?*
- *Look for a subjective, one-sided viewpoint.*
- *Look for opinions, often present in biased writing.*
- *If the author does not appear to have either a positive or a negative attitude toward the subject, the writing is objective, or unbiased.*

SECTION 2 ◆ DIAGNOSTIC: BIASED LANGUAGE

Read the passages and apply the strategies described above for finding biased language. When you are done, check your work with the answers immediately following the diagnostic. Even if you get a perfect score here, go ahead and complete the exercises in this section; they are designed to help build confidence and to give you practice for future test success.

Read the passages and answer the questions that follow.

PASSAGE #1

Managed care plans have agreements with certain physicians, hospitals, and health care providers to give a range of services to plan members at a reduced cost. There are three basic types of managed care plans: health maintenance organizations (HMOs), point-of-service plans (POSs), and preferred provider organizations (PPOs). The PPO, in my opinion, is the best type of managed care plan because it merges the best features of traditional health insurance and HMOs. As in traditional plans, participants in a PPO may pay premiums, deductibles, and co-payments, but the co-pay under a PPO is

5

lower. The best part of a PPO, though, is its flexibility: participants may choose their physicians and services from a list of preferred providers, or they may go outside the plan for care if they wish. (Adaped from Pruitt and Stein, *Healthstyles*, Boston: Allyn and Bacon, 2001.)   10

1. In the passage above, the author
   A. is biased against managed care plans.
   B. is biased in favor of HMO and POS plans.
   C. is unbiased.
   D. is biased in favor of PPOs.

PASSAGE #2

Plagiarism is a serious infraction in most settings. Students can be suspended or expelled from school. Researchers can lose their jobs and their standing in the academic community. More importantly, plagiarism is serious because it violates several of the reasonable criteria for ethical decision making. Plagiarism violates your obligation to yourself to be truthful, and it violates your obligation to other students and researchers.   5
(Adapted from Gurak and Lannon, *A Concise Guide to Technical Communication*, New York: Longman, 2001.)

2. In the passage above, the author
   A. is unbiased.
   B. is biased against plagiarism.
   C. is biased in favor of plagiarism.
   D. is biased against students and researchers.

PASSAGE #3

Tannen argues that the goal of a man in conversation is to be accorded respect, and so he seeks to display his knowledge and expertise even if he has to change the topic from one he knows little about to one he knows a great deal about. A woman, on the other hand, seeks to be liked, and so she expresses agreement and less frequently interrupts to take her turn as a speaker. (J. DeVito, *Essentials of Human Communication*, 3rd   5
ed., New York: Longman, 1999.)

3. In the passage above, the author
   A. is unbiased.
   B. is biased against men's style of conversation.
   C. is biased for women's style of conversation.
   D. is biased against women's style of conversation.

PASSAGE #4

Bush infuriated environmentalists, who had been pleased with Clinton's efforts to protect America's national heritage. And, catering to the interests of oil companies, he fought to promote drilling in the protected Arctic National Wildlife Refuge, even in the face of estimates that there was very little oil there to be found. When his own Environmental Protection Agency (EPA) issued a report in mid-2002 linking the use of fossil fuel to global warming, Bush dismissed the study by declaring that he had the "report put out by the bureaucracy," making it clear that he had no confidence in the judgments of the scientists working for the EPA. (G. Nash et al., *The American People: Creating a Nation and a Society*, 6th ed., New York: Longman, 2004.)

5

4. In this passage, the authors
   A. are unbiased.
   B. are biased in favor of the EPA.
   C. are biased against the actions of President George W. Bush.
   D. are biased against oil drilling.

PASSAGE #5

Clinton was an enormously successful politician. Not only had he escaped conviction in the highly visible—and embarrassing—impeachment case, but he also managed to co-opt Republican issues and seize the political center. When he moved to reconfigure the national welfare system, to limit the number of years a person could receive benefits and to pare down the number of people on welfare rolls, the conservatives were pleased while the liberals were furious. Yet in other ways, he quietly advanced liberal goals, with incremental appropriations, even when he was unable to push major programs, such as his medical insurance scheme, through Congress. (G. Nash et al., *The American People: Creating a Nation and a Society*, 6th ed., New York: Longman, 2004.)

5

5. In this passage, the authors
   A. are biased against welfare reform.
   B. are biased in favor of President Bill Clinton.
   C. are biased against Republicans.
   D. are unbiased.

PASSAGE #6

A report in 2000 observed that many Americans still saw Asian Americans as secretive and inscrutable. That kind of reaction was frustrating. "Too many people in this country continue to see us in simple stereotypes," complained Paul M. Ong, a social policy professor at the University of California at Los Angeles. (G. Nash et al., *The American People: Creating a Nation and a Society*, 6th ed., New York: Longman, 2004.)

6. In this passage, the authors
   A. are unbiased.
   B. are biased in favor of Asian Americans.
   C. are biased against stereotypes.
   D. are biased against Asian Americans.

PASSAGE #7

Along with self-education, employers could help by both providing the facts about sleep to employees and stressing how important an adequate amount of sleep is to everyday performance. Don't equate sleep with laziness; they're two totally different issues. Sleepy workers are more likely to cause accidents, make mistakes, and are more susceptible to heart attacks. Lazy workers, for whatever reason, just don't do their jobs. (Dorrit Walsh, "The Sandman is Dead—Long Live the Sleep-Deprived Walking Zombie," from K. McWhorter, *Reading Across the Disciplines*, New York: Longman, 2005.)

5

7. In the passage above, the author
   A. is biased against laziness.
   B. is unbiased.
   C. is biased against employers.
   D. is biased in favor of getting an adequate amount of sleep.

Answers to Diagnostic

1. D   2. B   3. A   4. C   5. B   6. C   7. D

SECTION 2 ◆ EXERCISES: BIASED LANGUAGE

Use the following exercises to practice reading for biased language.

PASSAGE #1

Read the passage and answer the questions that follow.

Many overweight and obese individuals are trying to lose weight. Although it took several months and years to put on the extra weight, many of them are looking for a quick way to lose that weight. This attitude results in choosing quick-weight-loss diets that are not effective and may be harmful. Some choose metabolic products, such as herbs or caffeine, to lose weight. Herbs have not been shown to speed the loss of fat, and caffeine shows little promise as a weight-loss aid.

5

Others go on very-low-calorie diets, which severely restrict nutrients and can result in serious metabolic imbalances. Weight can be lost on this type of diet; much of the weight lost will be lean protein tissue and/or water, not fat. This results in harm to the muscles (including the heart), loss of essential vitamins and minerals through the water loss, and dizziness and fatigue. Further, if one cuts calories, the metabolism slows; once this person goes off the diet, the metabolism remains slow and the body continues to use few calories—and the pounds come back.

10

Liquid-protein diets operate on the theory that insulin is controlled and therefore more fat is burned. With this type of diet, ketosis will result. Ketosis will increase blood levels of uric acid, a risk factor for gout and kidney stones. There is new research evidence that carbohydrates lead to fat storage and weight; further, the excessive protein in this diet can damage the kidneys and cause osteoporosis.

15

Prescription drugs, such as Redux and Pondimin (fen-phen), curb hunger by increasing the level of serotonin in the brain. These were intended for the obese, but they were banned in 1997 after the FDA found strong evidence that they could seriously damage the heart.   20

Some people try crash diets to lose a moderate amount of weight in a very short period. These types of diets can damage several body systems and have been proved not to work because most of these individuals regain their weight. This yo-yo dieting causes   25 many health problems and shortens lifespan. The best way to lose weight is to lose weight slowly (no more than one-half to one pound a week), eat properly and in moderation, and exercise. (Adapted from David J. Anspaugh and Gene Ezell, *Teaching Today's Health*, 7th ed., San Francisco: Benjamin Cummings, 2004.)

1. In this passage, the author expresses a bias in favor of
   A. taking prescription drugs to lose weight.
   B. controlling insulin levels to burn fat.
   C. restricting calories.
   D. losing weight slowly.

2. In this passage, the author is biased against
   A. harmful quick-weight-loss diets.
   B. moderating food choices.
   C. obesity.
   D. research evidence on quick weight-loss diets.

PASSAGE #2

Read the passage and answer the questions that follow.

Television's portrayal of courts and trials is almost as dramatic as its portrayal of detectives and police officers—both often vary from reality. Highly publicized trials are dramatic but rare. The murder trial of O. J. Simpson made headlines for months. Cable News Network even carried much of the pretrial and trial live. But in reality, most cases, even ones in which the evidence is solid, do not go to trial.   5

If you visit a typical American criminal courtroom, you will rarely see a trial complete with judge and jury. In American courts, 90 percent of all cases begin and end with a guilty plea. Most cases are settled through a process called **plea bargaining**. A plea bargain results from an actual bargain struck between a defendant's lawyer and a prosecutor to the effect that a defendant will plead guilty to a lesser crime (or fewer crimes)   10 in exchange for the state's not prosecuting that defendant for a more serious (or additional) crime.

Critics of the plea-bargaining system believe that it permits many criminals to avoid the full punishment they deserve. The process, however, works to the advantage of both sides; it saves the state the time and money that would otherwise be spent on a trial,   15 and it permits defendants who think they might be convicted of a serious charge to plead guilty to a lesser one. (George C. Edwards, Martin P. Wattenberg, and Robert L. Lineberry, *Government in America*, 9th ed., New York: Longman, 2000.)

3. In this passage, the authors are biased against
   A. live television trial coverage.
   B. the guilty plea.
   C. O. J. Simpson's verdict.
   D. spending money on trials.

4. In this passage, the authors express a bias in favor of
   A. television's portrayal of courts and trials.
   B. detective and police shows on television.
   C. plea bargaining.
   D. trial by jury for every criminal case.

PASSAGE #3

Read the passage and answer the question that follows.

The most common stimulant is caffeine, which is contained in coffee, tea, cola drinks, and even chocolate. Caffeine is a mild stimulant that is often abused. Nonetheless, it is a drug and should be recognized as one that can lead to health problems.

Caffeine is absorbed rather quickly into the bloodstream and reaches a peak blood level in about thirty to sixty minutes. It increases mental alertness and provides a feeling   5
of energy. However, high doses of caffeine can overstimulate and cause nervousness and increased heart rate. Caffeine can also cause sleeplessness, excitement, and irritability. In some cases, high doses of caffeine can induce convulsions.

Coffee or cola drinking, let alone chocolate eating, cannot be considered drug abuse by most commonly accepted standards. But some individuals seek out caffeine for its   10
own sake in over-the-counter products and in illegal substances to produce a caffeine "high." Because it is not considered a dangerous drug, the opportunities for caffeine abuse are often overlooked. (David J. Anspaugh and Gene Ezell, *Teaching Today's Health*, 7th ed., San Francisco: Benjamin Cummings, 2004.)

5. In this passage, the authors have a bias in favor of
   A. eating chocolate and drinking coffee and cola.
   B. considering caffeine a drug.
   C. using caffeine to produce a "high."
   D. using caffeine to increase mental alertness.

PASSAGE #4

Read the passage and answer the questions that follow.

Through the Equal Employment Opportunity Commission, the federal government has classified some interview questions as unlawful. Some of the more important areas about which unlawful questions are frequently asked concern age, marital status, race, religion, nationality, physical condition, and arrest and criminal records. For example, it's legal to ask applicants whether they meet the legal age requirements for the job and could   5
provide proof of that, but it's unlawful to ask their exact age, even in indirect ways.

One strategy to deal with unlawful questions is to answer the part you do not object to and to omit any information you do not want to give. For example, if you're asked the unlawful question concerning what language is spoken at home, you may respond with a statement such as "I have language facility in German and Italian" without specifying   10 a direct answer to the question. Generally, this type of response is preferable to the one that immediately tells the interviewer he or she is asking an unlawful question. In many cases, the interviewer may not even be aware of the legality of various questions and may have no intention of trying to get at information you're not obliged to give.

On the other hand, recognize that in many employment interviews, the unwritten in-   15 tention is to keep certain people out, whether it's people who are older or those of a particular nationality, religion, and so on. If you're confronted by questions that are unlawful and that you do not want to answer, and if the gentle method described above does not work and your interviewer persists, you might counter by saying that such information is irrelevant to the interview and to the position you're seeking. Be cour-   20 teous but firm. If the interviewer still persists, though it is doubtful that many would after these direct responses, you might note that these questions are unlawful and that you're not going to answer them. (Adapted from Joseph A. DeVito, *Essentials of Human Communication*, 3rd ed., New York: Longman, 1999.)

6. In this passage, the author is biased against
   A. answering unlawful questions.
   B. answering direct questions.
   C. answering closed questions.
   D. answering for proof of age.

7. In this passage, the author has a bias in favor of
   A. immediately telling the interviewer that he or she is asking an unlawful question.
   B. answering an unlawful question.
   C. developing strategies to deal with unlawful questions.
   D. turning in the employer for asking unlawful questions.

PASSAGE #5

Read the passage and answer the question that follows.

Hate sites began on the Internet in the mid-1990s, and their numbers expanded rapidly. Now hate groups in general across the nation are on the rise because of the Internet. Hate sites advocate violence toward immigrants, Jews, Arabs, gays, abortion providers, and others. Through the Internet, disturbed minds effectively fuel hatred, violence, sex- ism, racism, and terrorism. Never before has there been such an intensive way for de-   5 praved people to gather to reinforce their prejudices and hatred. In one analysis of hate speech sites, the researchers found sophisticated use of persuasive strategies. The hate sites generally started with an objective approach that was straightforward and neutral, in which they reinforced and strengthened the hate ideas that people already have. The Internet provides a forum for people with prejudicial attitudes to speak out and act   10 out. Hatemongers can create an online world where they reign supreme, a world of similar minds, where they can gather with others to feel that their way is right and where they can design severe disruption for the on-ground world. (Adapted from Leonard J. Shedletsky and Joan E. Aitken, *Human Communication on the Internet*, Boston: Allyn and Bacon, 2004.)

8. In this passage, the author is biased against
    A. online commentaries.
    B. online messages among terrorists.
    C. immigrants.
    D. hate sites.

PASSAGE #6

Read the passage and answer the questions that follow.

The thousands of McDonald's restaurants that dot the U.S. landscape—and increasingly the world—have a significance that goes far beyond the convenience of ready-made hamburgers and milk shakes. As sociologist George Ritzer says, our everyday lives are being "McDonaldized."

The McDonaldization of society, the standardization of everyday life, does not refer 5
just to the robotlike assembly of food. Shopping malls offer one-stop shopping in controlled environments. Travel agencies offer "package" tours. They will transport middle-class Americans to ten European capitals in fourteen days. All visitors experience the same hotels, restaurants, and other scheduled sites, and no one need fear meeting a "real" native. *USA Today* spews out McNews—short, bland, unanalytic pieces that 10
can be digested between gulps of the McShake or the McBurger.

Efficiency brings dependability. You can expect your burger and fries to taste the same whether you buy them in Los Angeles or Beijing. Efficiency also lowers prices. But efficiency does come at a cost. Predictability washes away spontaneity, changing the quality of our lives. It produces a sameness, a bland version of what used to be unique 15
experiences. For good or bad, our lives are being McDonaldized, and the predictability of packaged settings seems to be our social destiny. (Adapted from James M. Henslin, *Sociology*, 6th ed., Boston: Allyn and Bacon, 2003.)

9. In this passage, the author has a bias in favor of
    A. package travel tours.
    B. unique experiences.
    C. *USA Today* news reporting.
    D. consistency in food at McDonald's across the world.

10. In this passage, the author is biased against
    A. shopping at a mall.
    B. standardization of everyday life.
    C. McDonald's burgers.
    D. efficiency.

SECTION 3 ◆ AUTHOR'S TONE

An author's choice of words conveys his or her attitude toward the subject. Understanding the author's tone will help you comprehend the author's ideas and feelings toward the topic. To determine the tone, you must pay close attention to the language of the passage. Look for adjectives that describe nouns. Think about the connotation, the emotional tone of the words. Look for opinions and bias. Also think about the main idea and author's purpose. Knowing the author's main point and the purpose for writing can help identify the tone of the passage.

For the Exit Exam, questions about the author's tone can cause problems – not because it is difficult to determine an author's tone, but because the <u>vocabulary words</u> that the Exit Exam uses to describe tone are sometimes difficult. There is nothing worse than understanding clearly what an author's tone is only to get the question wrong because you don't understand the answer choices. Therefore, learning the meanings to as many tone words as you can is vital. Knowing what the tone words mean will help you to choose the correct tone.

Sometimes, students who lack confidence will select an answer to a tone question when they do not know what that tone word means. This happens simply because such students believe the test is harder than it really is, that the test writers are trying to trick them, or that they should choose the most difficult answer. <u>Do not make this mistake!!</u> If you do not know what some tone word means, do NOT select it as the answer unless you are 100% sure that the other answer choices are wrong. Most of the time, you will see an answer choice that matches fairly closely your own estimation of the author's tone.

*<u>NOTE</u>: The word "objective" has nothing to do with a goal or with making an argument against something. Objective means neutral, unbiased, or straightforward. Many academic texts are written in an objective tone because they are fact-based. Make sure that you know this tone word definition in particular because it shows up frequently on the Exit Exam.

COMMON TONE WORDS TO LEARN

Ambivalent	Docile	Ironic	Reverent
Apathetic	Earnest	Irreverent	Righteous
Awestruck	Eloquent	Malicious	Satiric
Callous	Enigmatic	Melancholic	Scornful
Caustic	Erudite	Melodramatic	Smug
Condescending	Farcical	Morose	Solemn
Contemplative	Flippant	Nostalgic	Somber
Contemptuous	Frenzied	Objective	Vindictive
Cynical	Frivolous	Obsequious	

Example:
Efficiency brings dependability. You can expect your burger and fries to taste the same whether you buy them in Los Angeles or Beijing. Efficiency also lowers prices. But efficiency does come at a cost. Predictability washes away spontaneity, changing the quality of our lives. It produces a sameness, a bland version of what used to be unique experiences. For good or bad, our lives are being McDonaldized, and the predictability of packaged settings seems to be our social destiny. (Henslin, *Sociology*, 6th ed., Boston: Allyn and Bacon, 2003.)

Topic: Efficiency

Main Idea: Efficiency is changing the quality of our lives to a bland version of what used to be unique experiences.

Author's Purpose: To criticize how efficiency has negatively changed the quality of our lives.

Author's Language: Notice the choice of words used to describe efficiency: "a *sameness*, a *bland* version."

1. What is the overall tone of this passage?
    A. Humorous
    B. Nostalgic
    C. Sarcastic
    D. Pessimistic

The author's feeling is more pessimistic than any of the other choices, so the correct answer is D. However, if you do not know what pessimistic means, you may have problems with this question. Based on the author's use of language, you may feel that the tone is negative or critical. However, those choices do not appear. You can see how important it is to learn the vocabulary words typically used to describe an author's tone.

> **Example #2**
> Plagiarism is a serious infraction in most settings. Students can be suspended or expelled from school. Researchers can lose their jobs and their standing in the academic community. More importantly, plagiarism is serious because it violates several of the reasonable criteria for ethical decision making. Plagiarism violates your obligation to yourself to be truthful, and it violates your obligation to other students and researchers. (Adapted from Gurak and Lannon, *A Concise Guide to Technical Communication*, New York: Longman, 2001.)

2. What is the overall tone of this passage?
    A. Detached
    B. Objective
    C. Concerned
    D. Reverent

Topic: Plagiarism

Main Idea: Plagiarism is a serious infraction in most settings for many reasons.

Author's Purpose: To show why plagiarism is a serious offense.

Author's Language: Note the language the author uses: "a *serious* infraction" and "*violates* your obligation."

The correct answer is choice C, concerned. Reverent means deeply respectful or worshipful. If you selected that answer because you did not know the meaning, please do not do that on the real Exit Exam! Study the tone words and do not select an answer unless you know what it means.

> **Example #3**
> Overt statements about the self as well as slips of the tongue, unconscious nonverbal move-ments, and public confessions would all be considered forms of self-disclosure. Self-dis-closure is information previously unknown by the receiver. This may vary from the relatively commonplace ("I'm really afraid of that French exam") to the extremely signif-icant ("I'm so depressed, I feel like committing suicide"). (DeVito, *Essentials of Human Communication*, 3rd ed., Boston: Allyn and Bacon, 1999.)

3. What is the overall tone of this passage?
   A. Objective
   B. Bitter
   C. Lighthearted
   D. Nostalgic

Topic: Self-disclosure

Main Idea: Self-disclosure is a type of communication in which you reveal information about yourself, in which you move information from the hidden self into the open self.

Author's Purpose: To define and explain self-disclosure and provide examples.

Author's Language: The author uses facts and very few adjectives with a positive or negative conno-tation. Do not consider quotes in examples as representing the author's feeling; the author is simply repeating what someone else has said. Focus on the author's own words.

The correct answer choice is A, objective. The tone is very factual and straightforward, and does not attempt to sway the reader's attitude about the topic. Again, objective is a very common tone word that has nothing to do with argument or a goal. Make sure you know what this tone word means.

▶▶| *Secrets to Success*

- *Learn the meanings to as many tone words as you can.*
- *Pay close attention to the language of the passage.*
- *Look for adjectives that describe nouns.*
- *Think about the connotation, the emotional tone of the words.*
- *Look for opinions.*
- *Think about the main idea and author's purpose.*

SECTION 3 ◆ DIAGNOSTIC: AUTHOR'S TONE

Read the passages and apply the strategies described above for determining the author's tone. When you are done, check your work with the answers immediately following the diagnostic. Even if you get a perfect score here, go ahead and complete the exercises in this section; they are designed to help build confidence and to give you practice for future test success.

Read the passages and choose the word that best describes the author's tone.

PASSAGE #1

> The baby died last winter. It was pretty terrible. Little Charlotte (not her real name) lay on a high white bed, surrounded by nurses and doctors pushing drugs into her

veins, tubes into her trachea and needles into her heart, trying as hard as they could to take over for her failing body and brain. She was being coded, as they say in ICU. It had happened several times before, but this time it would fail. Her parents, who were working, weren't there. (C. Mitchell, "When Living Is a Fate Worse Than Death," *Newsweek*, 2000, from *Reading Across the Disciplines*, New York: Longman, 2005.)

5

1. The overall tone of this passage is
   A. sorrowful.
   B. ambivalent.
   C. caustic.
   D. malicious.

PASSAGE #2

Nobody is arguing that the huge and growing global environmental and social crisis is entirely the fault of one high-profile burger chain, or even just the whole food industry. McDonald's is, of course, simply a particularly arrogant, shiny and self-important example of a system that values profits at the expense of anything else. Even if McDonald's were to close down tomorrow, someone else would simply slip straight into its position. There is a much more fundamental problem than Big Macs and French fries: capitalism. (Anonymous, "McDonald's Makes a Lot of People Angry for a Lot of Different Reasons," from *Reading Across the Disciplines*, New York: Longman, 2005.)

5

2. The overall tone of this passage is
   A. ironic.
   B. reverent.
   C. critical.
   D. objective.

PASSAGE #3

Harriet Tubman was born a slave in Maryland in 1820 and escaped to Philadelphia in 1849. Her own escape presumably required tremendous courage, but that was just the beginning. Through her work on the Underground Railroad, Harriet Tubman led more than 300 slaves to freedom. During the Civil War, Tubman continued her efforts toward the abolition of slavery by working as a nurse and a spy for the Union forces. Today, Americans of all races consider Harriet Tubman one of the most heroic figures in our country's history. (K. McWhorter, *Reading Across the Disciplines*, New York: Longman, 2005.)

5

3. The overall tone of this passage is
   A. optimistic.
   B. admiring.
   C. pessimistic.
   D. solemn.

PASSAGE #4

In Japan, married women are often supposed to stay at home and clean the house and raise the children. In fact, the Japanese word for wife means "Mrs. In-the-Back-of-the-House." There are even legal incentives to encourage married women to quit full-time jobs, and a married couple is legally required to use the same last name—almost always the husband's. Such an environment presents immense obstacles for women to overcome 5 in order to transform themselves into a meaningful force in Japanese politics. Women find it difficult to be taken seriously by voters, facing prejudice such as that reflected in one male candidate's taunt, "Women can't do anything. They should just shut up." (Edwards, Wattenberg, and Lineberry, *Government in America*, 9th ed., New York: Longman, 2000.)

4. The overall tone of this passage is
   A. serious.
   B. ironic.
   C. objective.
   D. critical.

PASSAGE #5

Inside those (television) networks, a growing number of people with Ph.D.'s are injecting the latest in child development theory into new programs. That's the good news. The bad news is that working these shows into kids' lives in a healthy way remains a challenge. Much of what kids watch remains banal or harmful. Many kids watch too much. There are also troubling socioeconomic factors at work. In lower income homes, 5 for instance, kids watch more and are more likely to have TV in their bedrooms, a practice pediatricians discourage. (Daniel McGinn, *Newsweek*, November 11, 2002.)

5. The overall tone of this passage is
   A. lighthearted.
   B. amused.
   C. angry.
   D. concerned.

Answers to Diagnostic
   1. A   2. C   3. B   4. D   5. D

SECTION 3 ◆ EXERCISES: AUTHOR'S TONE

Use the following exercises to practice reading for author's tone.

PASSAGE #1

Read the passage and answer the question that follows.

Efficiency brings dependability. You can expect your burger and fries to taste the same whether you buy them in Los Angeles or Beijing. Efficiency also lowers prices. But efficiency does come at a cost. Predictability washes away spontaneity, changing the qual-

ity of our lives. It produces a sameness, a bland version of what used to be unique experiences. For good or bad, our lives are being McDonaldized, and the predictability   5
of packaged settings seems to be our social destiny. (Adapted from James M. Henslin,
Sociology, 6th ed., Boston: Allyn and Bacon, 2003.)

1. What is the overall tone of this passage?
    A. Humorous
    B. Pessimistic
    C. Critical
    D. Nostalgic

PASSAGE #2

Read the passage and answer the question that follows.

Regardless of the type of job you have, you have to divide your time between work
and school. The following suggestions will help you balance these two segments of
your life. First of all, make sure that your supervisor knows you are attending college
and that your job helps pay for it. He or she may be more understanding and helpful
if he or she knows you are a serious student. In addition, try to find a coworker who   5
may be willing to switch work hours or take your hours if you need extra time to study.
Next, if possible, try to build a work schedule around your class schedule. For example,
if you have an eight-o'clock class on Tuesday mornings, try not to work until midnight
on Monday night. Finally, allow study time for each class. Make sure you have time
between class sessions to do homework and complete assigned readings. For example,   10
if you have a Tuesday/Thursday class, make sure you have some study time between
the two sessions. (Adapted from Kathleen T. McWhorter, *Study and Critical Thinking
Skills in College*, 5th ed., New York: Longman, 2003.)

2. The tone of this passage can best be described as
    A. instructive.
    B. authoritative.
    C. cautionary.
    D. sarcastic.

PASSAGE #3

Read the passage and answer the question that follows.

Each of the 2000 or so species of firefly has its own way to signal a mate. When a female
sees flashes of light from a male of her species, she reacts with flashes of her own. If the
male sees her flashes, he automatically gives another display and flies in the female's direction. Members of both sexes are responding to particular patterns of light flashes
characteristic of their species. Some flash more often than others or during different   5
hours, while other species give fewer but longer flashes. Many species produce light of
a characteristic color: yellow, bluish-green, or reddish. Mating occurs when the female's
display leads a male to her, and most females stop flashing after they mate. But in a few
species, a mated female will continue to flash, using a pattern that attracts males of other

firefly species. A veritable *femme fatale*, she waits until an alien male gets close, then   5
grabs and eats him. (Adapted from Neil A. Campbell, Lawrence G. Mitchell, and Jane
B. Reece, *Biology*, 3rd ed., San Francisco: Benjamin Cummings, 2000.)

3. What is the overall tone of this passage?
    A. Humorous
    B. Objective
    C. Critical
    D. Argumentative

PASSAGE #4

Read the passage and answer the question that follows.

Fungi have a number of practical uses for humans. Most of us have eaten mushrooms although we may not have realized that we were ingesting the fruiting bodies of subterranean
fungi. In addition, mushrooms are not the only fungi we eat. The distinctive flavors of
certain kinds of cheeses, including Roquefort and blue cheese, come from the fungi used
to ripen them. Highly prized by gourmets are truffles, the fruiting bodies of certain myc-   5
orrhizal fungi associated with tree roots. The unicellular fungi, the yeasts, are important
in food production. Yeasts are used in baking, brewing, and winemaking. Fungi are medically valuable as well. Some fungi produce antibiotics that are used to treat bacterial diseases. In fact, the first antibiotic discovered was penicillin, which is made by the common
mold called *Penicillium*. (Adapted from Neil A. Campbell, Lawrence G. Mitchell, and   10
Jane B. Reece, *Biology*, 3rd ed., San Francisco: Benjamin Cummings, 2000.)

4. The tone of this passage can best be described as
    A. neutral.
    B. respectful.
    C. excited.
    D. boring.

PASSAGE #5

Read the passage and answer the question that follows.

Plagiarism is a serious infraction in most settings. Students can be suspended or expelled
from school. Researchers can lose their jobs and their standing in the academic community. Most importantly, plagiarism is serious because it violates several of the reasonable criteria for ethical decision making. Plagiarism violates your obligation to
yourself to be truthful, and it violates your obligation to society to produce fair and   5
accurate information. It also violates your obligation to other students and researchers.
(Adapted from Laura J. Gurak and John M. Lannon, *A Concise Guide to Technical
Communication*, New York: Longman, 2001.)

5. What is the overall tone of this passage?
    A. Cautionary
    B. Defiant
    C. Annoyed
    D. Sad

PASSAGE #6

Read the passage and answer the question that follows.

Truman's critics argue that the war might have ended even without the atomic bombings. They maintain that the Japanese economy would have been strangled by a continued naval blockade and forced to surrender by conventional firebombing. The revisionists also contend that the President had options apart from using the bombs. They believe that it might have been possible to induce a Japanese surrender by a demonstration of 5 the atomic bomb's power or by providing a more specific warning of the damage it could produce or by guaranteeing the emperor's position in postwar Japan. (Adapted from James Kirby Martin et al., *America and Its Peoples*, 5th ed., New York: Longman, 2004.)

6. The tone of this passage can best be described as
   A. complaining.
   B. passionate.
   C. neutral.
   D. humorous.

PASSAGE #7

Read the passage and answer the question that follows.

On April 20, 1999, a school shooting of such immense proportions occurred which radically, if not permanently, altered public thinking and debate about student safety and security. After months of planning and preparation, 18-year-old Eric Harris and 17-year-old Dylan Klebold armed themselves with guns and explosives and headed off to Columbine High School in Littleton, Colorado, to celebrate Adolph Hitler's birthday in a manner fit- 5 ting their hero. By the time the assault ended with self-inflicted fatal gunshots, a dozen students and one teacher lay dead. (Adapted from Neil A. Campbell, Lawrence G. Mitchell, and Jane B. Reece, *Biology*, 3rd ed., San Francisco: Benjamin Cummings, 2000.)

7. What is the overall tone of this passage?
   A. Objective
   B. Tragic
   C. Excited
   D. Flattering

PASSAGE #8

Read the passage and answer the question that follows.

We, therefore, the Representatives of the United States of America, in General Congress, Assembled, appealing to the Supreme Judge of the world for the rectitude of our intentions, do, in the Name, and by the Authority of the good People of these Colonies, solemnly publish and declare, That these United Colonies are, and of Right ought to be Free and Independent States; that they are Absolved from all Allegiance to the British 5 Crown, and that all political connection between them and the State of Great Britain, is and ought to be totally dissolved; and that as Free and Independent States, they have full Power to levy War, conclude Peace, contract Alliances, establish Commerce, and

to do all other Acts and Things which Independent States may of right do. And for the
support of this Declaration, with a firm reliance on the protection of divine Providence,   5
we mutually pledge to each other our Lives, our Fortunes and our sacred Honor. (From
The Declaration of Independence, in George C. Edwards, Martin P. Wattenberg, and
Robert L. Lineberry, *Government in America*, 9th ed., New York: Longman, 2000.)

8. The tone of this passage can best be described as
   A. reverent.
   B. nostalgic.
   C. objective.
   D. formal.

PASSAGE #9

Read the passage and answer the question that follows.

September 11, 2001

Today, our fellow citizens, our way of life, our very freedom came under attack in a series
of deliberate and deadly terrorist acts. The victims were in airplanes or in their offices: secretaries, business men and women, military and federal workers, moms and dads, friends
and neighbors. Thousands of lives were suddenly ended by evil, despicable acts of terror.   5

The pictures of airplanes flying into buildings, fires burning, huge structures collapsing have
filled us with disbelief, terrible sadness and a quiet, unyielding anger. These acts of mass
murder were intended to frighten our nation into chaos and retreat. But they have failed.

Terrorist attacks can shake the foundations of our biggest buildings, but they cannot
touch the foundation of America. These acts shatter steel but they cannot dent the steel   10
of American resolve.

Today, our nation saw evil, the very worst of human nature, and we responded with
the best of America, with the daring of our rescue workers, with the caring for strangers
and neighbors who came to give blood and helped in any way they could. (From President George W. Bush's speech on September 11, 2001, in James Kirby Martin et al.,
America and Its Peoples, 5th ed., New York: Longman, 2004.)

9. What is the overall tone of this passage?
   A. Impartial
   B. Sympathetic
   C. Inspirational
   D. Graphic

PASSAGE #10

Read the passage and answer the question that follows.

It was a Tiwi custom when an old woman became too feeble to look after herself to
"cover her up." This could only be done by her sons and brothers, and all of them had
to agree beforehand so there would be no feud afterwards. My "mother" was now

completely blind, she was constantly falling over logs or into fires, and they, her senior clansmen, were in agreement that she would be better out of the way. The method was to dig a hole in the ground in some lonely place, put the old woman in the hole and fill it in with earth until only her head was showing. Everybody went away for a day or two and then went back to the hole to discover to their surprise that the old woman was dead, having been too feeble to raise her arms from the earth. Nobody had "killed" her; her death in Tiwi eyes was a natural one. She had been alive when her relatives last saw her. I had never seen it done, though I knew it was the custom, so I asked my brothers if it was necessary for me to attend the "covering up." They said no and that they would do it, but only after they had my agreement. Of course I agreed, and a week or two later we heard in our camp that my "mother" was dead, and we walked and put on the trimmings of mourning. (Adapted from James M. Henslin, *Sociology*, 6th ed., Boston: Allyn and Bacon, 2003.)

10. The tone of this passage can best be described as
    A. graphic.
    B. annoyed.
    C. argumentative.
    D. excited.

KEEP IN MIND ◆ SUMMARY OF CHAPTER 3

Using context clues correctly can help you to determine the meaning of an unfamiliar word. Context is the language that surrounds a word that helps to determine its meaning. To choose the correct meaning of the word in the question,

- Always go back and reread the sentence containing the word in the question to determine which meaning is the closest for the context of *that sentence*. If necessary, reread the entire paragraph.
- Knowing the part of speech (noun, verb, adjective, etc.) will help determine the correct meaning.
- Substitute a blank in place of the word, and ask which answer choice seems to make most sense when put into the blank.
- Use other information in the sentence as clues to what the word means. Look for synonyms, antonyms, examples, and definitions, and consider the general sense of the passage.
- Look for smaller words within bigger words. Use word structure (prefixes, roots, and suffixes) to determine the meaning of a word.
- Remember that the correct answer may not be the word's exact meaning, but is the **closest** of the four choices offered.
- Use a combination of **all** of the strategies listed above to determine the meaning of unfamiliar words.

Biased Language

Authors often choose words that reveal their attitudes toward their subjects. A bias is an attitude that is for or against the subject. This subjective point of view may have a negative attitude or a positive one. Being able to recognize the author's use of positive or negative language will help you to determine the author's bias for or against the topic.

If the author does not seem to have either a positive or a negative attitude, then the writing is considered unbiased. In unbiased writing, the author attempts to balance opposing views, without appearing to be for or against the topic. The tone is therefore neutral, objective, straightforward, or matter-of-fact. Consider the following when determining the author's bias:

- Look for biased language with positive or negative connotations.
- Is the author's language mostly positive toward the subject?
- Is the author's language mostly negative toward the subject?
- Does the author balance both the negative and the positive aspects of the topic? Or is the information presented about the topic decidedly one-sided?
- Does the author present mostly facts or opinions?
- Begin by stating the author's topic and main idea. They may give you a clue to the author's bias.
- If the author does not appear to have either a positive or a negative bias toward the subject, the writing is objective, or unbiased.

Author's Tone

Authors choose words to create a tone or feeling. Understanding the author's tone will help you to comprehend the author's ideas and attitude toward the topic.
- Learn the meanings of as many tone words as you can.
- Pay close attention to the language of the passage.
- Look for adjectives that describe nouns.
- Think about the connotation, the emotional tone of the words.
- Look for opinions.
- Think about the main idea and author's purpose.

Chapter 4: Reasoning Skills

In Reading texts and on tests of Reading Comprehension, there are several rules to keep in mind when determining whether a statement is a fact or an opinion. Learning the rules can help you choose the correct answer.

A *fact* is any statement that is verifiable, or provable. It does not necessarily have to be a true statement, but it must be provable by some means.

An *opinion* is not provable. It is a personal belief, a judgment, or an attitude.

All future events are considered opinions because, since they have not yet happened, they are not provable, even when they seem certain to happen.

> **Examples**
> Columbus died in 1506. (A provable fact.)
> He discovered America in 1493. (An incorrect but provable fact.)
> Columbus was a brave and heroic man. (A judgment and an opinion.)
> The discovery of the New World will be remembered throughout history. (Future event, an opinion.)

Beware of opinions in quotes:

"This is the most exciting book you can read," our instructor said.

Even though the statement contains an opinion, the sentence is provable by verifying that the instructor said it. Therefore, it's a fact.

Important: If a statement appears to be half fact and half opinion, and the choices available are only fact and opinion, then choose opinion. If a third option, "fact and opinion" is offered, then choose that one.

▶▶◀ *Secrets to Success*

- *Look for adjectives that describe people, places, things, or events.*
- *Ask: Is this provable?*
- *Don't confuse opinions in quotes with the fact that someone said it.*
- *If a sentence is both fact and opinion, consider it opinion unless you have an option to choose "fact and opinion."*

SECTION 1 ◆ DIAGNOSTIC: FACT AND OPINION

Read the passages and apply the strategies described above for fact and opinion. When you are done, check your work with the answers immediately following the diagnostic. Even if you get a perfect score here, go ahead and complete the exercises in this section; they are designed to help build confidence and to give you practice for future test success.

Read each sentence and choose A for "Fact" or B for "Opinion."

1. The meeting is scheduled for 9:00 a.m. on Wednesday morning.
   A. Fact
   B. Opinion

2. There will be several items on the agenda which we must discuss at the meeting.
   A. Fact
   B. Opinion

3. We have been unable to determine whether or not our e-mails have been received.
   A. Fact
   B. Opinion

4. Sending an e-mail to notify everyone on the committee is the most efficient way to communicate the information about the meeting.
   A. Fact
   B. Opinion

5. Several members of the committee will not be able to attend because of another sales meeting they must attend in Tokyo.
   A. Fact
   B. Opinion

6. The committee meets once a month to discuss important issues and resolve complicated business problems.
   A. Fact
   B. Opinion

7. When the Japanese attend our business meetings, they prefer to begin by socializing and getting to know the members of our committee.
   A. Fact
   B. Opinion

8. After September 11, 2001, many businesses faced extreme hardship and bankruptcy.
   A. Fact
   B. Opinion

9. The U.S. economy suffered one of the worst recessions in its economic history after 9/11.
   A. Fact
   B. Opinion

10. Despite the setbacks, both the stock market and real estate markets have rebounded to become effective investments.
    A. Fact
    B. Opinion

Answers to Diagnostic

1. A   2. B (future event)   3. A   4. B
5. A   6. B   7. A   8. B   9. A   10. A

SECTION 1 ◆ EXERCISES: FACT AND OPINION

Use the following exercises to practice reading for fact and opinion.

PASSAGE #1

Read the passage and answer the question that follows.

As a result of Robert Fulton's construction of the North River Steamboat in 1907, the day of the steamboat had dawned. In the 1820s its major effects were clear. The great Mississippi Valley, in the full tide of its development, was immensely enriched. Produce poured down to New Orleans, which soon ranked with New York and Liverpool among the world's great ports. Only 80,000 tons of freight reached New Orleans from the interior in 1816 and 1817. Later, in 1840 and 1841, more than 542,000 tons of freight were transported. Upriver traffic was affected even more spectacularly. Freight charges plummeted, in some cases to a tenth of what they had been after the War of 1812. Around 1818, coffee cost 16 cents a pound more in Cincinnati than in New Orleans, a decade later less than 3 cents more. The Northwest emerged from self-sufficiency with a rush and became part of the national market. (Adapted from John A. Garraty and Mark C. Carnes, *The American Nation*, 10th ed., New York: Longman, 2000.)

1. Which sentence is a statement of opinion?
   A. Only 80,000 tons of freight reached New Orleans from the interior in 1816 and 1817.
   B. Later, in 1840 and 1841, more than 542,000 tons of freight were transported.
   C. Upriver traffic was affected even more spectacularly.
   D. Around 1818, coffee cost 16 cents a pound more in Cincinnati than in New Orleans, a decade later less than 3 cents more.

PASSAGE #2

Read the passage and answer the question that follows.

The modern science of genetics began in the 1860s when an Augustinian monk named Gregor Mendel discovered the fundamental principles of genetics by breeding garden peas. Mendel lived and worked in an abbey in Brunn, Austria. In a paper published in 1866, Mendel correctly argued that parents pass on to their offspring discrete heritable factors. He stressed that the heritable factors (today called genes) retain their individuality generation after generation. Mendel probably chose to study garden peas because they were easy to grow and available in many readily distinguishable varieties. Also, with pea plants, Mendel was able to exercise strict control over plant matings. As a result, he was always sure of the parentage of new plants. (Adapted from Neil A. Campbell, Lawrence G. Mitchell, and Jane B. Reece, *Biology*, 3rd ed., San Francisco: Benjamin Cummings, 2000.)

2. Which sentence is a statement of opinion?
   A. The modern science of genetics began in the 1860s when an Augustinian monk named Gregor Mendel discovered the fundamental principles of genetics by breeding garden peas.
   B. Mendel lived and worked in an abbey in Brunn, Austria.
   C. Mendel probably chose to study garden peas because they were easy to grow and available in many readily distinguishable varieties.
   D. In a paper published in 1866, Mendel correctly argued that parents pass on to their offspring discrete heritable factors.

PASSAGE #3

Read the passage and answer the questions that follow.

Ignorance of African geography and environment has contributed greatly to the prevailing misconceptions about African culture and history. Many Americans, for instance, have thought of the continent as an immense "jungle." In reality, more than half of the area south of the Sahara consists of grassy plains known as *savanna*, whereas "jungle" or tropical rain forests take up just seven percent of the land surface.   5

The most habitable areas have been the savannas, their grasslands and trees favoring both human settlement and long-distance trade and agriculture. The northern savanna stretches across the continent just south of the central desert, the Sahara. Other patches of savanna are interspersed among the mountains and lakes of East Africa and another belt of grassland that runs east and west across southern Africa, north and east of the   10
Kalahari Desert.

Between the northern and southern savannas, in the region of the equator, is dense rain forest. Although the rain forest is lush, its soils are poor because torrential rains cause soil erosion and intense heat leaches the soil of nutrients and burns off humus or organic matter that is essential for soil fertility. The rain forests also harbor insects that   15
carry deadly diseases. Mosquitoes transmit malaria and yellow fever, and the tsetse fly is a carrier of sleeping sickness to which both humans and animals such as horses and cattle are susceptible. (Brummet, Palmira, et al., *Civilization*, 9th ed., New York: Longman, 2000.)

3. "Ignorance of African geography and environment has contributed greatly to the prevailing misconceptions about African culture and history." (lines 1–2)

   The above sentence is a statement of

   A. fact.
   B. opinion.

4. "Mosquitoes transmit malaria and yellow fever, and the tsetse fly is a carrier of sleeping sickness to which both humans and animals such as horses and cattle are susceptible." (lines 17–19)

The above sentence is a statement of

A. fact.
B. opinion.

5. "Many Americans, for instance, have thought of the continent as an immense 'jungle.'" (lines 2–3)

The above sentence is a statement of

A. fact.
B. opinion.

PASSAGE #4

Read the passage and answer the questions that follow.

Though most precincts now use computer punch cards to record votes, the high-tech age has not yet made much impact on the voting process. There is good reason to expect that this will change in the twenty-first century.

The National Mail Voter Registration Form is available to download on the Federal Election Commission website. Twenty-two states currently accept copies of this application printed from the computer image, signed by the applicant, and mailed in the old-fashioned way. As e-mail becomes ever more popular and "snail mail" fades into a method reserved for packages, the entire voter registration process may someday be conducted mostly through electronic means. In an age where personal computers in the home will be as common as television sets are today, this technology would clearly make registering to vote more user-friendly.

If people can register by computer, the next step is naturally voting by e-mail. A growing trend in the Pacific Coast states has been voting by mail. In 1998, Oregon voters approved a referendum to eliminate traditional polling places and conduct all future elections by mail. In California, 25 percent of the votes cast currently come in via the post office. Again, as e-mail takes the place of regular mail, why not have people cast their votes via cyberspace? It would be less costly for the state, as well as easier for the average citizen—assuming that computer literacy reaches near-universal proportions sometime in the future. The major concerns, of course, are currently being addressed by some of the world's top computer programmers, as commercial enterprises look toward using the Internet to conduct business.

Making voting more user-friendly should encourage turnout, but people will still have to be interested enough in the elections of the future to send in their e-mail ballots. If everyone votes electronically in the convenience of his or her home, the sense of community on election day may be lost, which could lead to lower turnout. (Adapted from George C. Edwards, Martin P. Wattenberg, and Robert L. Lineberry, *Government in America*, 9th ed., New York: Longman, 2000.)

6. "In California, 25 percent of the votes cast currently come in via the post office." (lines 15–16)

   The above sentence is a statement of

   A. fact.
   B. opinion.

7. "If everyone votes electronically in the convenience of his or her home, the sense of community on election day may be lost, which could lead to lower turnout." (lines 23–25)

   The above sentence is a statement of

   A. fact.
   B. opinion.

8. "If people can register by computer, the next step is naturally voting by e-mail." (line 12)

   The above sentence is a statement of

   A. fact.
   B. opinion.

9. The National Mail Voter Registration Form is available to download on the Federal Election Commission website. (lines 4–5)

   The above sentence is a statement of

   A. fact.
   B. opinion.

PASSAGE #5

Read the passage and answer the question that follows.

There is no military conscription at present. The United States has had a volunteer force since 1973. However, President Jimmy Carter asked Congress to require both men and women to register for the draft after the Soviet Union invaded Afghanistan in 1979. Registration was designed to facilitate any eventual conscription. In 1980, Congress reinstated registration for men only, a policy that was not universally popular. Federal courts ordered registration suspended while several young men filed suit. These men argued that the registration requirement was gender-based discrimination that violated the due process clause of the Fifth Amendment.

5

The Supreme Court ruled in 1981 in *Rostker v. Goldberg* that male-only registration did not violate the Fifth Amendment. The Court found that male-only registration bore a substantial relationship to Congress's goal of ensuring combat readiness and that Congress acted well within its constitutional authority to raise and regulate armies and navies when it authorized the registration of men and not women. Congress, the Court said, was allowed to focus on the question of military need, rather than "equity." (Adapted from George C. Edwards, Martin P. Wattenberg, and Robert L. Lineberry, *Government in America*, 9th ed., New York: Longman, 2000.)

10

10. Which sentence is a statement of opinion?
    A. The United States has had a volunteer force since 1973.
    B. In 1980, Congress reinstated registration for men only, a policy that was not universally popular.

C. These men argued that the registration requirement was gender-based discrimination that violated the due process clause of the Fifth Amendment.
D. The Supreme Court ruled in 1981 in *Rostker v. Goldberg* that male-only registration did not violate the Fifth Amendment.

SECTION 2 ◆ INFERENCES AND CONCLUSIONS

Inference and conclusion questions are among the most difficult to answer correctly. This is because they generally require a full reading of the text with complete comprehension, and because they require the reader to "read between the lines" in a logical way to locate the correct answer. To make an **inference** or understand an **implication** means to come to a logical conclusion based upon the facts that are given. Information that is implied is not stated. Therefore, you must look at the facts and details to arrive at a logical conclusion.

One technique to help determine which statement is a logical conclusion in a multiple choice test is to treat each answer choice as if it were a true/false question. Go back and reread to determine whether the answer choices could be true or false based upon the information that is presented in the passage. Be careful not to assume more than what is stated, but rely upon what is stated and your own background knowledge to help you make the right choice. Also, **be especially careful to read the question!** Sometimes, you will be asked to locate an inference that <u>cannot</u> be reached. In that case, you must look for the <u>false</u> answer rather than the true answer.

When drawing conclusions and making inferences, be sure that you understand the literal meaning of the passage. Begin by stating the topic and main idea. Pay close attention to the details. Think like a detective and use the details (clues) to arrive at the correct conclusion.

Also, be careful not to call a statement an inference or a conclusion simply because you strongly agree with that statement. In other words, do not let your own biases cause you to see things in the text that are not there or to jump too far with your logic.

Example
Truman's critics argue that the war might have ended even without the atomic bombings. They maintain that the Japanese economy would have been strangled by a continued naval blockade and forced to surrender by conventional firebombing. The revisionists also contend that the President had options apart from using the bombs. They believe that it might have been possible to induce a Japanese surrender by a demonstration of the atomic bomb's power or by providing a more specific warning of the damage it could produce or by guaranteeing the emperor's position in postwar Japan. (Adapted from J. Martin et al., *America and Its Peoples*, 5th ed., New York: Longman: 2004.)

A conclusion that can be drawn from this passage is

A. Truman was not a popular president.
B. The navy did not blockade Japan.
C. The Japanese witnessed a demonstration of the atomic bomb.
D. After the atomic bombing, the war with Japan ended.

Look at each choice carefully, rereading the passage to determine if each statement is true or false.

A. *Truman was not a popular president.* Is there any information in the passage to support the idea that Truman was either popular or unpopular? The passage mentions Truman's critics, but every president, even popular ones, has critics. This statement is not supported by the passage. (False)

B. *The navy did not blockade Japan.* The passage does not say whether the navy blockaded Japan or not. It simply says, "the Japanese economy would have been strangled by a continued naval blockade." This statement is not supported by information in the passage. (False)

C. *The Japanese witnessed a demonstration of the atomic bomb.* This statement is the opposite of what the passage stated. In the passage, the argument states that the atomic bombing of Japan may not have been necessary because "it might have been possible to induce a Japanese surrender by a demonstration of the atomic bomb's power." Obviously, this did not happen. (False)

D. *After the atomic bombing, the war with Japan ended.* The passage states, "Truman's critics argue that the war might have ended even without the atomic bombings." The phrase "even without the atomic bombings" implies that the bombings took place and ended the war. This statement is true, and the correct answer.

▶▶▎ *Secrets to Success*

- *Look at the facts and details to arrive at a logical conclusion.*
- *Treat each answer choice as if it were a true/false question.*
- *Read the question very carefully to make sure you are being asked to locate true rather than false answers.*
- *Go back and reread to determine whether the answer choices could be true or false based upon the information that is presented in the passage.*
- *Do not assume more than what is stated in the passage, and do not select an inference simply because you agree with that statement.*
- *Rely upon your own background knowledge to help you make the right choice.*

SECTION 2 ◆ DIAGNOSTIC: INFERENCES AND CONCLUSIONS

Read the passages and apply the strategies described above for inferences and conclusions. When you are done, check your work with the answers immediately following the diagnostic. Even if you get a perfect score here, go ahead and complete the exercises in this section; they are designed to help build confidence and to give you practice for future test success.

Read the passages and answer the questions that follow.

PASSAGE #1

Time is especially linked to status considerations, and the importance of being on time varies with the status of the individual you are visiting. If the person is extremely important, you had better be there on time or even early just in case he or she is able to see you before schedule. Junior executives, for example, must be on time for conferences with senior executives, but it is even more important to be on time for the company president or the CEO. Senior executives, however, may be late for conferences with their juniors but not for conferences with the president. (DeVito, *Interpersonal Communication*, 6th ed.)

5

1. Which of the following conclusions can be drawn from the passage?
   A. The higher a person's status, the more important it is for a visitor to be on time for a meeting with that person.
   B. The higher a person's status, the less likely it is that they will wait for you.
   C. People with lower status must wait longer than people with higher status.
   D. Making people wait a long time will give a low status person higher status.

2. According to the passage, which of the following conclusions cannot be true?
   A. Junior executives must be on time for all persons of higher status.
   B. Even senior executives must be on time for some meetings.
   C. Senior executives have equal status with the company president or CEO.
   D. A CEO has as much status as a company president.

PASSAGE #2

In one experiment, Daniel Lehrman of Rutgers University found that when a male blond ring dove was isolated from females, it soon began to bow and coo to a stuffed model of a female—a model that had previously been ignored. When the model was replaced by a rolled-up cloth, he began to court the cloth; and when this was removed the sex-crazed dove distracted his attention to a corner of the cage, where it could at least focus its gaze. (R. Wallace, *Biology: The World of Life*, 4th ed., Glenview, NJ: Scott Foresman, 1987.)

5

3. Which of the following conclusions can be drawn from the passage?
   A. The experiment shows how all blond ring doves mate.
   B. Male ring doves have a very strong instinct to court.
   C. All male ring doves will court by bowing and cooing.
   D. Male blond ring doves do not have a high level of intelligence.

4. According to the passage, which of the following conclusions cannot be true?
   A. A male blond ring dove will try to court another female even if it is a model.
   B. The male blond ring dove has a strong drive to mate.
   C. The male blond ring dove cannot tell the difference between a live mate and a stuffed model.
   D. The male blond ring dove will exhibit mating behaviors even without a live female present.

PASSAGE #3

Bush infuriated environmentalists, who had been pleased with Clinton's efforts to protect America's national heritage. And, catering to the interests of oil companies, the new administration fought to promote drilling in the protected Arctic National Wildlife

Refuge, even in the face of estimates that there was very little oil there to be found.
When his own Environmental Protection Agency (EPA) issued a report in mid-2002   5
linking the use of fossil fuel to global warming, Bush dismissed the study by declaring
that he had "read the report put out by the bureaucracy," making it clear that he had
no confidence in the judgments of the scientists working for the EPA. (G. Nash et al.,
The American People: Creating a Nation and a Society, 6th ed., New York: Longman,
2004.)

5. Which of the following conclusions can be drawn from the passage?
   A. Environmentalists wanted to help oil companies drill in protected areas.
   B. The EPA's report was inaccurate.
   C. Research has been conducted regarding the presence of oil in the Arctic National Wildlife
      Refuge.
   D. Bush didn't want the EPA to study global warming.

6. What does the following sentence suggest about the environmentalists? "Bush infuriated en-
   vironmentalists, who had been pleased with Clinton's efforts to protect America's national
   heritage."
   A. Environmentalists approved of the EPA's report.
   B. In comparison to Bush, Clinton was considered a better environmental president by envi-
      ronmentalists.
   C. America's national heritage is infuriating environmentalists.
   D. Because of Bush's actions, environmentalists were angry at Clinton's efforts to protect the
      environment.

PASSAGE #4

Managed care plans have agreements with certain physicians, hospitals, and health
care providers to give a range of services to plan members at a reduced cost. There are
three basic types of managed care plans: health maintenance organizations (HMOs),
point-of-service plans (POSs), and preferred provider organizations (PPOs). The PPO,
in my opinion, is the best type of managed care plan because it merges the best features   5
of traditional health insurance and HMOs. As in traditional plans, participants in a
PPO may pay premiums, deductibles, and co-payments, but the co-pay under a PPO is
lower. The best part of a PPO, though, is its flexibility: participants may choose their
physicians and services from a list of preferred providers, or they may go outside the
plan for care if they wish. (Adapted from Pruitt and Stein, *Healthstyles,* Boston: Allyn   10
and Bacon, 2001.)

7. Which of the following conclusions can be drawn from the passage?
   A. A PPO costs less overall than an HMO.
   B. People with HMO and POS plans may not be able to choose their own physician.
   C. Traditional plans pay no deductibles.
   D. People in PPOs must choose their physicians only from a list of preferred providers.

Answers to Diagnostic
   1. A   2. C   3. B   4. C   5. C   6. B   7. B

SECTION 2 ◆ EXERCISES: INFERENCES AND CONCLUSIONS

Use the following exercises to practice reading for inferences and conclusions.

PASSAGE #1

Read the passage and answer the questions that follow.

During the seventeenth and eighteenth centuries, the process of childbirth in colonial America was conducted by women. The typical woman gave birth to her children at home, while female relatives and neighbors clustered at her bedside to offer support and encouragement.

Most women were assisted in childbirth not by a doctor but by a midwife. Most   5
midwives were older women who relied on practical experience in delivering children. One midwife, Martha Ballard, who practiced in Augusta, Maine, delivered 996 babies with only 4 recorded fatalities. Skilled midwives were highly valued. Communities tried to attract experienced midwives by offering a salary or a rent-free house. In addition to assisting in childbirth, midwives helped deliver the offspring   10
of animals, attended the baptisms and burials of infants, and testified in court cases of illegitimate babies.

During labor, midwives administered no painkillers except for alcohol. Pain in childbirth was considered God's punishment for Eve's sin of eating the forbidden fruit in the Garden of Eden. Women were merely advised to have patience, to pray, and during   15
labor, to restrain their groans and cries which upset the people near them.

After delivery, new mothers were often treated to a banquet. At one such event, visitors feasted on boiled pork, beef, poultry, roast beef, turkey pie, and tarts. Women from well-to-do families were then expected to spend three to four weeks in bed convalescing. Their attendants kept the fireplace burning and wrapped them in a heavy blanket in   20
order to help them sweat out "poisons." Women from poorer families were generally back at work in one or two days. (Adapted from James Kirby Martin et al., *America and Its Peoples*, New York: Longman, 2004.)

1. A conclusion that can be drawn from this passage is that during the seventeenth and eighteenth centuries,
   A. midwives had children themselves.
   B. midwives received high salaries.
   C. doctors did not want to deliver babies.
   D. women from different social classes had different post-childbirth experiences.

2. What does the following sentence from the second paragraph suggest about midwives?

   "Skilled midwives were highly valued." (line 8)

   A. Skilled midwives were superior to doctors.
   B. Skilled midwives delivered babies without medicating the mothers.
   C. Skilled midwives were scarce.
   D. Midwives gave religious guidance to mothers.

PASSAGE #2

Read the passage and answer the question that follows.

In the 1980s, a long-running TV public service advertisement showed a father confronting his son with what is obviously the boy's drug paraphernalia. The father asks his son incredulously, "Where did you learn to do this?" The son, half in tears, replies, "From you, okay? I learned it from watching you!" Observational learning, which results simply from watching others, clearly appears to be a factor in an adolescent's willingness to experiment with drugs and alcohol.   5

Andrews and her colleagues found that adolescents' relationships with their parents influence whether they will model the substance use patterns of the parents. Specifically, they found that adolescents who had a positive relationship with their mothers modeled her use (or nonuse) of cigarettes, and those who had a close relationship   10
with their fathers modeled the father's marijuana use (or nonuse). Similarly, those who had a negative relationship with their parents were less likely to model their parents' use of drugs or alcohol. Although some of the more complex results of this study depended on the age and sex of the adolescent, the general findings can be understood by thinking about them from the three levels of analysis and their   15
interactions.

At the level of the brain, observing someone engage in a behavior causes you to store new memories, which involves the hippocampus and related brain systems. These memories later can guide behavior, as they do in all types of imitation. At the level of the person, if you are motivated to observe someone, you are likely to   20
be paying more attention to him or her and, therefore, increasing the likelihood of your learning from that person and remembering what you learn. At the level of the group, you are more likely to be captivated by models who have certain attractive characteristics.

In this case, adolescents who had a positive relationship with their parents were more   25
likely to do what their parents did; if their parents didn't smoke, the adolescents were less likely to do so. The events at these levels interact. Children who enjoy a positive relationship with their parents may agree with their parents' higher status than do children who have a negative relationship with their parents. Thus, the former group of children probably increases the amount of attention they give to their parents' behavior.   30
(Adapted from Stephen M. Kosslyn and Robin S. Rosenberg, *Psychology,* 2nd ed., Boston: Allyn and Bacon, 2004.)

3. A conclusion that can be drawn from this passage is that
    A. adolescents model their parents' behavior.
    B. the more a child pays attention to his or her parents, the more likely it is that the child will pick up the parents' bad habits.
    C. parents who drink set a poor example for their children.
    D. adolescents are willing to experiment with drugs and alcohol.

PASSAGE #3

Read the passage and answer the questions that follow.

Deborah Tannen, sociologist and author, explains the differences in the listening behavior of men and women. Women seek to build rapport and establish a closer relationship and so use listening to achieve these ends. For example, women use more listening cues that let the other person know they are paying attention and are interested. On the other hand, men not only use fewer listening cues but interrupt more and will often change the topic to one they know more about or one that is less relational or people-oriented to one that is more factual, for example, sports, statistics, economic developments, or political problems. Men, research shows, play up their expertise, emphasize it, and use it to dominate the conversation. Women play down their expertise. Research shows that men communicate with women in the same way they do with other men. Men are not showing disrespect for their female conversational partners, but are simply communicating as they normally do. Women, too, communicate as they do not only with men but also with other women.

Tannen argues that the goal of a man in conversation is to be accorded respect, and so he seeks to display his knowledge and expertise even if he has to change the topic from one he knows little about to one he knows a great deal about. A woman, on the other hand, seeks to be liked, and so she expresses agreement and less frequently interrupts to take her turn as speaker.

Men and women also show that they are listening in different ways. A woman is more apt to give lots of listening cues, such as interjecting, "yeah, uh-uh," nodding in agreement, and smiling. A man is more likely to listen quietly, without giving lots of listening cues as feedback. Tannen also argues, however, that men do listen less to women than women listen to men. The reason is that listening places the person in an inferior position whereas speaking places the person in a superior position. There is no evidence to show that these differences represent any negative motives on the part of men to prove themselves superior or of women to ingratiate themselves. Rather, these differences in listening are largely the result of the way in which men and women have been socialized. (Adapted from Joseph A. DeVito, *Essentials of Human Communication*, 3rd ed., New York: Longman, 1999.)

5

10

15

20

25

4. A conclusion that can be drawn from this passage is that
   A. men are naturally more aggressive than women, a fact that influences their listening styles.
   B. women and men do not communicate well.
   C. men are less likely than women to tolerate being uncomfortable in a conversation.
   D. in conversation, women are more likely to discuss people and relationships than men are.

5. What does the following suggest about the way people listen?

   "Rather, these differences in listening are largely the result of the way in which men and women have been socialized." (lines 26–27)

   A. Men and women have inherently different listening styles.
   B. People could change their bad listening habits if they seek professional help.
   C. Men disrespect women because society tells them to.
   D. Men's and women's listening styles are learned rather than natural.

PASSAGE #4

Read the passage and answer the questions that follow.

On April 20, 1999, a school shooting of such immense proportions occurred which radically, if not permanently, altered public thinking and debate about student safety and security. After months of planning and preparation, 18-year-old Eric Harris and 17-year-old Dylan Klebold armed themselves with guns and explosives and headed off to Columbine High School in Littleton, Colorado, to celebrate Adolph Hitler's birthday in a manner fitting their hero. By the time the assault ended with self-inflicted fatal gunshots, a dozen students and one teacher lay dead. 5

In understanding the horrific actions of schoolyard snipers, it is as important to examine friendships as it is to delve into family background. At Columbine, Harris and Klebold were generally seen as geeks or nerds, from the point of view of any of the large student cliques—the jocks, the punks, etc. Though excluded from mainstream student culture, they banded together and bonded together with several of their fellow outcasts in what they came to call the "Trench Coat Mafia." The image they attempted to create was clearly one of power and dominance—the barbaric incivility, the forces of darkness, the preoccupation with Hitler, the celebration of evil and villainy. Harris and Klebold desperately wanted to feel important; and in the preparations they made to murder their classmates, the two shooters got their wish. For more than a year, they plotted and planned, colluded and conspired to put one over on their schoolmates, teachers, and parents. They amassed an arsenal of weapons, strategized about logistics, and made final preparations—yet, until it was too late, not a single adult got wind of what Harris and Klebold intended to do. 10 ... 15 ... 20

Birds of a feather may kill together. Harris, the leader, would likely have enjoyed the respect and admiration from Klebold, who in turn would have felt uplifted by the praise he received from his revered buddy. In their relationship, the two boys got from one another what was otherwise missing from their lives—they felt special, they gained a sense of belonging, they were united against the world. As Harris remarked, as he and his friend made last-minute preparations to commit mass murder: "This is just a two-man war against everything else." (Adapted from James Alan Fox and Jack Levin, *The Will to Kill*, Boston: Allyn and Bacon, 2001.) 25

6. A conclusion that can be drawn from this passage is that
   A. it is important to understand family background and friendships of students who commit school shootings.
   B. students who are outcasts are likely to commit acts of violence.
   C. schools are not safe.
   D. young people who are preoccupied with Hitler are mentally unstable.

7. What does the following sentence from the third paragraph suggest about Harris and Klebold's motivation to commit mass murder?

   "This is just a two-man war against everything else." (lines 26–27)

   A. They might not have gone on their murderous rampage if they had been able to join the military or to go to military school.
   B. They wanted to show that they were important.

C. Their rage was reasonable.
D. They thought they could win.

PASSAGE #5

Read the passage and answer the question that follows.

Few people work constantly at their jobs. Most of us take breaks and, at least once in a while, goof off. We meet fellow workers at the water cooler, and we talk in the hallway. Much of this interaction is good for the company, for it bonds us to fellow workers and ties us to our jobs. Our personal lives may even cross over into our workday. Some of us make personal calls from the office. Bosses know that we need to check in with   5
our child's preschool or make arrangements for a babysitter. They expect such calls. Some even wink as we make a date or nod as we arrange to have our car worked on. And most bosses make personal calls of their own from time to time. It's the abuse that bothers bosses, and it's not surprising that they fire anyone who talks on the phone all day for personal reasons.   10

The latest wrinkle at work is *cyberslacking*, using computers at work for personal purposes. Most workers fritter away some of their workday online. They trade stocks, download music, gamble, and play games. They read books, shop, exchange jokes, send personal e-mail, and visit online red-light districts. Some cyberslackers even operate their own businesses online. Others spend most of their "working" hours battling   15
virtual enemies. One computer programmer became a national champion playing *Starcraft* at work. Companies have struck back. Xerox fired 40 employees for downloading pornography at work. Dow Chemical fired 200 "workers" for cyberloafing. Then there is the cybersleuth. With specialized software, cybersleuths can examine everything employees read online, everything they write, and every web site they visit. They can even   20
bring up every word they've erased. What some workers don't know (and what some of us forget) is that "delete" does not mean *delete*. Our computer keeps a hidden diary, even of what we've erased. With a few clicks, the cybersleuth, like magic ink, makes our "deleted" information visible, exposing our hidden diary for anyone to read. (Adapted from James M. Henslin, *Sociology*, 6th ed., Boston: Allyn and Bacon, 2003.)

8. A conclusion that can be drawn from this passage is that
    A. most employees are expected to work the entire time they are on the premises.
    B. employers are probably unaware of how much time employees use to make personal phone calls at work.
    C. with the right software, an employer can view all of an employee's e-mails, even the personal ones.
    D. viewing pornography online is tolerated if it does not interfere with work.

PASSAGE #6

Read the passage and answer the questions that follow.

The analysis of DNA from fossils provides an opportunity to better understand extinct life and to trace the ancestry of genes found in modern organisms, including humans. Scientists have reported finding fragments of ancient DNA from many fossils, including a 40-million-year-old insect preserved in amber (fossilized plant resin), a 65-million-year-old dinosaur fossil, and a 30,000-year-old fossil arm bone of an extinct member of the human family tree (one of a group found in northern Europe called the Neanderthals).   5

In early autumn of 1991, two hikers working their way along the edge of a melting glacier in the high Alps of northern Italy found what seemed to be the weathered remains of an unlucky mountain climber. It was a man clothed in hand-sewn leather, frozen in glacial ice. Next to him were a bow and several arrows, a wooden backpack,   10
and a metal ax. A closer look turned up a leather pouch and other tools. The "Ice Man" turned out to be a leftover from the Stone Age, a young hunter who may have died from exhaustion and exposure some 5000 years ago.

Although scientists knew that the Ice Man was ancient, they did not know where he was from. In 1994, researchers reported that mitochondrial DNA from the Ice Man   15
closely matched that of modern central and northern Europeans, not Native Americans. Currently, the Ice Man remains frozen in the anatomy department of the University of Innsbruck. Continuing analysis of his DNA may provide more clues about his place in human evolution.

Science advances by the ebb and flow of ideas. Hypotheses are proposed, predictions   20
made, and test results evaluated. Too often, however, the advance is highlighted by the popular press as though it involves only a forward march, and the importance of disproving a hypotheses is lost. Some of the research on fossilized DNA illustrates this key aspect of science. Because it is difficult to obtain uncontaminated samples from fossils, ancient DNA is very challenging. Every report of success in isolating ancient   25
DNA has been met with skepticism and further analyses to make sure the DNA traces were not contaminated with DNA from bacteria, fungi, or other organisms. DNA is unlikely to remain intact, except when organisms fossilize in extremely cold or dry places where organic material tends to be preserved. Contamination is a potential pitfall even in ideal conditions. (Adapted from Neil A. Campbell, Lawrence G. Mitchell, and   30
Jane B. Reece, *Biology*, 3rd ed., San Francisco: Benjamin Cummings, 2000.)

9. It can be inferred that
   A. the Ice Man was probably out hunting when he was overcome by a snowstorm.
   B. the mitochondrial DNA of central and northern Europeans has changed very little over the last 5000 years.
   C. Neanderthals were not as well adapted to the earth as homo sapiens, and so they died off.
   D. the discovery of the Ice Man disproved many scientists' theories about ancient man.

10. A conclusion that can be drawn from this passage is that
    A. scientists would be more skeptical of DNA obtained from a fossil found in a rainforest than of DNA from a fossil found in the desert.
    B. the Ice Man is one of the oldest humans ever discovered.
    C. global warming must have caused the melting of the glacier where the Ice Man was found.
    D. the DNA of ancient insects preserved in amber is unlikely to be contaminated by other organisms.

PASSAGE #7

Read the passage and answer the questions that follow.

Today television is the most prevalent means used by candidates to reach voters. Thomas Patterson stresses that "today's presidential campaign is essentially a mass media campaign. . . . It is not exaggeration to say that, for the majority of voters, the campaign has little reality apart from its media version."

The most important goal of any media campaign is simply to get attention. Media coverage is determined by two factors: (1) how candidates use their advertising budget, and (2) the "free" attention they get as newsmakers. The first, obviously, is relatively easy to control; the second is more difficult but not impossible. Almost every logistical decision in a campaign—where to eat breakfast, whom to include on the rostrum, when to announce a major policy proposal—is calculated according to its intended media impact. About half the total budget for a presidential or senatorial campaign will be used for television advertising.

Candidates attempt to manipulate their images through advertising and image building, but they have less control over the other aspect of the media, news coverage. To be sure, most campaigns have press aides who feed "canned" news releases to reporters. Still, the media largely determine for themselves what is happening in a campaign. Campaign coverage seems to be a constant interplay between hard news about what candidates say and do and the human interest angle, which most journalists think sells newspapers or interests television viewers. (Adapted from George C. Edwards, Martin P. Wattenberg, and Robert L. Lineberry, *Government in America*, 9th ed., New York: Longman, 2000.)

11. A conclusion that can be drawn from this passage is that
    A. presidential candidates who do not receive much "free" media attention are unlikely to reach enough voters to win the election.
    B. most people are more interested in hard news about candidates than in personal stories about them.
    C. the press looks for opportunities to discredit presidential candidates.
    D. presidential candidates often criticize each other in their television advertisements.

12. What does the following sentence suggest about political campaigns?

    "It is not exaggeration to say that, for the majority of voters, the campaign has little reality apart from its media version." (lines 3–4)

    A. Campaigns are like television shows.
    B. Voters believe everything they see on television and read in the newspapers.
    C. The media's coverage of a campaign is very influential.
    D. Most people are too lazy to check sources other than the media for information about presidential candidates.

PASSAGE #8

Read the passage and answer the question that follows.

The most common stimulant is caffeine, which is contained in coffee, tea, cola drinks, and even chocolate. Caffeine is a mild stimulant that is often abused. Nonetheless, it is a drug and should be recognized as one that can lead to health problems.

Caffeine is absorbed rather quickly into the bloodstream and reaches a peak blood level in about thirty to sixty minutes. It increases mental alertness and provides a feeling   5
of energy. However, high doses of caffeine can overstimulate and cause nervousness and increased heart rate. Caffeine can also cause sleeplessness, excitement, and irritability. In some cases, high doses of caffeine can induce convulsions.

Coffee or cola drinking, let alone chocolate eating, cannot be considered drug abuse by most commonly accepted standards. But some individuals seek out caffeine for its   10
own sake in over-the-counter products and in illegal substances to produce a caffeine "high." Because it is not considered a dangerous drug, the opportunities for caffeine abuse are often overlooked. (David J. Anspaugh and Gene Ezell, *Teaching Today's Health*, 7th ed., San Francisco: Benjamin Cummings, 2004.)

13. A conclusion that can be drawn from this passage is that
    A. caffeine should be regulated by the Food and Drug Administration like other drugs are.
    B. people can get addicted to the caffeine in chocolate.
    C. some people abuse caffeine.
    D. caffeine is not dangerous.

PASSAGE #9

Read the passage and answer the question that follows.

Hate sites began on the Internet in the mid-1990s, and their numbers expanded rapidly. Now hate groups in general across the nation are on the rise because of the Internet. Hate sites advocate violence toward immigrants, Jews, Arabs, gays, abortion providers, and others. Through the Internet, disturbed minds effectively fuel hatred, violence, sexism, racism, and terrorism. Never before has there been such an intensive way for deprived   5
people to gather to reinforce their prejudices and hatred. In one analysis of hate speech sites, the researchers found sophisticated use of persuasive strategies. The hate sites generally started with an objective approach that was straightforward and neutral in which they reinforced and strengthened the hate ideas that people already have. The Internet provides a forum for people with prejudicial attitudes to speak out and act out. Hate-   10
mongers can create an online world where they reign supreme, a world of similar minds, where they can gather with others to feel that their way is right and where they can design severe disruption for the on-ground world. (Adapted from Leonard J. Shedletsky and Joan E. Aitken, *Human Communication on the Internet*, Boston: Allyn and Bacon, 2004.)

14. A conclusion that can be drawn from this passage is that
    A. the Internet has made it easier for hate groups to gather like-minded people.
    B. Internet hate sites are developed by unsophisticated or uneducated people.
    C. hate sites encourage people to kill Jews, Arabs, gays, and abortion providers.
    D. terrorists use the Internet to encourage suicide bombings.

PASSAGE #10

Read the passage and answer the questions that follow.

Evaluation research on drug education prevention programs done over the last thirty years indicates that these programs have not been effective. In fact, the findings state that these programs essentially had no effect on the drug problem. Although studies of the more recently developed programs are more optimistic, the findings still do not provide strong evidence of highly effective programs.   5

The goals of these programs have been to affect three basic areas: knowledge, attitudes, and behavior. The programs have had some success in increasing knowledge and, to a lesser extent, attitudes towards drugs; however, increases in knowledge and changed attitudes do not mean much if the actual drug behavior is not affected. In fact, those programs that only increase knowledge tend to reduce anxiety and fear of drugs and   10 may actually increase the likelihood of drug use. For example, one approach in the past was to provide students with complete information about all the possibilities of drug abuse, from the names of every street drug, to how the drugs are usually ingested, to detailed descriptions of possible effects of drugs and possible consequences of an overdose. Given the inquiring nature of children, such an approach could well amount   15 to a primer on how to take drugs, not how to avoid them.

The only effective approach to drug education is one in which children come to see that drug abuse constitutes unnecessary and self-abusive consequences. Too often, the real appeal of such drugs as marijuana or alcohol is dismissed by asking children to take up a sport or go bike riding or learn to play a musical instrument. Such suggestions   20 are fine as far as they go, but they often fail to take into account the personal problems that may tempt children into drug abuse.

Education programs that address social influence show the most promise in reducing or delaying the onset of drug use. Psychological approaches in which social influences and skills are stressed are more effective than other approaches. The most effective   25 programs in influencing both attitudes and behavior are peer programs that include either refusal skills—with more direct emphasis on behavior—or social and life skills, or both.

The use of scare tactics in any health education program, including drug abuse education programs, is counterproductive. Children soon learn to recognize the difference   30 between fact and possible fiction. Attempts to equate the dangers of marijuana with those of heroin, suggestions that any drug can kill or permanently impair an individual, and other dire warnings, no matter how true, are often disregarded as propaganda. (David J. Anspaugh and Gene Ezell, *Teaching Today's Health*, 7th ed., San Francisco: Benjamin Cummings, 2004.)

15. A conclusion that can be drawn from this passage is that
    A. telling children to take up a sport instead of drugs is an effective tactic.
    B. sometimes, drug prevention programs provide misleading information about drugs.
    C. the best approach for drug education is to avoid approaching it at all.
    D. programs that increase knowledge about drugs are very successful.

16. What conclusion can be reached regarding the following statement about scare tactics?

   "The use of scare tactics in any health education program, including drug abuse education programs, is counterproductive." (lines 28–29)

   A. Frightening children can cause psychological problems.
   B. Scare tactics may make drugs appealing.
   C. Children know more about drugs than their teachers do.
   D. The most successful drug abuse education programs do not use scare tactics.

PASSAGE #11

Read the passage and answer the questions that follow.

Matt Drudge was 30 years old when he broke his first story about Monica Lewinsky's relationship with President Clinton, which would become the biggest political scandal of the 1990s. Drudge had never been trained in journalism nor hired by any media outlet. He had neither verified the story nor done any extensive research on it. All he had to go on was the rumor that *Newsweek* had been working on this story and had decided not to print it in that week's issue. But for Drudge, a rumor was good enough to report on. No editor was going to tell him that he needed confirmation, as Drudge worked on his own. He didn't have to worry about the damage to his publication because he didn't have one; he relied instead on getting the "Drudge Report" out through an e-mail list and by posting it on his web site. When Drudge hit the enter button on his computer to post the Lewinsky story, he knew his life would be changed forever, and for quite some time so would the nation's.

Matt Drudge and his brand of cyber reporting have changed the whole news cycle in America. Journalists who are working on a scoop know they can quickly lose an exclusive story if someone like Drudge gets wind of it and posts the headline on the Internet. As a result, a number of newspapers immediately post their most important stories on their web site rather than waiting until the next morning. The *Dallas Morning News* made big headlines when they rushed a story onto the web about a White House steward testifying that he had seen President Clinton and Monica Lewinsky in a compromising position. The next day the paper had egg on its face, however, when the steward's lawyer strongly denied the story and the paper was forced to retract it. Similarly, Drudge found himself in trouble when he accused White House aide Sidney Blumenthal of spouse abuse. He quickly pulled the story and apologized when he realized it was planted by politically motivated Republican operatives, but not before Blumenthal hit him with a $30 million libel suit.

Opinions on Matt Drudge and his reporting techniques vary widely. Because of his penchant for reporting rumors and gossip, the *New York Times* called him "the nation's chief mischief maker." Others have dubbed him the first Internet superstar and praised how he has paved the way for communication power to be transferred from media giants to anyone with a modem. However one views him, it is clear that Matt Drudge has made a difference. (Adapted from George C. Edwards, Martin P. Wattenberg, and Robert L. Lineberry, *Government in America*, 9th ed., New York: Longman, 2000.)

17. A conclusion that can be drawn from this passage is that
    A. Matt Drudge made the Internet a player in news reporting.
    B. Matt Drudge is an entertainer.
    C. Matt Drudge gets away with libel.
    D. Power players appreciate seeing stories about themselves on Drudge's site.

18. A conclusion that can be drawn from the first paragraph of this passage is that
    A. Matt Drudge is a troublemaker.
    B. Drudge does not always confirm stories before publishing them.
    C. Drudge enjoyed gathering and spreading rumors.
    D. Drudge broke the story about Monica Lewinsky's relationship with President Clinton.

PASSAGE #12

Read the passage and answer the questions that follow.

Forest decline is not a new phenomenon. During the past two centuries, our forests have experienced several declines, with different species affected. What sets the current decline apart from all others is differences among the symptoms in the past and the similarity of symptoms among species today. Past declines could be attributed to natural stresses, such as drought and disease. What causes forest decline and dieback today is not established, but the widespread similarity of symptoms suggests a common cause—air pollution. All of the affected forests are in the path of pollutants from industrial and urban sources.   5

Forests close to the point of origin of pollutants experience the most direct effects of air pollution, and their decline and death can be directly attributed to it. Little evidence exists that acid precipitation alone is the cause of forest decline and death at distant points. The effects of acid deposition, however, can so weaken trees that they succumb to other stresses such as drought and insect attack. The stressed forests of Fraser fir in the Great Smoky Mountains succumbed to the attacks of the introduced balsam woolly adelgid. The once deep, fragrant stands of Fraser fir, especially on the windward side and peaks of the Great Smoky Mountains, are now stands of skeleton trees.   10   15

Air pollution and acid rain also are altering succession by changing the species composition of forests. Just as the chestnut blight shifted dominance in the central hardwood forest from chestnut to oaks, so is air pollution shifting dominance from pines and other conifers to leaf-shedding trees more tolerant of air pollution. (Adapted from Robert Leo Smith and Thomas M. Smith, *Elements of Ecology*, 5th ed., San Francisco: Benjamin Cummings, 2003.)   20

19. An inference that <u>cannot</u> be made from this passage is that
    A. the balsam woolly adelgid is an insect.
    B. pine trees are susceptible to the effects of air pollution.
    C. forest decline cannot be directly attributed to air pollution.
    D. healthy trees can sometimes fight off attacks of disease and drought.

20. What does the following sentence suggest?

"All of the affected forests are in the path of pollutants from industrial and urban sources." (lines 7–8)

A. Air pollution is probably responsible for the damage to these forests.
B. All of the other forests beyond the reach of these pollutants are healthy.
C. Eventually, all trees in the path of these pollutants will die.
D. The polluters should be held responsible for the damage to the forests.

SECTION 3 ◆ ASSESSING SUPPORT FOR REASONING AND ARGUMENT

When an author makes a claim about something, it is expected that the claim will be supported with details that are relevant and logical, and it will provide sufficient factual information. Critical thinkers evaluate the author's support, looking for data and facts that prove the author's point.

This section tests your ability to recognize the difference between *adequate* and *inadequate* support, *relevant* and *irrelevant* support, and *objective* and *emotional* support for an argument. You will be given a passage to read; you will then be expected to choose a statement that offers the best support for an author's claim or an option that describes a support as *adequate, inadequate, relevant,* or *irrelevant*.

Check details against the main pattern of organization. The same event will provide different relevant details based on how the ideas are organized. For example, narrative passages may include different time order details than a process that relies on ordered steps in a series.

Check to match that generalized or broad statements are followed by specific examples or illustrations.

Check the logic of inferences and implications by matching conclusions to evidence.

What kind of support is offered in the following examples?

Example #1
Year-round schools have been huckstered as a way to raise students' achievement and a cure-all for what ails education. The year-round school proposal, however, does not get to the heart of our educational difficulties. It just relieves some school officials from attacking the real problems that plague their school systems. I am fed up with fads and with all self-aggrandizing individuals who, like vultures, have targeted the rich educational terrain looking to pick its bones at the expense of our students, parents and all taxpayers. The school system should not be used as a political smokescreen to buy time for those school officials who need to show taxpayers that they are doing "something." (Dorothy Rubin, "Should Students Attend School Year Round? No," from K. McWhorter, *Reading Across the Disciplines*, New York: Longman, 2005.)

Topic: Year-Round Schooling

Main Idea: Students should not attend school year round.

What kind of support is offered for the author's claim that students should not attend school year round?

A. Objective (factual)
B. Emotional (opinions)

The support given to the author's claim is B, Emotional. Rather than presenting logical and relevant reasons why year-round school is a bad idea, the author has simply given her own opinions. Some of the details have little to do with the topic and are therefore irrelevant. The supporting details must be related to the topic.

> **Example #2**
> Year-round school offers two important benefits. The most important is continuity of instruction that currently is split by a two-month summer break. Everyone who has attended school, and certainly everyone who has taught school, recognizes that much is forgotten over the summer and that tedious review in the fall wastes time. Not surprisingly, a great deal of research substantiates this observation. Research also shows that the vast majority of the more than 2,700 year-round schools show improved academic success. (Daniel Domenech, "Should Students Attend School Year Round? Yes," from K. McWhorter, *Reading Across the Disciplines*, New York: Longman, 2005.)

Topic: Year-Round Schooling

Main Idea: Students should attend school year round.

The author's claim that students should attend school year round is

 A. inadequately supported because it lacks evidence and explanation.
 B. adequately supported by factual details.

The author presents facts and data to support his claim, pointing out two important benefits of year-round school, and cites that research done on this issue shows that 2,700 year-round schools show improved academic success. The correct answer is B, adequately supported by factual details.

Which sentence offers the best support for the author's claim, "Year-round school offers two important benefits"?

 A. Not surprisingly, a great deal of research substantiates this observation.
 B. Everyone who has attended school, and certainly everyone who has taught school, recognizes that much is forgotten over the summer and that tedious review in the fall wastes time.
 C. Research also shows that the vast majority of the more than 2,700 year-round schools show improved academic success.

The correct answer is C, Research also shows that the vast majority of the more than 2,700 year-round schools show improved academic success. This statement offers proof that year-round schooling has benefits. Choices A and B are not as strong in their evidence that year-round school has important benefits.

▶▶│ *Secrets to Success*

- *Make sure that the literal meaning of the passage is clearly understood by stating the topic, the main idea, and the author's claim.*
- *Go back into the passage and look for supporting details that prove or support the author's claim.*
- *Look for specific examples or illustrations of the author's claim.*
- *Look for opinions.*
- *Check to make sure that the supporting details are related to the issue.*
- *Check to make sure the author's claim is logical and based on facts and not opinions.*

SECTION 3 ◆ DIAGNOSTIC: ASSESSING SUPPORT FOR REASONING AND ARGUMENT

Read the passages and apply the strategies described above for reasoning and argument. When you are done, check your work with the answers immediately following the diagnostic. Even if you get a perfect score here, go ahead and complete the exercises in this section; they are designed to help build confidence and to give you practice for future test success.

Read the passages and answer the questions that follow.

PASSAGE #1

Forest decline is not a new phenomenon. During the past two centuries, our forests have experienced several declines, with different species affected. What sets the current decline apart from all others is differences among the symptoms in the past and the similarity of symptoms among species today. Past declines could be attributed to natural stresses, such as drought and disease. What causes forest decline and dieback today is not established,   5
but the widespread similarity of symptoms suggests a common cause—air pollution. All of the affected forests are in the path of pollutants from industrial and urban sources.

Forests close to the point of origin of pollutants experience the most direct effects of air pollution, and their decline and death can be directly attributed to it. Little evidence exists that acid precipitation alone is the cause of forest decline and death at distant   10
points. The effects of acid deposition, however, can so weaken trees that they succumb to other stresses such as drought and insect attack. The stressed forests of Fraser fir in the Great Smoky Mountains succumb to the attacks of the introduced balsam woolly adelgid. The once deep, fragrant stands of Fraser fir, especially on the windward side and peaks of the Great Smoky Mountains, are now stands of skeleton trees.   15

Air pollution and acid rain also are altering succession by changing the species composition of forests. Just as the chestnut blight shifted dominance in the central hardwood forest from chestnut to oaks, so is air pollution shifting dominance from pines and other conifers to leaf-shedding trees more tolerant of air pollution. (Adapted from Robert Leo Smith and Thomas M. Smith, *Elements of Ecology*, 5th ed., San Francisco: Benjamin Cummings, 2003.)

1. The author's claim that, "What causes forest decline and dieback today is not established, but the widespread similarity of symptoms suggests a common cause—air pollution," is
   A. inadequately supported based upon opinion.
   B. adequately supported based upon facts.

2. Throughout the passage, which type of support is offered for the author's claim that, "What causes forest decline and dieback today is not established, but the widespread similarity of symptoms suggests a common cause—air pollution"?
   A. Objective
   B. Emotional

3. Which statement offers the best support for the author's claim that, "What causes forest decline and dieback today is not established, but the widespread similarity of symptoms suggests a common cause—air pollution"?
   A. All of the affected forests are in the path of pollutants from industrial and urban sources.
   B. The effects of acid deposition, however, can so weaken trees that they succumb to other stresses such as drought and insect attack.
   C. Air pollution and acid rain also are altering succession by changing the species composition of forests.
   D. During the past two centuries, our forests have experienced several declines, with different species affected.

PASSAGE #2

September 11, 2001

Today, our fellow citizens, our way of life, our very freedom came under attack in a series of deliberate and deadly terrorist acts. The victims were in airplanes or in their offices: secretaries, business men and women, military and federal workers, moms and dads, friends and neighbors. Thousands of lives were suddenly ended by evil, despicable acts of terror.   5

The pictures of airplanes flying into buildings, fires burning, and huge structures collapsing have filled us with disbelief, terrible sadness and a quiet, unyielding anger. These acts of mass murder were intended to frighten our nation into chaos and retreat. But they have failed.   10

Terrorist attacks can shake the foundations of our biggest buildings, but they cannot touch the foundation of America. These acts shatter steel but they cannot dent the steel of American resolve.

Today, our nation saw evil, the very worst of human nature, and we responded with the best of America, with the daring of our rescue workers, with the caring for strangers   15
and neighbors who came to give blood and helped in any way they could. (From President George W. Bush's speech on September 11, 2001, in James Kirby Martin et al., *America and Its Peoples*, 5th ed., New York: Longman, 2004.)

4. The authors' claim that, "These acts of mass murder were intended to frighten our nation into chaos and retreat. But they have failed" is
   A. inadequately supported based upon opinion.
   B. adequately supported based upon facts.

5. Throughout the passage, which type of support is offered for the authors' claim that, "Terrorist attacks can shake the foundations of our biggest buildings, but they cannot touch the foundation of America"?
   A. Objective
   B. Emotional

6. Which statement offers the best support for the authors' claim that, "These acts shatter steel but they cannot dent the steel of American resolve"?

A. These acts of mass murder were intended to frighten our nation into chaos and retreat.

B. The victims were in airplanes or in their offices: secretaries, business men and women, military and federal workers, moms and dads, friends and neighbors.

C. The pictures of airplanes flying into buildings, fires burning, and huge structures collapsing have filled us with disbelief, terrible sadness and a quiet, unyielding anger.

D. Today, our nation saw evil, the very worst of human nature, and we responded with the best of America, with the daring of our rescue workers, with the caring for strangers and neighbors who came to give blood and helped in any way they could.

7. The authors' claim that, "Terrorist attacks can shake the foundations of our biggest buildings, but they cannot touch the foundation of America" is

A. inadequately supported based upon opinion.

B. adequately supported based upon facts.

Answers to Diagnostic

1. B   2. A   3. A   4. A   5. B   6. D   7. A

SECTION 3 ◆ EXERCISES: ASSESSING SUPPORT FOR REASONING AND ARGUMENT

Use the following exercises to practice reading for assessing support for reasoning and argument.

PASSAGE #1

Read the passage and answer the questions that follow.

Everywhere it occurred, industrialization drove society from an agricultural to an urban way of life. The old system, in which peasant families worked the fields during the summer and did their cottage industry work in the winter to their own standards and at their own pace, slowly disappeared. In its place came urban life tied to the factory system. The factory was a place where for long hours people did repetitive tasks using   5
machines to process large amounts of raw materials. This was an efficient way to make a lot of high-quality goods cheaply. But the factories were often dangerous places, and the lifestyle connected to them had a terrible effect on the human condition.

In the factory system, the workers worked, and the owners made profits. The owners wanted to make the most they could from their investment and to get the most work   10
they could from their employees. The workers, in turn, felt that they deserved more of the profits because their labor made production possible. This was a situation guaranteed to produce conflict, especially given the wretched conditions the workers faced in the first stages of industrialization.

The early factories were miserable places, featuring bad lighting, lack of ventilation,   15
dangerous machines, and frequent breakdowns. Safety standards were practically non-existent, and workers in various industries could expect to contract serious diseases; for example, laborers working with lead paint developed lung problems, pewter work-

ers fell ill to palsy, miners suffered black lung disease, and operators of primitive machines lost fingers, hands, and even lives. Not until late in the nineteenth century did health and disability insurance come into effect. In some factories workers who suffered accidents were deemed to be at fault; and since there was little job security, a worker could be fired for almost any reason.

The demand for plentiful and cheap labor led to the widespread employment of women and children who worked long hours. Girls as young as 6 years old were used to haul carts of coal in Lancashire mines, and boys and girls of 5 years of age worked in textile mills, where their nimble little fingers could easily untangle jams in the machines. When they were not laboring, the working families lived in horrid conditions in Manchester, England. There were no sanitary, water, or medical services for the workers, and working families were crammed 12 and 15 individuals to a room in damp, dark cellars. Bad diet, alcoholism, cholera, and typhus reduced lifespans in the industrial cities. (Brummet, Palmira, et al., *Civilization: Past and Present*, New York: Longman, 2000.)

1. Throughout the passage, which type of support is offered for the authors' conclusion that "But the factories were often dangerous places, and the lifestyle connected to them had a terrible effect on the human condition"? (lines 7–8)
   A. Objective
   B. Emotional

2. The authors' claim that "This was a situation guaranteed to produce conflict, especially given the wretched conditions the workers faced in the first stages of industrialization" (lines 12–14) is
   A. inadequately supported because it lacks evidence and explanation.
   B. adequately supported by factual details.

3. Which statement offers the best support for the authors' claim that "The demand for plentiful and cheap labor led to the widespread employment of women and children who worked long hours" (lines 24–25)?
   A. Women made up the majority of the workplace in textile mills.
   B. Children were fast workers.
   C. Women worked in textile mills from 5 a.m. to 7:30 p.m., 14½ hours, 6 days a week.
   D. Women earned higher wages in factories than they could in other jobs.

PASSAGE #2

Read the passage and answer the questions that follow.

If you have ever stayed up late, say, studying or partying, and then awakened early the next morning, you have probably experienced sleep deprivation. In fact, you may be sleep deprived right now. If so, you have company. Many adults do not get enough sleep (defined as 8 hours). Sleep deprivation affects us in at least three important psychological areas: attention, mood, and performance.

Sleep deprivation affects the ability to perform tasks requiring sustained attention. Young adults who volunteered for a sleep deprivation study were allowed to sleep for only 5 hours each night, for a total of 7 nights. After 3 nights of restricted sleep, volunteers complained of cognitive, emotional, and physical difficulties. Moreover, their performance on a visual motor task declined after only 2 nights of restricted sleep. Visual motor tasks usually require participants to concentrate on detecting a change in a particular stimulus, and then to respond as quickly as they can after they perceive the change by pressing a button. Although you may be able to perform short mental tasks normally when sleep deprived, if a task requires sustained attention and a motor response, your performance will suffer. Driving a car is an example of such a task. In fact, in a survey by the National Sleep Foundation, 25% of the respondents reported that they had at some time fallen asleep at the wheel; sleepy drivers account for at least 100,000 car crashes each year.   10   15

Moods are also affected by sleep deprivation. Those who sleep less than 6 hours each weekday night are more likely to report being impatient or aggravated when faced with common minor frustrations such as being stuck in traffic or having to wait in line, and they were more dissatisfied with life in general, according to the National Sleep Foundation. The loss of even one night's sleep can lead to increases in the next day's level of cortisol. Cortisol helps the body meet the demands of stress. However, sleep deprivation can lead to a change in cortisol levels that, in turn, alters other biological functions. Regularly increased cortisol levels affect memory and cause a decrease in the immune system.   20   25

And what about a series of all-nighters, when you get no sleep at all, as might occur during finals period? Results from volunteers who have gone without sleep for long stretches (finally sleeping after staying awake anywhere from 4 to 11 days) show profound psychological changes, such as hallucinations, feelings of losing control or going crazy, anxiety, and paranoia. Morevoer, going without sleep alters the normal circadian rhythms of changes in temperature, metabolism, and hormone secretion. Results of a study on sleep-deprived humans found a different pattern of brain activation when learning verbal material, compared to the pattern of activation when not sleep deprived, suggesting an attempt to compensate for the brain changes induced by sleep deprivation. (Adapted from Stephen M. Kosslyn and Robin S. Rosenberg, *Psychology*, Boston: Allyn and Bacon, 2004.)   30   35

4. The authors' claim that "Sleep deprivation affects the ability to perform tasks requiring sustained attention" (line 6) is
   A. inadequately supported based on personal opinion.
   B. adequately supported based on factual details.

5. Throughout the passage, which type of support is offered for the authors' conclusion that "Sleep deprivation affects us in at least three important psychological areas: attention, mood, and performance"? (lines 4–5)
   A. Objective
   B. Emotional

6. Which statement offers the best support for the authors' claim that "Many adults do not get enough sleep (defined as 8 hours)"? (lines 3–4)
   A. In today's world of overscheduled lives and 10-hour workdays, no one can claim to be getting a natural amount of sleep.
   B. Older adults sleep less than younger adults and children.

C. Many adults claim to be so sleepy during the day that their daily activities are affected.

D. A 2002 survey by the National Sleep Foundation found that two out of three people are sleeping fewer than 6 hours each night.

PASSAGE #3

Read the passage and answer the questions that follow.

Almost everyone agrees that the use of drugs to enhance sports performance is unfair. Safeguards have been put in place, and the detection of drugs in a winner's body disqualifies that person from competition.

Now comes genetic engineering. With the human genome mapped and technology following rapidly, it is likely that inserting genetic materials in athletes can increase their bulked-up muscle mass or their oxygen-carrying capacity. They will be able to run faster, to jump higher, and to throw further. Where the record for the 26.2 mile marathon is about 2 hours, someone may be able to run it in an hour and a half. The record for the 100-meter sprint, currently at 9.79 seconds, could drop to 6 seconds. The risks to health would be high. As the president of a biomedical ethics research institute said, inserting genetic materials "is like firing at the bull's-eye of a target with shotgun pellets." When you inject the material, you don't know its exact effects. You might want to strengthen the shoulder muscles of a javelin thrower, for example, but you might enlarge that person's heart, too. Suppose that you add the gene for human growth hormone, but it turns out that you can't regulate it. The individual could end up with a gigantic head, jaw, hands, and feet. 5

10

15

With health risks high, would athletes take the risk? There is no doubt about the answer. Nearly 200 U.S. athletes who were aspiring for the Olympics were asked if they would take a banned substance that would guarantee them victory in every competition for the next five years—but at the end of the five years it would cause their death. More than half said they would take it. 20

As genetic manipulation becomes more like a rifle shot than a shotgun blast—and we are closing in on that day—some athletes will seize the opportunity to increase their advantage. Others, seeing this, will do the same. The rush for genetic manipulation will be on. (James M. Henslin, *Sociology*, 6th ed., Boston: Allyn and Bacon, 2003.) 25

7. Throughout the passage, which type of support is offered for the author's conclusion that "As genetic manipulation becomes more like a rifle shot than a shotgun blast—and we are closing in on that day—some athletes will seize the opportunity to increase their advantage"? (lines 22–24)
A. Objective
B. Emotional

8. The author's claim that "When you inject the material, you don't know its exact effects" (line 12) is
A. inadequately supported because it lacks evidence.
B. adequately supported with relevant details.

9. The author's claim that "With the human genome mapped and technology following rapidly, it is likely that inserting genetic materials in athletes can increase their bulked-up muscle mass or their oxygen-carrying capacity" (lines 4–6) is
    A. adequately supported by factual detail.
    B. inadequately supported because it is based on generalizations.

10. Which statement offers the best support for the author's claim that "The risks to health would be high"? (line 10)
    A. When you inject the material, you don't know its exact effects.
    B. Genetic modifications to make muscles strong may put a strain on bones.
    C. Injecting red blood cells improves endurance, but the risks are blood clots, bacterial infection, and congestive heart failure.
    D. Injecting artificial genes to help a sprinter's muscles bulge with energy could result in pulled muscles and broken bones.

KEEP IN MIND ◆ SUMMARY OF CHAPTER 4

Fact and Opinion

In reading texts and on tests of reading comprehension, there are several rules to keep in mind when determining whether a statement is a fact or an opinion. Learning the rules can help you choose the correct answer.

*   Look for adjectives that describe people, places, things, or events.
*   Ask: Is this provable?
*   Look for attitudes, prejudices, and beliefs.
*   Don't confuse opinions in quotes with the fact that someone said it.
*   If a sentence is both fact and opinion, consider it opinion unless you have an option to choose "fact and opinion."

Inferences and Conclusions

To make an inference means to come to a logical conclusion based upon the facts that are given. Information that is implied is not stated. To arrive at a logical conclusion:

*   Look at the facts and details to arrive at a logical conclusion.
*   Treat each answer choice as if it were a true/false question.
*   Go back and reread to determine whether the answer choices could be true or false based upon the information that is presented in the passage.
*   Do not assume more than what is stated in the passage.
*   Rely upon your own background knowledge to help you make the right choice.

Part Three: Test-Taking Strategies

"It's not that I'm so smart; it's just that I stay with problems longer."

—Albert Einstein

The word "test" conjures up all kinds of different ideas, many of which are negative. Keep in mind, however, that a test is not intended to be a judgment of you as a person; it is simply a measurement of what information you know.

The best way to overcome the fear and anxiety you may have about passing this test is to become test-wise, that is, to learn the format of the questions that are on the test, to work through practice questions that are similar to those on the test, and to review the competencies that you will be tested on. *Thinking Through the Test* has everything you need to get ready for the exam.

The Reading Exit Exam consists of <u>36 multiple-choice questions</u> over four multi-paragraph readings. Each reading usually has approximately nine questions associated with it. The readings are usually fairly academic in nature but quite accessible. In other words, the subject matter of the readings is something one might encounter in a textbook, but it is often quite interesting, and the language and sentence structure of the readings is usually not overly academic. Sometimes, a narrative or even a humorous essay is used as one of the readings, but overall, the readings are similar to what one might see in a high-interest textbook on some subject. The questions concern the reading skills you have been learning as you go through the exercises in this book: Main Idea, Supporting Detail, Author's Purpose, Author's Tone, Patterns of Organization, Inferences and Conclusions, Vocabulary, and Fact and Opinion. Knowing as much as you can about the test before you take it can really reduce your test anxiety and make it much more likely that you will pass the test.

How to Prepare for the Exit Exam

1. Take the sample Pretest at the beginning of the book to find out what your strengths and weaknesses are before you begin working on the individual skills. This way, you will know which skills you need to spend more time acquiring.

2. Work through the sections of *Thinking Through the Test,* and make sure you understand the correct answers to the exercises. Be sure to follow the tips given in each section.

3. <u>Learn</u> the Patterns of Organization and the transitional words (key words) that accompany them from Chapter 2. There are more questions addressing this skill on the Exit Exam than any other, so make sure you comprehend this skill thoroughly.

4. <u>Learn</u> the most common words used to describe the author's tone in Chapter 3, section 3 of this text. Tone questions are not difficult as long as you know what the answer choices mean.

5. Take the practice Exit Exams in Part Four. After you score each test, analyze which skills you still need to work on. At the end of Part Five in this book, you'll find charts that show the skill tested in each of the questions as well as a Tracking Sheet to record your progress, strengths, and weaknesses. Use these tools to determine which skills need the most work.

6. Find extra help if you need it. Some people are uncomfortable about asking for help and want to tough it out alone. You don't have to! Go to your campus writing center; talk to an academic tutor. And most importantly, talk to your instructor!

7. Form a study group. You'll find that each person in the group has a particular strength to share. Studying with others not only helps academically, but also emotionally. You become a team in which the members support each other.

What to Do on the Day of the Test

1. **Get a Good Night's Sleep:** The night before the test, get a good night's sleep. Don't try to stay up all night studying. Pulling an "all-nighter" will disrupt your ability to think clearly. Overdosing on caffeinated products will make you shaky and hyper, and you won't be able to concentrate.

2. **Food:** Don't take your test on an empty stomach. You may not be hungry before the exam, but sooner or later your hunger is going to kick in and cloud your thinking. Eat something light but avoid foods that can increase stress, like caffeine and sugar-laden products. Another thing you can do is bring a snack with you, like a health bar.

3. **Time:** Arrive early. You don't want to get stuck in a traffic jam and risk being late. Bring something interesting with you to read so the wait won't be so nerve-wracking.

4. **Relaxation:** Try the square breathing technique while you wait. Practice relaxation techniques so that when the day of the test comes, you will be able to overcome your anxiety. Square breathing is one easy relaxation technique to master. Here's how you do it:

   • Close your eyes.
   • Take a slow, deep breath through your nose while you count to three.
   • Hold your breath while you count to three slowly.
   • Breathe out through your mouth, again counting to three slowly.
   • Hold your breath for three slow counts.

   Repeat this several times. You will be surprised to see how well this works to get rid of stress. Use it any time you feel anxious—and remember to use this method on the day of the test.

5. **Seating:** If you can, choose a seat away from distractions like doors or windows. Turn off your cell phone and put it out of sight so you won't be tempted to check for calls or messages. Also, avoid others in the room who show negative behavior, are not prepared, or are anxious.

6. **Materials:** Be sure to bring the materials required, such as a number 2 pencil and a scantron sheet.

7. **Anxiety:** Most people feel some anxiety at test time. Use that energy to motivate you to do your best. Don't turn that anxiety into negative self-talk. Turn negative thoughts, such as "I never do well on tests" or "Everyone else will do better than I will," into positive thoughts. When you find yourself thinking a negative thought, stop and replace it with a positive one. "I can pass this test with ease."

Specific Strategies for the Reading Skills Exit Exam

There are some specific tips you can follow to reduce your anxiety and improve your score on the Reading Skills Exit Exam.

1. **Note the TIME the test ends** so that you will finish the test on time.

2. **Look over the test to see how many questions and reading passages there are**—Usually there are 4 readings and 36 questions.

3. **Read the directions**—It's a good habit to make sure you understand what the test is measuring and how you should approach the test.

4. **PREVIEW each paragraph before you actually read it**—When you preview, you read the entire introductory paragraph, the first and last sentences of the body paragraphs, and the entire concluding paragraph. This technique usually helps you capture the main ideas (thesis statement for the reading as well as the topic sentences of the body paragraphs), which helps you focus on the most important information in the text. It also helps activate any background knowledge you may possess about the topic so that you are more ready to read new information about it.

5. **If you do not understand a reading passage, READ IT AGAIN**—One of the most common causes of anxiety on the Reading Skills Exit Exam is lack of comprehension of a particular reading passage. It can cause students to become insecure and miss even relatively easy questions from that passage. If you do not comprehend some passage, do not move on to the questions. Instead, read it again. If the reading is still incomprehensible, mark your spot on the answer key and move on to the next reading. Perhaps after successfully completing a different reading, you will be able to relax enough to come back to the one that was giving your problems and read it with ease.

6. **Focus on the QUESTIONS, not on the readings**—For each reading passage on the Reading Skills Exit Exam, more than half of the questions can usually be answered with minimal reading. Questions such as Relationship Within or Between Sentences, Fact and Opinion, and Word Choice can be answered by just reading the questions themselves.

7. **Know where to find the Main Ideas**—Main idea is <u>vital</u>. Misunderstanding the main idea can cause you to also miss the author's purpose, the overall pattern of organization, and supporting detail questions. Review Chapter 1, Part 1. If you are not sure about where the main idea is located, assume it is either the last sentence of the first paragraph, the first sentence of the first paragraph, or the first sentence of the second paragraph. If the reading is a narrative, you can expect to find the main idea somewhere in the conclusion.

8. **Purpose is VERY closely related to Main Idea**—Very often, the author's purpose is simply a restatement of the main idea. If a reading selection contains both an overall main idea question and a purpose question, compare the answers in the two questions to look for similarities.

9. **Locate the answers to Supporting Detail questions directly in the text**—Do NOT guess, and do not rely on memory. Before you select an answer to a supporting detail question, make sure you locate it directly in the text.

10. **Do NOT select a Tone Word answer if you do not know what it means**—Insecure students tend to select what looks like the hardest answer choice. Only do this if you can eliminate the other answer choices with 100% certainty.

11. **Fact and Opinion have NOTHING to do with True and False**—A fact is not necessarily true. It is just checkable. Similarly, an opinion is not necessarily wrong. It's just not verifiable the way it is written. Also, don't forget that reported speech (saying that someone else said something) is FACT.

12. **Watch out for Subtle Bias**—Does the author consider anything to be inherently positive or negative? If so, that's a subtle bias.

13. **Watch out for Personal Bias when doing Inference and Conclusion questions**—Do not call something an inference simply because you strongly believe it to be true. The text itself must support that inference. Also, do not leap too far in your logic when making an inference or reaching a conclusion. Again, the text itself must support any inference or conclusion that you draw.

Marking Your Answer Sheet

Most tests in college are taken with automatic scoring answer sheets. An answer sheet is usually made up of a line of bubbles or bars that you fill in with a pencil—NEVER USE A PEN. Also, many students do not realize that when the answer sheets are scanned for scores, any stray mark will be counted as a wrong answer; therefore, NEVER MARK OUTSIDE OF YOUR ANSWER CHOICES. Little marks, such as question marks or dashes, in the margins or anywhere on the test answer sheet, will all be read by the scanner as multiple answers and will be marked as wrong. If you must mark a question on your answer sheet, follow this suggestion: Once you have narrowed down your answer to two possible choices, make a diagonal slash in *one* of the bubbles, *but do not fill it in*. This way, when you have finished your test, you can go back and review the answers that have a slash. Also, if you run out of time, you will have one answer marked which may possibly be right. There are no penalties for guessing, but a blank will be marked as an incorrect answer.

Example

	A	B	C	D
1.	0	0	0	0

When you have completed the test, go back to the answers with a slash in them and reread the sections necessary to make a decision, looking for support for the answer.

Remember to fill in each bubble or bar neatly and completely. Do not bear down on the pencil to make a heavy mark. Answer sheet scanners can read ordinary pencil marks. If your mark is too dark, it makes it difficult to erase, and smudges can be read as wrong answers. For this reason, use a number 2 or higher pencil. A softer lead is more difficult to erase and leaves smudges.

Always bring to the test two sharpened pencils with good erasers that don't leave smudges when you erase an answer. A good pencil may cost a few pennies more, but the results make it worth the added minimal expense.

Choosing Answers

The best strategy for test taking is to answer all the questions, going once through the entire test without spending too much time on any one question. Narrow down your answer choices to the best two answers, and then go back into the reading selection to find support for one of the two. If the question is on one paragraph of the test, just reread that particular paragraph, do not read the entire passage again unless it is necessary.

After rereading, if you are still having difficulty answering a question, make an educated guess from the two best answers. The odds of getting it right are 50-50. Do not use "eeny-meeny-miney-moe" to decide. Remember, all the answers to the questions are in the passages. You just have to find them.

Keep Cool

If you find yourself getting frustrated over a question—or if you "blank," don't get upset—just make a slash through one of the possible correct answers and *move on*. Do all the easiest questions, then go back and revisit the hardest ones later.

Do not allow yourself to become angry, frustrated, or anxious over test questions. Keep a positive mental attitude by telling yourself, "The answer is there and I *will* find it." Sometimes leaving a passage and coming back to it later can actually help you to understand it better.

If you are feeling overwhelmed, take a few seconds for some deep breaths, and visualize yourself in a pleasant place, just long enough to relax your body. A relaxed body and mind can think much more clearly than one that is tense or worried. If you have problems dealing with stressful situations, like tests, then do some research on relaxation techniques and learn some strategies to help reduce your anxiety.

When you have finished the test, go back once more to make sure you have answered every question with one (and only one) answer. Make sure you have ended up on the correct number on your last answer. If you find that you are short by one or over by one number, work backwards, beginning at the end of the test, and go back over each answer until you find the one that you skipped or answered twice. Make slashes for your corrected answers, then go back and erase the answers you marked and fill in the slashes.

Always check your test over before you hand it in. However, this *does not* mean that you should retake the test or change your answers. Also, *never change an answer* unless you *are sure that the answer you have chosen is wrong*; your first choice on an answer is usually correct.

Avoid choosing answers that use words like *always, never, all*, or *none*. Unless the passage states that this is indeed the case, one cannot assume it to be true. For example, if a question were to ask:

A good testing strategy is:

A. skip questions that you don't know the answer to.
B. mark in the margins of your answer sheet.
C. never change an answer.
D. use a slash for an answer that you want to review later.

The correct answer is D, "use a slash for an answer that you want to review later." The paragraph stated, "Never change an answer unless you are sure that the answer you have chosen is wrong." So, there can be times when you will need to change an answer.

Also, when you see answer choices like "All of the above," "None of the above," or "No change is necessary," consider it as a possible correct answer, especially on tests where these options are not used often. They tend to be the correct answer. But always go back to check each of the other choices by rereading before choosing "all" or "none of the above."

Keep an Eye on the Clock

Monitor the time you have left to make sure you finish the test on time. Before reading each passage, look at the clock and estimate how much time you have left. If you have 30 minutes left and two passages to read and answer questions for, this allows you 10 to 15 minutes per passage.

If others finish before you, don't try to hurry to finish too. When you think you are done, and you still have time left, use that time to make sure that you have answered every question and to go over your answers. Try to allow yourself at least 5 to 10 minutes at the end of the test to check your answers.

It is not surprising that many good readers do poorly on tests. They tend to over-analyze the questions, thinking that the test is out to trick them, and the question is actually harder than it seems. This is rarely the case. Most test questions are very straightforward. If the answer you have chosen seems like the obvious choice, it is most likely the correct answer. Reading tests are not mind games; they are simply a measurement of your comprehension skills.

After you have checked over your answers, hand in your test. If you have followed the suggestions and applied the strategies in this book, you can hand in your paper with confidence, knowing that you were well prepared for success.

Finally, remember to congratulate yourself!

"Difficulties mastered are opportunities won."

—Winston Churchill

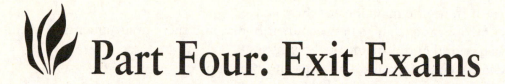

Part Four: Exit Exams

Instructions: This Exit Exam has 36 questions. Read each passage below and answer the questions that follow.

Snakes, like all reptiles, are cold-blooded. They need to maintain a certain body temperature to survive. Although snakes depend on the outside environment to give them the energy they need to maintain their body temperature within the range necessary for life processes, they are not passive prisoners of the constant variations in temperature. Snakes can control heat exchange between their bodies and their environments by a combination of behavioral and physiological processes. For instance, a snake can control its absorption of the heat from the sun—and thereby its body temperature—by altering the color of its skin or changing the exposure of its body to the sun.

5

Many snakes can change their color. Because dark skin substantially increases the amount of solar energy that is absorbed, many snakes living in cooler parts of an area are darker than those that live in warmer climates. Additionally, many snakes that live in warmer regions can change their color according to the amount of sun they get during changes in seasons. Some snakes use their color changing ability to increase sun exposure by having dark skin on their heads which they expose to the sun before other parts of their body. Warming the brain and the sensory organs such as the eyes and the tongue first enhances a snake's ability to detect both danger and food. Finally, pregnant females of some species are darker than males and non-pregnant females to maintain warmer-than-normal body temperatures that speed up the development of embryos.

10

15

A second way that snakes control their absorption of the sun is by increasing or decreasing the amount of body area exposed to the sun. The snake can make its temperature warmer than the outside air by lying at right angles to the direction of the sun and spreading and flattening to increase its body's surface area. When a snake's body has reached a suitable temperature, it avoids further heating by lightening its skin color, changing its position, and eventually moving underground. In addition, the temperature of the surface that the snake is in contact with is also important because a cool snake

20

25

can crawl on a warm rock or other surface and absorb its heat. (Adapted from Robert Leo Smith and Thomas M. Smith, *Elements of Ecology*, 5th ed., San Francisco: Benjamin Cummings, 2003.)

1. Which sentence best states the main idea of the passage?
   A. Snakes can control heat exchange between their bodies and their environments by a combination of behavioral and physiological processes.
   B. Snakes can change color to control absorption of the sun.
   C. Snakes, like all reptiles, are cold-blooded.
   D. Although snakes depend on the outside environment to give them the energy they need to maintain their body temperature, they are not passive prisoners of the constant variations in temperature.

2. In this passage, the author's purpose is
   A. to describe the ways that snakes can change color to control their absorption of the sun.
   B. to persuade readers that snakes are not passive prisoners of variations in temperature.
   C. to explain how snakes can change their color to control their absorption of the sun.
   D. to describe the ways that snakes can control heat exchange between their bodies and their environments.

3. The overall pattern of organization is
   A. listing.
   B. compare and contrast.
   C. cause and effect.
   D. illustration.

4. What is the relationship within this sentence from paragraph two? "Finally, pregnant females of some species are darker than males and non-pregnant females to maintain warmer-than-normal body temperatures that speed up the development of embryos."
   A. Illustration
   B. Listing
   C. Cause and effect
   D. Compare and contrast

5. According to the passage, which statement is true?
   A. Pregnant female snakes are lighter than non-pregnant females.
   B. A snake can alter the exposure of its body to the sun.
   C. Cool rocks will absorb the heat from the snakes' body.
   D. A snake can store body heat for long periods.

6. Is the following sentence a fact or an opinion? "Warming the brain and the sensory organs such as the eyes and the tongue first enhances a snake's ability to detect both danger and food."
   A. Fact
   B. Opinion

7. The author's claim that "Snakes can control heat exchange between their bodies and their environments by a combination of behavioral and physiological processes" is
   A. adequately supported by factual details.
   B. inadequately supported based upon opinions.

8. The tone of this passage can best be described as
    A. admiring.
    B. nostalgic.
    C. objective.
    D. ironic.

9. A conclusion that can be drawn from the passage is
    A. Snakes do not like to live in cold regions.
    B. Snakes can change color at will simply by deciding to do it.
    C. Snakes have a temperature that remains relatively constant.
    D. Snakes must constantly seek to find warmer or cooler environments to maintain their body temperature.

Read the passage below and answer the questions that follow.

Spielberg's journey is one version of the universal story of human development: A skinny kid beset by fears and with few friends becomes one of the most powerful figures in the global entertainment industry; from a family with a fragmented family life develops a man's resolve to make the best possible life for his own family.

Steven Spielberg was a perpetual new kid on the block. His father, Arnold, a pioneer   5
in the use of computers in engineering, was hardly ever around and, to make matters
worse, frequently uprooted his family, moving from Ohio to New Jersey, to Arizona,
and finally to Northern California. He was also, by all accounts, an unusual child, both
in his appearance (he had a large head and protruding ears) and in his fearful and awk-
ward behavior. Spielberg himself has said that he "felt like an alien" throughout his   10
childhood. He desperately wanted to be accepted but didn't fit in. So, at age 12 he
began making films. Spielberg continued to make movies as a teenager, which helped
him gain acceptance by his peers.

When he was 16, Spielberg's parents divorced, and Spielberg blamed his father's constant traveling for the breakup. His father remarried, which deepened Spielberg's un-   15
happiness; he couldn't stand his father's second wife. Although he withdrew from his
father, he remained close with his mother, Leah, a concert pianist and artist. His split
with his father lasted some 15 years.

In many ways, Spielberg's films, like the rest of his life, are shaped by his childhood.
Spielberg himself has said about *E.T., The Extra-Terrestrial*, "The whole movie is really   20
about divorce. . . . Henry's (the main character's) ambition to find a father by bringing
E.T. into his life to fill some black hole—that was my struggle to find somebody to replace the dad who I felt had abandoned me." Many of Spielberg's other films include
children who are separated from their parents (such as the girl in *Poltergeist* and the
boy in *Close Encounters of the Third Kind*). *Back to the Future* might represent his   25
longings to change the past, if only he could. As he matured, Spielberg's identification
with oppressed people in general, not just oppressed children, led him to make movies
such as *The Color Purple*, *Schindler's List*, and *Amistad*.

Steven Spielberg married and had a child, but eventually divorced his first wife, actress
Amy Irving. His own experiences made him extremely sensitive to the effect of the di-   30

vorce on his son, Max, and he made every attempt to ensure that Max did not feel abandoned. When he married again, he became deeply involved with his family, which includes seven children, some of them adopted. His father Arnold became a well-loved grandfather as well. (Adapted from Stephen M. Kosslyn and Robin S. Rosenberg, *Psychology*, 2nd ed., Boston: Allyn and Bacon, 2004.)

10. The sentence which best states the main idea of the passage is
    A. The separation of Spielberg's parents caused him to make movies with characters who were divorced or abandoned.
    B. Spielberg's childhood influenced his career as a filmmaker and his personal life as a husband and a father.
    C. Spielberg's journey is one version of the universal story of human development.
    D. Spielberg's identification with oppressed people in general, not just oppressed children, led him to make movies.

11. What is the relationship within the following sentence? "He desperately wanted to be accepted but didn't fit in."
    A. Listing
    B. Time order
    C. Contrast
    D. Comparison

12. What is the relationship between these sentences? "He desperately wanted to be accepted but didn't fit in. So, at age 12 he began making films."
    A. Summary
    B. Time order
    C. Listing
    D. Cause and effect

13. The overall pattern of organization for this passage is
    A. cause and effect.
    B. time order.
    C. listing.
    D. illustration.

14. The author's purpose in writing this passage is
    A. to summarize Spielberg's career.
    B. to show how Spielberg's childhood affected his filmmaking career.
    C. to analyze the effect of divorce on children.
    D. to illustrate examples of the many films that Spielberg has made.

15. A conclusion that can be drawn from this passage is that
    A. Spielberg was not a good student in school.
    B. Spielberg's family moved frequently during his childhood because his parents had divorced.
    C. Spielberg expresses many of his feelings about his own life through his film characters.
    D. Spielberg's mother did not approve of his career in movies.

16. Which statement provides the best support for the author's claim that "In many ways, Spielberg's films, like the rest of his life, are shaped by his childhood"?
   A. Many of Spielberg's other films include children who are separated from their parents (such as the girl in *Poltergeist* and the boy in *Close Encounters of the Third Kind*).
   B. When he was 16, Spielberg's parents divorced, and Spielberg blamed his father's constant traveling for the breakup.
   C. He desperately wanted to be accepted but didn't fit in.
   D. Spielberg himself has said that he "felt like an alien" throughout his childhood.

17. According to the passage, Spielberg
   A. always knew he would be famous some day.
   B. got his ideas for the movie *The Color Purple* from observing his parents.
   C. became interested in filmmaking after his parents' divorce.
   D. modeled the character Henry in *E.T., The Extra-Terrestrial*, after himself as a child.

18. Is the following sentence a fact or an opinion? "Spielberg himself has said about *E.T., The Extra-Terrestrial*, 'The whole movie is really about divorce. . . . Henry's (the main character's) ambition to find a father by bringing E.T. into his life to fill some black hole—that was my struggle to find somebody to replace the dad who I felt had abandoned me.'"
   A. Fact
   B. Opinion

Read the passage below and answer the questions that follow.

There had been great athletes before; indeed probably the greatest all-around athlete of the twentieth century was Jim Thorpe, a Sac and Fox Indian who won both the pentathalon and the decathalon at the 1912 Olympic Games, made Walter Camp's All-American football team in 1912 and 1913, then played major league baseball for several years before becoming a pioneer founder and player in the National Football League. 5
But what truly made the 1920s a golden age was a coincidence—the emergence in a few short years of a remarkable collection of what today would be called superstars.

In football there was the University of Illinois's Harold "Red" Grange, who averaged over 10 yards a carry during his college career and who in one incredible quarter during the 1924 game between Illinois and Michigan carried the ball four times and scored a 10 touchdown each time, gaining in the process 263 yards. In prizefighting, heavyweight champion Jack Dempsey, the "Manassas Mauler," knocked out a succession of challengers in bloody battles only to be **deposed** in 1927 by "Gentleman Gene" Tunney, who gave him a 15-round boxing lesson and then, according to Tunney's own account, celebrated by consuming "several pots of tea." 15

During the same years, William "Big Bill" Tilden dominated tennis, winning the national singles title every year from 1920 to 1925 along with nearly every other tournament he entered. Beginning in 1923, Robert T. "Bobby" Jones ruled over the world of golf with equal authority, his climactic achievement being his capture of the amateur and open championships of both the United States and Great Britain in 1930. 20

A few women athletes dominated their sports during the Golden Age in similar fashion. In tennis Helen Wills was three times United States singles champion and the winner of the women's singles at Wimbledon eight times in the late 1920s and early 1930s. The swimmer Gertrude Ederle, holder of 18 world records by the time she was 17, swam the English Channel on her second attempt, in 1926. She was not only the first woman to do so, but she did it faster than any of the four men who had previously made it across.   25

However, the sports star among stars was "the Sultan of Swat," baseball's Babe Ruth. Ruth not only dominated baseball, he changed it from a game ruled by pitchers and low scores to one in which hitting was more greatly admired. Originally himself a brilliant pitcher, his incredible hitting ability made him more valuable in the outfield, where he could play every day. Before Ruth, John "Home Run" Baker was the most famous slugger; his greatest home run total was 12, achieved shortly before the Great War. Ruth hit 29 in 1919 and 54 in 1920, his first year with the New York Yankees. By 1923, he was so feared that he was given a base on balls more than half the times he appeared at the plate. (John A. Garraty and Mark C. Carnes, *The American Nation*, New York: Longman, 2000.)   30 · 35

19. The main idea of this passage is that
    A. many superstars dominated the field of football and baseball in the 1920s.
    B. women athletes were relatively new during the Golden Age of superstars.
    C. the 1920s were the Golden Age of athletic superstars.
    D. Jim Thorpe was one of the greatest athletes of all time.

20. The author's purpose in writing this passage is
    A. to give examples of the numerous superstar athletes in the 1920s.
    B. to analyze why so many athletes were superstars in the 1920s
    C. to compare women athletes to men athletes in the 1920s.
    D. to inform the reader about the history of athletic superstars.

21. A conclusion that can be drawn from the passage is that
    A. there were fewer female superstar athletes than male superstar athletes.
    B. Gertrude Ederle was the first person to swim the English Channel.
    C. William "Big Bill" Tilden won every tournament he entered.
    D. Jack Dempsey defeated "Gentleman Gene" Tunney for the world boxing championship.

22. The overall pattern of organization of this passage is
    A. statement and clarification.
    B. compare and contrast.
    C. spatial order.
    D. illustration.

23. The overall tone of this passage can best be described as
    A. ironic.
    B. sarcastic.
    C. nostalgic.
    D. irreverent.

24. What is the meaning of the word **deposed** in the following sentence? "In prizefighting, heavy-weight champion Jack Dempsey, the "Manassas Mauler," knocked out a succession of challengers in bloody battles only to be **deposed** in 1927 by "Gentleman Gene" Tunney, who gave him a 15-round boxing lesson and then, according to Tunney's own account, celebrated by consuming "several pots of tea"?
    A. Fought
    B. Defeated
    C. Challenged
    D. Taught

25. In this passage, the author is
    A. biased against the boxer "Gentleman Gene" Tunney.
    B. biased in favor of the New York Yankees.
    C. biased in favor of the superstar athletes of the 1920s.
    D. unbiased.

26. What is the relationship between the following sentences? "Before Ruth, John 'Home Run' Baker was the most famous slugger; his greatest home run total was 12, achieved shortly before the Great War. Ruth hit 29 in 1919 and 54 in 1920, his first year with the New York Yankees."
    A. Comparison
    B. Listing
    C. Example
    D. Contrast

27. What is the relationship within the following sentence? "She was not only the first woman to do so, but she did it faster than any of the four men who had previously made it across."
    A. Listing
    B. Contrast
    C. Comparison
    D. Time order

Read the passage below and answer the questions that follow.

Public opinion polling sounds scientific with its talk of random samples and sampling error; it is easy to take results for solid fact. But being an informed consumer of polls requires more than just a nuts-and-bolts knowledge of how they are conducted; you should think about whether the questions are fair and unbiased before making too much of the results. The good—or the harm—that polls do depends on how well the data are collected and how thoughtfully the data are interpreted.   5

Political scientist Benjamin Ginsberg has even argued that polls weaken democracy. He says that polls permit the government to think that it has taken public opinion into account when only passive, often ill-informed opinions have been counted. Polls substitute passive attitudes for active expressions of opinion, such as voting and letter writing, which take work. Responding to a poll taker is a lazy way to claim that "my voice has been heard."   10

Polls can also weaken democracy by distorting the election process. They are often accused of creating a *bandwagon effect*. This term refers to voters who support a candi-   15 date merely because they see that others are doing so. Although only 2 percent of people in a recent CBS/*New York Times* poll said that poll results had influenced them, 26 percent said they thought others had been influenced (showing that Americans feel "It's always the other person who's susceptible.") Beyond this, polls play to the media's interest in who's hot and who's not. The issues of recent presidential campaigns have sometimes been drowned out by a steady flood of poll results.   20

Perhaps the most extensive criticism of polling is that by altering the wording of a question, pollsters can get pretty much the results they want. Sometimes subtle changes in question wording can produce dramatic differences. For example, a month before the start of the Gulf War, the percentage of the public who thought we should go to war was 18 percentage points higher in the ABC/*Washington Post* poll than the CBS/*New York Times* poll. The former poll asked whether the United States should go to war "at some point after January 15 or not," a relatively vague question; in contrast, the latter poll offered an alternative to war, asking whether the "U.S. should start military actions against Iraq, or should the U.S. wait longer to see if the trade embargo and other economic **sanctions** work." It is, therefore, important to evaluate carefully how questions are posed when reading public opinion data. (Adapted from George C. Edwards, Martin P. Wattenberg, and Robert L. Lineberry, *Government in America*, 9th ed., New York: Longman, 2000.)   25   30   35

28. The implied main idea of the passage is
   A. Critics of polls believe that polls can be harmful, depending on how the data is collected, interpreted, and used.
   B. Polls can get the results they want depending on how the questions are worded.
   C. Public opinion polling sounds scientific with its talk of random samples and sampling error; it is easy to take results for solid fact.
   D. Polls can weaken democracy because they create a bandwagon effect.

29. The overall pattern of organization for this passage is
   A. statement and clarification.
   B. compare and contrast.
   C. time order.
   D. listing.

30. What is the relationship between the following sentences? "Responding to a poll taker is a lazy way to claim that 'my voice has been heard.' Polls can also weaken democracy by distorting the election process."
   A. Classification
   B. Compare and contrast
   C. Addition
   D. Statement and clarification

31. In this passage, the author is
   A. biased in favor of using poll results as solid fact.
   B. biased in favor of understanding how poll data is collected and interpreted.
   C. biased against the media using poll results on television.
   D. unbiased.

32. What is the relationship between these sentences? "They are often accused of creating a *band-wagon effect*. This term refers to voters who support a candidate merely because they see that others are doing so."
    A. Addition
    B. Illustration
    C. Definition
    D. Statement and clarification

33. What does the word **sanctions** mean in the sentence, "The former poll asked whether the United States should go to war 'at some point after January 15 or not,' a relatively vague question; in contrast, the latter poll offered an alternative to war, asking whether the 'U.S. should start military actions against Iraq, or should the U.S. wait longer to see if the trade embargo and other economic **sanctions** work.'"
    A. Penalties
    B. Exports
    C. Businesses
    D. Situations

34. What is the relationship within the following sentence? "Although only 2 percent of people in a recent CBS/*New York Times* poll said that poll results had influenced them, 26 percent said they thought others had been influenced."
    A. Cause and effect
    B. Illustration
    C. Spatial order
    D. Compare and contrast

35. Throughout the passage, which type of support is offered for the author's claim that "The good—or the harm—that polls do depends on how well the data are collected and how thoughtfully the data are interpreted"?
    A. Objective
    B. Emotional

36. A conclusion that can be drawn from this passage is
    A. People can be influenced to vote for a candidate based upon the results of polls.
    B. Polls help the government find out what the people are thinking on many issues.
    C. The media uses polls to persuade the viewing public on certain issues.
    D. People who conduct polls are not honest about reporting the results correctly.

EXIT EXAM #2

Instructions: This Exit Exam has 36 questions. Read each passage below and answer the questions that follow.

On average, American adults consume about 22 gallons of beer, 2 gallons of wine, and 1.5 gallons of spirits a year. Despite these high rates of consumption, many people are unaware of the harm excessive use of alcohol can cause. To combat these dangers, the United

States spends approximately $130 billion annually on problems related to alcoholism. However, alcoholism still creates serious problems for those who drink and their families.   5

Alcoholics can expect to live 10 to 12 years fewer than non-alcoholics. There are several reasons for this shortened life span. First, alcohol contains a high number of calories and no vital nutrients. Thus, alcoholics generally have a reduced appetite for nutritious food and inevitably suffer from vitamin deficiencies; as a result, their resistance to infectious diseases is lowered. Second, over a long period, large amounts of alcohol destroy liver   10
cells, which are replaced by scar tissue. This condition, called cirrhosis of the liver, is the cause of more than 27,000 deaths each year in the United States. Heavy drinking also contributes to heart ailments, and there is some evidence that alcohol contributes to the incidence of cancer. Finally, alcohol is implicated in thousands of suicides each year.

In 2004 more than 1,160,000 arrests, or about 12 percent of all non-serious crimes,   15
involved drunkenness or an offence related to violation of liquor laws. These criminal acts were minor, such as breaches of the peace, disorderly conduct, and vagrancy. In arrests for major crimes, drunkenness does not generally appear in the charges, although alcohol often contributes to criminal acts. Each year thousands of homicides are linked to alcohol use. In many homicide cases, alcohol is found in the victim, the   20
offender, or both. A significant percentage of male sex offenders are chronic alcoholics or were drinking at the time of the offense. The reasons for the strong link between drinking and arrests for serious crimes are not fully understood. It has been pointed out that alcohol, by removing inhibitions, may cause people to behave in unusual ways.

If only the victims of alcoholism were the alcoholics themselves, but other people, espe-   25
cially the families of alcoholics, also suffer. The emotional effect, which is part of any family crisis, is heightened when the crisis itself is socially defined as shameful. The effects of "acts of God," such as fires, illnesses, and accidents, on a family **elicit** sympathy, but those of alcoholism produce negative reactions. The children of an alcoholic parent frequently develop severe physical and emotional illnesses, and marriage to an alcoholic frequently   30
ends in divorce or desertion. Finally, because alcoholics are often unable to hold jobs, the outcome may be poverty for their families. (Adapted from William Kornblum and Joseph Julian, *Social Problems*, 13th ed., Upper Saddle River, NJ: Pearson Prentice Hall, 2009.)

1. Which sentence best states the main idea of the passage?
   A. American adults consume about 22 gallons of beer, 2 gallons of wine, and 1.5 gallons of spirits a year.
   B. The United States spends approximately $130 billion annually on problems related to alcoholism.
   C. Many people are unaware of the harm excessive use of alcohol can cause.
   D. Alcoholism creates serious problems for those who drink and their families.

2. The overall pattern of organization is
   A. compare and contrast.
   B. chronological
   C. listing.
   D. classification.

3. The implied main idea of paragraph 2 is that
    A. There are several reasons alcoholics do not live as long as non-drinkers.
    B. Vitamin deficiencies cause alcoholics to have little resistance to infectious diseases.
    C. Alcoholism can cause many serious problems.
    D. Cirrhosis of the liver leads to more than 27,000 deaths each year in the United States.

4. What is the relationship between the following sentences? "Each year thousands of homicides are linked to alcohol use. In many homicide cases, alcohol is found in the victim, the offender, or both."
    A. Cause and Effect
    B. Addition
    C. Statement and Clarification
    D. Generalization and Example

5. The author's purpose in writing this passage is
    A. to warn the reader about the damage alcohol can do to a person's health.
    B. to contrast the lives of alcoholics and non-alcoholics.
    C. to persuade the reader not to drink alcohol in excess.
    D. to give examples of some of the problems alcoholism can cause.

6. What is the meaning of the word **elicit** in the following sentence? "The effects of 'acts of God,' such as fires, illnesses, and accidents, on a family **elicit** sympathy, but those of alcoholism produce negative reactions."
    A. Require
    B. Create
    C. Exclude
    D. Justify

7. According to the passage, alcoholism
    A. can be passed down from parent to child.
    B. is the cause of more than 27,000 deaths each year in the United States.
    C. is more common in the United States than in other countries.
    D. can make a person more likely to develop an infectious disease.

8. A conclusion that can be drawn from the passage is
    A. The United States spends too little money on solving the problems associated with alcoholism.
    B. Vitamins help to build resistance to infectious diseases.
    C. Children of alcoholics grow up to be alcoholics themselves.
    D. Americans drink more alcohol than they should.

9. The author's claim that "alcoholism still creates serious problems for those who drink and their families" is
    A. adequately supported with relevant details.
    B. inadequately supported because it lacks evidence.

Read the passage below and answer the questions that follow.

Anyone from San Francisco who knew him believed that Charles E. Bolton was a gentleman. Mild-mannered and considerate, he always tucked a decorative handkerchief into his
waistcoat pocket. Bolton made frequent trips to check on his mining property—the sign,
people believed, of a savvy, well-to-do businessman. His friends, therefore, were stunned
to learn of Bolton's arrest and true identity. He was, in reality, the notorious Black Bart, a   5
highwayman who stalked northern California between 1875 and 1883. In all, Bart robbed
twenty-seven stagecoaches for the gold they carried. In classic English highwayman fashion, he sat astride a horse and greeted drivers with the demand, "Throw down the box!"

Black Bart was never vicious during his robberies. He extended great civility to lady passengers and always respected the sanctity of their purses. In fact, he left travelers alone   10
and stole only from large, impersonal institutions such as Wells Fargo and Company and
the U.S. Postal Service. He carried a large shotgun to threaten drivers, but evidence later
revealed that he kept it unloaded, fearing that it might accidentally go off and injure
somebody. Bart also had a sense of humor and a somewhat skewed taste for the literary.
Following each robbery, he left behind a poem usually deposited in the empty strongbox.   15

Wells Fargo detective James B. Hume tracked down Bart after he left behind one of his
handkerchiefs. Hume discovered that Bart's real name was Bolles and not Bolton. Bart
was arrested in 1883 and served jail time. After his release in 1888, he disappeared but
may have managed one final heist of Wells Fargo money. His deeds reveal a frequent
trend in the nineteenth-century West. Because railroads, mining companies, large cattle   20
outfits, bonanza farms, and banks often acquired vast wealth, some outlaws attacked
the very institutions that offered others jobs.

Even so, the motives for western banditry, crime, and violence remain complex. Possibly
for all his poetry and exaggerated manners, dandy Black Bart simply needed money to
live on and robbed a stage when he found his wallet empty. Maybe he reveled in the   25
adventure and the notoriety. Perhaps like Robin Hood he targeted the rich and powerful
that so often unjustly gained favor. Regardless, Bart hardly represents the typical western bandit. (Adapted from Gary Clayton Anderson and Kathleen P. Chamberlain,
Power and Promise: The Changing American West, Prentice Hall, 2008.)

10. What is the implied main idea of this passage?
A. Black Bart was able to trick his neighbors into thinking he was a respectable businessman.
B. Many bandits in the nineteenth-century West only robbed because they truly needed the
money.
C. The motives for western banditry, crime, and violence remain complex.
D. Black Bart was a very unusual western outlaw.

11. What is the relationship within the following sentence? "Because railroads, mining companies,
large cattle outfits, bonanza farms, and banks often acquired vast wealth, some outlaws at-
tacked the very institutions that offered others jobs."
A. Listing
B. Cause and effect
C. Contrast
D. Statement and clarification

12. What is the relationship between the following sentences? "Bolton made frequent trips to check on his mining property—the sign, people believed, of a savvy, well-to-do businessman. His friends, therefore, were stunned to learn of Bolton's arrest and true identity."
   A. Contrast
   B. Cause and effect
   C. Enumeration
   D. Generalization and example

13. According to the passage, which statement is NOT true about Black Bart?
   A. His neighbors thought he was a respectable businessperson before he was caught.
   B. He always left a poem after he committed a robbery.
   C. His real name was Charles E. Bolton.
   D. He never searched a lady's purse.

14. Which statement does NOT support the idea that "Black Bart was considerate to the people on the stagecoaches that he robbed?
   A. In fact, he left travelers alone and stole only from large, impersonal institutions such as Wells Fargo and Company and the U.S. Postal Service.
   B. Following each robbery, he left behind a poem usually deposited in the empty strongbox.
   C. He extended great civility to lady passengers and always respected the sanctity of their purses.
   D. He carried a large shotgun to threaten drivers, but evidence later revealed that he kept it unloaded, fearing that it might accidentally go off and injure somebody.

15. A conclusion that can be drawn from the passage is that Black Bart was
   A. not a violent man despite being an outlaw.
   B. not just looking for money and fame, but also the chance to avenge the poor.
   C. loved by his neighbors before they found out he was really a notorious bandit.
   D. well educated and an exceptionally good poet.

16. The tone of this passage can best be described as
   A. informative.
   B. reverent.
   C. satiric.
   D. nostalgic.

17. In this passage, the author is
   A. biased in favor of the bandits of the nineteenth-century West.
   B. biased in favor of the railroads, mining companies, large cattle outfits, bonanza farms, and banks.
   C. biased against Black Bart.
   D. unbiased.

18. Is the following sentence a fact or an opinion? "Perhaps like Robin Hood he targeted the rich and powerful that so often unjustly gained favor."

   A. Fact
   B. Opinion

Read the passage below and answer the questions that follow.

No biotechnology issue has raised more debate than that of genetically modified (GM) crops. What is this controversy about? In a nutshell, proponents of GM crops see in them the exciting potential to feed a hungry world and to lessen the environmental damage caused by such human practices as pesticide application. Overly cautious opponents of them only see the unlikely potential to harm human health and the possible disruption to the Earth's ecosystems.   5

One example of this debate can be seen in cotton plants. The genetically modified cotton plants contain genes from a bacterium called *Bacillus thuringienis* that is found naturally in the soil and produces proteins that are toxic to a number of insects. Collectively these proteins form a natural insecticide known as *Bt*, which has been sprayed on crops for years.   10
In the 1990's, biotech firms were able to **splice** *Bt* genes into cotton crops with the result that these plants now produce their *own* insecticide. The results are clearly an environmentalist's dream. In one survey conducted in the American Southeast, farmers who planted *Bt* cotton reduced the amount of chemical pesticides they applied to their fields by 72 percent. They did this, moreover, while increasing cotton yields by more than 11 percent.   15

Despite such obvious benefits, some environmentalists are uneasy about the use of *Bt* seeds. They claim that those few insects that survive in *Bt*-enhanced fields are likely to produce offspring resistant to the natural toxin. This raises the prospect of the insecticide losing its effectiveness against insects over the long run. In order to calm those critics, the U.S. Environmental Agency requires that at least 20 percent of any farmer's   20
crops must be non-*Bt* plants. This creates non-*Bt* "refugees" near the *Bt* fields that will provide habitat for bugs that will then mate with the *Bt*-resistant bugs, thus helping to ensure that the *Bt*-resistance does not spread. (Adapted from David Krogh, *Biology*, 3rd ed., Upper Saddle River, NJ: Pearson Prentice Hall, 2005.)

19. The implied main idea of this passage is that
   A. creating genetically modified crops can have unforeseen consequences.
   B. natural bacteria, such as *Bacillus thuringieni*s, can be combined with crops like cotton to produce a plant with its own insecticide.
   C. there are two sides to the debate about genetically modified crops that can be seen in the example of modified cotton.
   D. genetically modified crops will solve both human needs and environmental concerns.

20. The overall pattern of organization for this passage is
   A. cause and effect.
   B. compare and contrast.
   C. classification.
   D. simple listing.

21. What is the relationship within the sentence, "In the 1990's, biotech firms were able to splice *Bt* genes into cotton crops with the result that these plants now produce their *own* insecticide"?
   A. Addition
   B. Time order

C. Cause and effect

D. Compare and contrast

22. What is the relationship between these sentences? "In one survey conducted in the American Southeast, farmers who planted *Bt* cotton reduced the amount of chemical pesticides they applied to their fields by 72 percent. They did this, moreover, while increasing cotton yields by more than 11 percent."

A. Process

B. Addition

C. Cause and effect

D. Compare and contrast

23. The author's purpose is to

A. present two views on a controversial topic.

B. criticize the genetic modification of crops.

C. explain how biotech firms can create genetically modified crops.

D. persuade the reader to buy genetically modified foods.

24. In describing the opponents of genetically modified crops, the author's tone is

A. apathetic.

B. straightforward.

C. skeptical.

D. sympathetic.

25. In this passage, the author

A. is biased in favor of genetically modifying crops.

B. is biased against genetically modifying cotton plants.

C. is biased against biotech firms.

D. is unbiased.

26. Which of the following statements is an opinion?

A. Some environmentalists are uneasy about the use of *Bt* seeds.

B. The results are clearly an environmentalist's dream.

C. The genetically modified cotton plants contain genes from a bacterium called *Bacillus thuringienis*.

D. They claim that those few insects that survive in *Bt*-enhanced fields are likely to produce offspring resistant to the natural toxin.

27. As used in this sentence from paragraph two, "In the 1990's, biotech firms were able to **splice** *Bt* genes into cotton crops with the result that these plants now produce their *own* insecticide," the word **splice** most nearly means

A. grow.

B. join.

C. transform.

D. separate.

Read the passage below and answer the questions that follow.

One of the most important components of social structure is *status*. **Status** is a recognized position that a person occupies in society. A person's status determines where he or she fits in society in relationship to everyone else. Status may be based on or accompanied by wealth, power, prestige, or a combination of all of these.

Sociologists recognize two types of status. An **ascribed status** is one that is attached to   5
a person from birth or that a person assumes involuntarily later in life. The most prevalent ascribed statuses are based on family and kinship relations (for example, daughter or son), sex (male or female), and age. In addition, in some societies ascribed statuses are based on one's race or ethnicity. For example, skin color was used to designate ascribed status differences in South Africa under the system of apartheid.   10

In contrast, an **achieved status** is one based at least in part on a person's voluntary actions. Examples of achieved statuses in the United States are one's profession and level of education. Of course, one's family and kinship connections may influence one's profession and level of education. George W. Bush's and John Kerry's educational level and status are interrelated to their family of birth. However, these individuals had to   15
act voluntarily to achieve their status. (Adapted from Raymond Scupin and Christopher R. DeCorse, *Anthropology: A Global Perspective*, 6th ed., Upper Saddle River, NJ: Pearson Prentice Hall, 2007.)

28. Which sentence best states the main idea of the passage?
    A. Status may be based on or accompanied by wealth, power, prestige, or a combination of all of these.
    B. One of the most important components of social structure is *status*.
    C. An **ascribed status** is one that is attached to a person from birth or that a person assumes involuntarily later in life.
    D. Sociologists recognize two types of status.

29. Which sentence best states the main idea of the second paragraph?
    A. All societies recognize both *ascribed* and *achieved* statuses.
    B. An **ascribed status** is one that is attached to a person from birth or that a person assumes involuntarily later in life.
    C. The most prevalent ascribed statuses are based on family and kinship relations (for example, daughter or son), sex (male or female), and age.
    D. In addition, in some societies ascribed statuses are based on one's race or ethnicity.

30. The overall pattern of organization for this passage is
    A. spatial order.
    B. definition and example.
    C. classification.
    D. cause and effect.

31. What is the relationship within the following sentence? "Many anthropologists use the term *socioeconomic status* to refer to how a specific position is related to the division of labor, the political system, and other cultural variables."
    A. Comparison
    B. Definition

C. Contrast
D. Process

32. What is the relationship between the following sentences? "In contrast, an **achieved status** is one based at least in part on a person's voluntary actions. Examples of achieved statuses in the United States are one's profession and level of education."
    A. Statement and clarification
    B. Addition
    C. Cause and effect
    D. Generalization and example

33. The author's purpose in writing this passage is
    A. to describe two types of statuses.
    B. to define the meaning of status.
    C. to contrast different cultures' definition of status.
    D. to show how achieved status is superior to ascribed status.

34. A conclusion that can be drawn from the passage is that
    A. all cultures measure status in the same way.
    B. a person's achieved status is often influenced by their ascribed status.
    C. achieved status is superior to ascribed status.
    D. Americans value achieved status over ascribed.

35. The overall tone of this passage can best be described as
    A. persuasive.
    B. objective.
    C. superior.
    D. farcical.

36. Is the following sentence a fact or an opinion? "Examples of achieved statuses in the United States are one's profession and level of education."
    A. Fact
    B. Opinion

READING SKILLS EXIT EXAM #3

Instructions: This Exit Exam has 36 questions. Read each passage below and answer the questions that follow.

Although humans are omnivorous creatures with the ability to digest many types of plants and animals for nutrition, there are many differences in eating behaviors and food preferences throughout the world. Most Americans would be repulsed by the thought of eating insects and insect larvae, but many societies consider them to be delicacies. American culture also distinguishes between pets, which are not eaten, and farm animals, such as chickens, cows, and pigs, which can be eaten. However, other cultures of the world do not necessarily share these food preferences. Pigs, for example, are forbidden food in Jewish and most Arab cultures. This particular food taboo has several possible explanations.

5

One is that the Jews classify reality by placing things into distinguishable "mental   10
boxes" based on their reading of the Bible. However, some things do not fit neatly into
these distinguishable mental boxes. Some items are anomalous or ambiguous, so they
fall between the basic categories that are used to define cultural reality. These anomalous items are usually treated as unclean, impure, unholy, polluted, or defiling. Edible
animals are those that fit the description of the animals God created in the first chapter   15
of the Bible, Genesis. Such animals include those that have cloven hoofs and chew cud.
Pigs do have cloven hooves. However, since they do not chew cud, they fail to fit into
the cultural classification of reality accepted by the ancient Israelites and are considered
dirty or unfit to eat. Similarly, the "fish" that God created in Genesis swim in the water
and have scales and fins, so they are fit to eat. However, since shellfish and eels lack   20
fins and scales, they are considered unclean and unfit to eat.

Another possible explanation for the pig taboo is more practical and economic. In the
hot, dry regions of the world, such as the Middle East, pigs are poorly adapted and extremely costly to raise. This is because unlike goats, sheep, or cattle, pigs are hard to
herd and are not grazing animals. In places like Israel and some Arabic countries, the   25
meat of pigs became forbidden. In contrast, in the cooler, wetter areas of the world
that are more appropriate for pig raising, such as China and New Guinea, pig taboos
are unknown, and pigs are the prized foods in those regions. (Adapted from Raymond
Scupin and Christopher R. DeCorse, *Anthropology A Global Perspective*, 6th ed.,
Upper Saddle River, New Jersey: Pearson Education, Inc., 2008.)

1. Which sentence best states the implied main idea of the passage?
   A. Cultures have different food preferences and taboos.
   B. The Jewish and Arabic prohibition of pork can be explained by religion and economics.
   C. God's description of the animals He created in the book of Genesis led Jews to their
      food laws.
   D. Food preferences result from the circumstances under which the culture developed.

2. In this passage, the author's purpose is
   A. to explain why certain cultures have certain food preferences.
   B. to describe Middle Eastern food taboos.
   C. to explain why Jews and other Middle Easterners prohibit pork from their diets.
   D. To convince readers that food preferences and taboos are cultural and not universally ac-
      cepted.

3. What is the overall pattern of organization of the passage?
   A. Compare and contrast
   B. Statement and clarification
   C. Process
   D. Simple listing

4. The author's claim that, "One is that the Jews classify reality by placing things into distin-
   guishable 'mental boxes' based on their reading of the Bible," is
   A. adequately supported by a mix of fact and opinion.
   B. inadequately supported by opinion.

5. What is the relationship within this sentence in paragraph one? "Most Americans would be repulsed by the thought of eating insects and insect larvae, but many societies consider them to be delicacies."
   A. Cause and effect
   B. Compare and contrast
   C. Definition
   D. Addition

6. The tone of the passage can best be described as
   A. flippant.
   B. persuasive.
   C. reverent.
   D. objective.

7. What is the meaning of the word **anomalous** in the following sentence? "Some items are **anomalous** or ambiguous, so they fall between the basic categories that are used to define cultural reality."
   A. Unusual
   B. Dirty
   C. Unacceptable
   D. Detailed

8. Is the following statement from paragraph 3 a fact or an opinion? "In the hot, dry regions of the world, such as the Middle East, pigs are poorly adapted and extremely costly to raise"?
   A. Fact
   B. Opinion

9. A conclusion that can be drawn from the passage is
   A. Jews believe that God wrote the Bible.
   B. China and New Guinea would be inappropriate places to raise cattle, sheep, or goats.
   C. In some parts of the world, people eat animals that Americans would consider to be pets.
   D. If a person eats pork, he or she cannot be Jewish.

Read the passage below and answer the questions that follow.

In December 1347, rats infested with fleas carrying bubonic plague arrived on the island of Sicily, Italy. Soon these fleas began biting the people who lived on the island, infecting them with the plague. The disease began in the lymph glands of the groin or armpits, which slowly filled with pus and turned black. The inflammations were called buboes—hence the name bubonic plague—and their black color lent the plague its other name, the Black Death. Since it was carried by rodents, which were commonplace even in wealthy homes, hardly anyone was spared. It was an egalitarian disease—archbishops, dukes, lords of the manor, merchants, laborers, and peasants fell equally before it. For those who survived the pandemic, life seemed little more than an ongoing burial service. In many towns, traditional funeral services were abandoned, and the dead were buried in mass graves. By 1350, all of Europe, with the exception of a few territories far from traditional trade routes, was devastated by the disease. In Tuscany, the death

5

10

rate in the cities was near 60 percent. In Florence, on June 24, 1348, the feast day of the city's patron saint, John the Baptist, 1,800 people reportedly died, and another 1,800 the next day—about 4 percent of the city's population in two days' time. Severe outbreaks of the plague erupted again in 1363, 1388-1390, and 1400.   15

Accounts of the time describe the surreal atmosphere of death and fear. Before the plague, it was common for friends and neighbors to gather in the house of someone who had died to mourn there and comfort the family. However, as the plague gained violence, these customs were either modified or laid aside altogether. More wretched   20 still were the circumstances of the common people and of much of the middle class. Because they were confined to their homes either by hope of safety, by poverty, or by customary restriction to their own sections, they fell sick daily by the thousands. A great many died in the public streets, day and night; a large number perished in their homes, and it was only by the stench of their decaying bodies that they proclaimed   25 their death to their neighbors. More out of fear of contagion rather than any charity they felt toward the dead, the neighbors would drag the corpses out of their homes and pile them in front of the doors to be collected. Huge trenches were dug in the crowded churchyards, and the new dead were piled in them, layer upon layer. Those writing during the plague years describe a world in virtual collapse as the Black Death   30 stalked the streets. (Adapted from Henry M. Sayre, *Discovering the Humanities*, Upper Saddle River, New Jersey: Pearson Education, Inc., 2008.)

10. Which sentence best states the implied main idea of the passage?
    A. The plague was an equal-opportunity illness.
    B. Outbreaks of bubonic plague in 14th-century Europe devastated the population and culture.
    C. The bubonic plague led to many changes in European burial rites.
    D. Outbreaks of plague caused people to lose sympathy for their affected neighbors.

11. What is the relationship within the following sentence? "Huge trenches were dug in the crowded churchyards, and the new dead were piled in them, layer upon layer."
    A. Spatial order
    B. Addition
    C. Cause and effect
    D. Time order

12. What is the relationship between the following sentences? "More wretched still were the circumstances of the common people and of much of the middle class," and "A great many died in the public streets, day and night; a large number perished in their homes, and it was only by the stench of their decaying bodies that they proclaimed their death to their neighbors."
    A. Compare and contrast
    B. Definition and example
    C. Listing
    D. Statement and clarification

13. According to the passage,
    A. mourning a death was a private, family affair in pre-plague Europe.
    B. plague victims were buried in mass graves.

    C. the Black Death turned people's armpits black.
    D. wealthier classes had fewer rodents in their homes than poorer classes.

14. It can be inferred from the passage that
    A. the city of Florence was Christian during the time of the plague.
    B. nobody who contracted the plague survived.
    C. the Europeans knew the plague was spread by rodents and their fleas.
    D. big cities were better able to handle plague than smaller communities.

15. The tone of the passage can best be described as
    A. farcical.
    B. contemptuous.
    C. grim.
    D. optimistic.

16. Is the following sentence fact or opinion? "In Tuscany, the death rate in the cities was near 60 percent."
    A. Fact
    B. Opinion

17. In this passage, the author is
    A. biased against writers who describe the Black Death.
    B. biased in favor of pre-plague culture.
    C. biased against the effects of sudden and widespread death.
    D. unbiased.

18. What is the meaning of the word **pandemic** in the following sentence? "For those who survived the **pandemic,** life seemed little more than an ongoing burial service."
    A. Grief and despair caused by death
    B. A widespread disease outbreak
    C. Starvation
    D. A curse brought by God

Read the passage below and answer the questions that follow.

Grandparents usually take great pleasure in their grandchildren. The new role of grandparent gives their lives a sense of purpose and provides them with new experiences. There are a number of different grandparenting styles, however. Some of the most common are remote or detached, companionate and supportive, and involved and influential.

In the *remote or detached* relationship, the grandparents and grandchildren live far apart and see each other infrequently, maintaining a largely ritualistic, symbolic relationship. For example, grandparents who are "distant figures" may see their grandchildren only on holidays or special occasions. Such relationships may be cordial but are also uninvolved and fleeting. While the biggest barrier to face-to-face contacts is living too far away, in other cases, grandparents are remote or detached because they're experiencing health problems or their grandchildren's busy schedule makes it difficult to get together.

    5

    10

In the *companionate and supportive* style of grandparenting, grandparents see their grandchildren often, frequently do things with them, and offer them emotional and instrumental support (such as providing money), but they don't seek authority in the grandchild's life. These grandparents are typically on the maternal side of the family, are younger, and have more income than other grandparents—characteristics that might encourage meddling—but they avoid getting involved in parental child-rearing decisions. This style of grandparenting is the most common pattern. According to a national survey, most grandparents (68%) see a grandchild every one or two weeks. Eight in ten grandparents contact a grandchild by telephone at least once every couple of weeks, and 19% chat with a grandchild by e-mail every few weeks.

In the *involved and influential* grandparenting style, grandparents play an active role in their grandchildren's lives. They may be spontaneous and playful, but they also exert substantial authority over their grandchildren, imposing definite—and sometimes tough—rules. Black grandmothers, especially, say that they are concerned with teaching their grandchildren the value of education, providing emotional support, and involving them in the extended family and community activities. In general, grandparents are more likely to be involved if their grandchildren are struggling in school. They are also twice as likely to be influential in their grandchildren's lives if they had close relationships with their own grandparents. (Adapted from Nijole V. Benokraitis, *Marriages and Families, Changes, Choices, and Constraints*, 6th ed., Upper Saddle River, NJ: Pearson Education, Inc., 2008.)

19. Which sentence best states the main idea of paragraph 3?
    A. This style of grandparenting is the most common pattern.
    B. According to a national survey, most grandparents (68%) see a grandchild every one or two weeks.
    C. In the *companionate and supportive* style of grandparenting, grandparents see their grandchildren often, frequently do things with them, and offer them emotional and instrumental support (such as providing money), but they don't seek authority in the grandchild's life.
    D. These grandparents are typically on the maternal side of the family, are younger, and have more income than other grandparents—characteristics that might encourage meddling—but they avoid getting involved in parental child-rearing decisions.

20. In this passage, the author's purpose is
    A. to describe the best types of grandparenting.
    B. to persuade grandparents to be more involved with their grandchildren.
    C. to describe grandparents.
    D. to define and describe the most common grandparenting styles.

21. What is the relationship within the following sentence? "While the biggest barrier to face-to-face contacts is living too far away, in other cases, grandparents are remote or detached because they're experiencing health problems or their grandchildren's busy schedule makes it difficult to get together."
    A. Time order
    B. Compare and contrast
    C. Listing
    D. Spatial order

22. What is the overall pattern of organization of the passage?
    A. Process
    B. Generalization and example
    C. Classification
    D. Comparison and contrast

23. Is the following sentence fact or opinion? "The *companionate and supportive* style of grand-parenting is the most common pattern."
    A. Fact
    B. Opinion

24. According to the passage,
    A. less than 10% of grandparents communicate with their grandkids by e-mail.
    B. grandparents are more likely to be involved if their grandchildren are doing well in school.
    C. *involved and influential* grandparents are playful and supportive but not authoritative.
    D. health problems cause some grandparents to be *remote or detached*.

25. It can be inferred from the passage that
    A. there are other grandparenting styles that are not described in this passage.
    B. the *involved and influential* style is superior to the other styles.
    C. a person's own experiences with grandparents rarely influences his or her own grandpar-enting style.
    D. *companionate and supportive* grandparents tend to come from the father's side of the family.

26. In this passage, the author is
    A. biased against *remote or detached* grandparents.
    B. biased in favor of *involved and influential* grandparents.
    C. biased in favor of black grandmothers.
    D. unbiased.

27. The statement, "The *companionate and supportive* style of grandparenting is the most com-mon pattern," is
    A. adequately supported by mostly facts.
    B. inadequately supported by mostly opinions.

Read the passage below and answer the questions that follow.

We often hear a great deal about the trend toward globalization, but the term and its meanings are often not defined. Economic globalization means the growing tendency for goods and services to be produced in one nation or region and consumed in another. The largest of the companies that produce these goods and services are multinational corporations, often with many subsidiary corporations, that have their headquarters in one country but pursue business activities and profits in one or more foreign nations.   5

The growth of multinational corporations is associated with the tendency to export capital and jobs overseas where labor is cheaper and more plentiful. During the 1970s and 1980s, U.S. plants, factories, mills, and other industrial facilities suffered as capital was diverted abroad. Unable to maintain their competitive edge, many manufacturing   10 facilities closed. Especially hard hit were plants in the nation's older, single-industry cities and towns, most of which were located in the manufacturing belt of the Midwest.

The biggest losers in the decline in manufacturing have been industrial towns and cities in the Northeast and Midwest. When rubber mills in Akron, Ohio, and steel mills in Youngstown, Ohio, and the Pittsburgh areas shut their doors, the local economies were devastated. With few secondary industries to fall back on, these cities experienced severe economic and social upheavals during the recessions of the mid-1970s and early 1980s and 1990s. In the1970s, the steel mills in Gary, Indiana, employed almost 28,000 workers in relatively well-paid jobs with good benefits. Today, fewer than 8,000 workers are employed in the Gary mills. Nevertheless, modernization of the steel industry, leading to greater efficiency and quality control, may produce a turnaround. Steel exports are rising, and steel companies' profits are improving. (Adapted from William Kornblum and Joseph Julian, *Social Problems*, 13th ed., Upper Saddle River, NJ: Pearson Prentice Hall, 2009.)

15

20

28. Which of the following sentences best states the <u>implied</u> main idea of the passage?
   A. Although globalization initially devastated the U.S. steel industry, the industry is now experiencing a turnaround.
   B. As multinational corporations moved their production overseas, cities and industries of the American Mid- and Northwest declined.
   C. Globalization has many benefits for multinational corporations.
   D. Globalization has all but devastated the American Midwest.

29. What is the relationship between the following sentences? "In the1970s, the steel mills in Gary, Indiana, employed almost 28,000 workers in relatively well-paid jobs with good benefits. Today, fewer than 8,000 workers are employed in the Gary mills."
   A. Statement and clarification
   B. Compare and contrast
   C. Time order
   D. Cause and effect

30. What is the overall pattern of organization of the SECOND paragraph?
   A. Listing
   B. Cause and effect
   C. Spatial order
   D. Compare and contrast

31. The author's purpose in writing this passage is
   A. to show how the rise in multinational corporations impacted American industrial cities.
   B. to persuade the reader that globalization is negative for U.S. industry.
   C. to describe the post-globalization Midwest.
   D. to argue for sanctions against multinational corporations.

32. The author's tone in this passage can best be described as
   A. optimistic.
   B. morose.
   C. condescending.
   D. neutral.

33. The statement, "The biggest losers in the decline in manufacturing have been industrial towns and cities in the Northeast and Midwest," from the third paragraph is
   A. adequately supported by mostly facts.
   B. inadequately supported by mostly opinions.

34. Which of the following is a conclusion that can be reached regarding this passage?
   A. Multinational corporations tend to concentrate on just one industry.
   B. Before the 1970s, the American manufacturing belt had no economic or social problems.
   C. Multinational corporations pay their workers less than they would pay an American worker.
   D. If it weren't for multinational corporations, the manufacturing industries of the Midwest would be thriving.

35. Is the statement, "Nevertheless, modernization of the steel industry, leading to greater efficiency and quality control, may produce a turnaround" fact or opinion?
   A. Fact
   B. Opinion

36. What does the word **capital** mean in the sentence, "The growth of multinational corporations is associated with the tendency to export **capital** and jobs overseas where labor is cheaper and more plentiful"?
   A. Headquarters
   B. Culture
   C. Money and equipment
   D. Employees

Part Five: Correspondence Charts for Test Questions

PRETEST CORRESPONDENCE CHART ◆ BY QUESTION NUMBER		
Ques. No.	**Skills**	
1	Main Idea	
2	Patterns of Organization	
3	Author's Purpose	
4	Relationships Between Sentences	
5	Support for Reasoning and Argument	
6	Relationships Within a Sentence	
7	Author's Tone	
8	Main Idea	
9	Inferences and Conclusions	
10	Main Idea	
11	Inferences and Conclusions	
12	Supporting Details	
13	Word Meaning	
14	Fact and Opinion	
15	Support for Reasoning and Argument	
16	Patterns of Organization	
17	Relationships Within a Sentence	
18	Author's Purpose	

Ques. No.	Skills
19	Main Idea
20	Fact and Opinion
21	Relationships Within a Sentence
22	Patterns of Organization
23	Author's Bias
24	Author's Tone
25	Support for Reasoning and Argument
26	Relationships Between Sentences
27	Inferences and Conclusions
28	Main Idea
29	Relationships Within a Sentence
30	Patterns of Organization
31	Author's Bias
32	Word Meaning
33	Inferences and Conclusions
34	Author's Tone
35	Fact and Opinion
36	Author's Purpose

PRETEST CORRESPONDENCE CHART ◆ BY SKILLS				
Skills	**Question Numbers**			
Main Idea	1	8	10	19	28
Supporting Details	12			
Author's Purpose	3	18	36	
Patterns of Organization	2	16	22	30
Relationships Within a Sentence	6	17	21	29
Relationships Between Sentences	4	26		
Context Clues	13	32		
Author's Bias	23	31		
Author's Tone	7	24	34	
Fact and Opinion	14	20	35	
Inferences and Conclusions	9	11	27	
Support for Reasoning and Argument	5	15	25	

EXIT EXAM #1 QUESTION CORRESPONDENCE CHART ◆ BY QUESTION NUMBER

Ques. No.	Skills	Ques. No.	Skills
1	Main Idea	19	Main Idea
2	Author's Purpose	20	Author's Purpose
3	Patterns of Organization	21	Inferences and Conclusions
4	Relationships Within a Sentence	22	Patterns of Organization
5	Supporting Details	23	Author's Tone
6	Fact and Opinion	24	Word Meaning
7	Support for Reasoning and Argument	25	Author's Bias
8	Author's Tone	26	Relationships Between Sentences
9	Inferences and Conclusions	27	Relationships Within a Sentence
10	Main Idea	28	Main Idea
11	Relationships Within a Sentence	29	Patterns of Organization
12	Relationships Between Sentences	30	Relationships Between Sentences
13	Patterns of Organization	31	Author's Bias
14	Author's Purpose	32	Relationships Between Sentences
15	Inferences and Conclusions	33	Word Meaning
16	Support for Reasoning and Argument	34	Relationships Within a Sentence
17	Supporting Details	35	Support for Reasoning and Argument
18	Fact and Opinion	36	Inferences and Conclusions

EXIT EXAM #1 CORRESPONDENCE CHART ◆ BY SKILLS

Skills	Question Numbers			
Main Idea	1	10	19	28
Supporting Details	2	14	20	
Author's Purpose	5	17		
Patterns of Organization	3	13	22	29
Relationships Within a Sentence	4	11	27	34
Relationships Between Sentences	12	26	30	32
Word Meaning	24	33		
Author's Bias	25	31		
Author's Tone	8	23		
Fact and Opinion	6	18		
Inferences and Conclusions	9	15	21	36
Support for Reasoning and Argument	7	16	35	

EXIT EXAM #2 QUESTION CORRESPONDENCE CHART
◆ BY QUESTION NUMBER

Ques. No.	Skills	Ques. No.	Skills
1	Main Idea	19	Implied Main Idea
2	Patterns of Organization	20	Patterns of Organization
3	Implied Main Idea	21	Relationships Within a Sentence
4	Relationships Between Sentences	22	Relationships Between Sentences
5	Author's Purpose	23	Author's Purpose
6	Context Clues	24	Author's Tone
7	Supporting Details	25	Author's Bias
8	Inferences and Conclusions	26	Fact and Opinion
9	Support for Reasoning and Argument	27	Context Clues
10	Implied Main Idea	28	Main Idea
11	Relationships Within a Sentence	29	Main Idea
12	Relationships Between Sentences	30	Patterns of Organization
13	Supporting Details	31	Relationships Within a Sentence
14	Support for Reasoning and Argument	32	Relationships Between Sentences
15	Inferences and Conclusions	33	Author's Purpose
16	Author's Tone	34	Inferences and Conclusions
17	Author's Bias	35	Author's Tone
18	Fact and Opinion	36	Fact and Opinion

EXIT EXAM #2 CORRESPONDENCE CHART ◆ BY SKILLS

Skills	Question Numbers					
Main Idea	1	3	10	19	28	29
Supporting Details	7	13				
Author's Purpose	5	23	33			
Patterns of Organization	2	20	30			
Relationships Within a Sentence	11	21	31			
Relationships Between Sentences	4	12	22	32		
Word Meaning	6	27				
Author's Bias	17	25				
Author's Tone	16	24	35			
Fact and Opinion	18	26	36			
Inferences and Conclusions	8	15	34			
Support for Reasoning and Argument	9	14				

EXIT EXAM #3 QUESTION CORRESPONDENCE CHART
◆ BY QUESTION NUMBER

Ques. No.	Skills	Ques. No.	Skills
1	Main Idea	19	Main Idea
2	Author's Purpose	20	Author's Purpose
3	Patterns of Organization	21	Relationships Within a Sentence
4	Support for Reasoning and Argument	22	Patterns of Organization
5	Relationships Within a Sentence	23	Fact and Opinion
6	Author's Tone	24	Supporting Details
7	Word Meaning	25	Inferences and Conclusions
8	Fact and Opinion	26	Author's Bias
9	Inferences and Conclusions	27	Support for Reasoning and Argument
10	Main Idea	28	Main Idea
11	Relationships Within a Sentence	29	Relationships Between Sentences
12	Relationships Between Sentences	30	Patterns of Organization
13	Supporting Details	31	Author's Purpose
14	Inferences and Conclusions	32	Author's Tone
15	Author's Tone	33	Support for Reasoning and Argument
16	Fact and Opinion	34	Inferences and Conclusions
17	Author's Bias	35	Fact and Opinion
18	Word Meaning	36	Word Meaning

EXIT EXAM #3 CORRESPONDENCE CHART ◆ BY SKILLS

Skills	Question Numbers			
Main Idea	1	10	19	28
Supporting Details	13	24		
Author's Purpose	2	20	31	
Patterns of Organization	3	22	30	
Relationships Within a Sentence	5	11	21	
Relationships Between Sentences	12	29		
Word Meaning	7	18	36	
Author's Bias	17	26		
Author's Tone	6	15	32	
Fact and Opinion	8	16	23	35
Inferences and Conclusions	9	14	25	34
Support for Reasoning and Argument	4	27	33	

TRACKING SHEET ◆ READING PRACTICE EXIT EXAMS

DIRECTIONS: Every time you take a Practice Exit Exam, you will fill in the number of errors you made for each type of skill. This way, you see which skills you need to practice before you take the real Exit Exam. Look at the correspondence charts in this chapter to determine which skill each question addresses. Then, mark the number of questions you missed for each skill on each exam. This should help you see what your strengths and weaknesses are for the real Exit Exam.

Reasoning/Supported Argument				
Inferences and Conclusions				
Fact and Opinion				
Tone				
Bias				
Meaning of Word in Context				
Relationship Between Sentences				
Relationship Within a Sentence				
Pattern of Organization				
Purpose				
Supporting Details				
Main Idea				
	Pretest	Practice Exam #1	Practice Exam #2	Practice Exam #3
	_____	_____	_____	_____

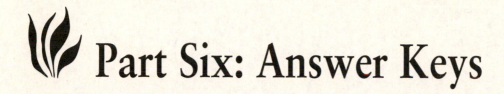

Part Six: Answer Keys

PRETEST – READING SKILLS

1.	C	2.	B	3.	C	4.	D	5.	B	6.	C
7.	A	8.	B	9.	A	10.	C	11.	B	12.	A
13.	C	14.	B	15.	A	16.	D	17.	C	18.	A
19.	A	20.	B	21.	D	22.	C	23.	D	24.	D
25.	B	26.	C	27.	C	28.	A	29.	B	30.	D
31.	A	32.	C	33.	C	34.	B	35.	A	36.	C

READING WORKBOOK

CHAPTER 1: CONCEPT SKILLS

1. The Main Idea

1.	A	2.	D	3.	C	4.	C	5.	A
6.	D	7.	B	8.	D	9.	A	10.	C

2. Supporting Details

1.	B	2.	D	3.	A	4.	B	5.	A
6.	C	7.	D	8.	C	9.	B	10.	B

3. Author's Purpose

1.	C	2.	B	3.	D	4.	A	5.	D
6.	D	7.	B	8.	A	9.	C	10.	C

CHAPTER 2: STRUCTURAL SKILLS

1. Patterns of Organization

1.	D	2.	B	3.	A	4.	C	5.	C
6.	D	7.	B	8.	A	9.	C	10.	D
11.	B	12.	A	13.	C	14.	B	15.	D
16.	C	17.	A	18.	B	19.	B	20.	D

2. Relationships *Within* a Sentence

1.	B	2.	D	3.	D	4.	A	5.	C
6.	A	7.	D	8.	B	9.	C	10.	C

3. Relationships *Between* Sentences

1.	D	2.	C	3.	C	4.	B	5.	A
6.	B	7.	D	8.	D	9.	D	10.	A

CHAPTER 3: LANGUAGE SKILLS

1. Word Choice: Context Clues

1.	B	2.	C	3.	D	4.	B	5.	A
6.	D	7.	A	8.	C	9.	B	10.	C

2. Biased Language

1.	D	2.	A	3.	D	4.	C	5.	B
6.	A	7.	C	8.	D	9.	B	10.	B

3. Tone of Passage

1.	C	2.	A	3.	B	4.	A	5.	A
6.	C	7.	B	8.	D	9.	C	10.	A

CHAPTER 4: REASONING SKILLS

1. Fact and Opinion

1.	C	2.	C	3.	B	4.	A	5.	B
6.	A	7.	B	8.	B	9.	A	10.	B

2. Inferences and Conclusions

1.	D	2.	C	3.	B	4.	D	5.	D
6.	A	7.	B	8.	C	9.	B	10.	A
11.	A	12.	C	13.	C	14.	A	15.	B
16.	D	17.	A	18.	B	19.	C	20.	B

3. Assessing Supports for Reasoning and Argument

1.	B	2.	A	3.	C	4.	B	5.	A
6.	D	7.	B	8.	A	9.	B	10.	C

Exit Exam #1 – Reading Skills

1.	A	2.	D	3.	A	4.	D	5.	B	6.	A
7.	A	8.	C	9.	D	10.	B	11.	C	12.	D
13.	A	14.	B	15.	C	16.	A	17.	D	18.	A
19.	C	20.	A	21.	A	22.	D	23.	C	24.	B
25.	C	26.	D	27.	B	28.	A	29.	D	30.	C
31.	B	32.	C	33.	A	34.	D	35.	B	36.	A

Exit Exam #2 – Reading Skills

1.	D	2.	C	3.	A	4.	C	5.	D	6.	B
7.	D	8.	B	9.	A	10.	D	11.	B	12.	B
13.	C	14.	B	15.	A	16.	A	17.	D	18.	B
19.	C	20.	B	21.	C	22.	B	23.	A	24.	C
25.	A	26.	B	27.	B	28.	D	29.	B	30.	C
31.	B	32.	D	33.	A	34.	B	35.	B	36.	A

Exit Exam #3 – Reading Skills

1.	B	2.	C	3.	D	4.	A	5.	B	6.	D
7.	A	8.	B	9.	C	10.	B	11.	B	12.	D
13.	B	14.	A	15.	C	16.	A	17.	C	18.	B
19.	C	20.	D	21.	B	22.	C	23.	A	24.	D
25.	A	26.	D	27.	A	28.	B	29.	C	30.	B
31.	A	32.	D	33.	A	34.	C	35.	B	36.	C

ANSWERS TO READING PRETEST *WITH* EXPLANATIONS

Pretest Answers with Explanations

1. Answer   C

Choices A, B, and D are details and do not cover everything discussed in the passage.

2. Answer   B

The information is organized by the type of carnivorous plant. Active trappers are discussed in paragraph two and passive trappers are discussed in paragraph three. Although some cause-and-effect examples are given, the overall pattern of how the information is presented is by classifying the types of carnivorous plants.

3. Answer   C

The author offers a detailed explanation of how the insects become trapped inside carnivorous plants. The author does more than give a definition; his focus is mostly upon the process that happens after the prey lands on the plant. Choice A is too narrow, dealing only with one type of carnivorous plant, and choice D is incorrect because the passage does not explain all of the effects (how the digestion of the insect helps the plant) of trapping prey.

4. Answer   D

The sentences describe two steps in the process of how a bladderwort traps its prey. It does not compare or contrast the two ideas, nor does it show a relationship of location (spatial order). The second statement doesn't clarify or explain the first.

5. Answer   B

The author supports his claim that carnivorous plants fall into two groups by giving examples of both active trappers and passive trappers and presenting facts about both types of plants.

6. Answer   C

The cause is the prey touching the tactile cells, and the effect is the trap door opening. It does not give an example of the first idea (when the prey touches the tactile cells) nor is it a summary of the process. The relationship is more than just listing facts in random order. In this sentence, the first action causes the second to happen.

7. Answer   A

Objective means an unbiased presentation of the facts. The author does not use emotional language to support the other tones, such as admiring, nostalgic, or reverent.

8. Answer   B

A is incorrect because it infers that the process is complicated, which is an opinion that may not be shared by others. Choice C only refers to one type of active trapper that is discussed in the paragraph. Choice D is incorrect

because the passage does not state that <u>all</u> active trappers have nectar glands.

9. Answer   A

In paragraph one, the author states that active trappers use rapid plant movements to open trap doors or to close traps. Since the Pitcher plant is a passive trapper, and a bladderwort is an active trapper, the pitcher plant would be slower at trapping its prey. Choice B is not discussed. Choice C is not accurate according to the passage. The passage does not state that <u>all</u> passive trappers have small trigger hairs to trap their prey, so D is incorrect.

10. Answer   C

Choice A presents a detail from the passage, not the implied main idea of the entire passage. Choice B does not have enough evidence from the text to support and does not capture the full main idea. Choice D is close, but it is a bit too narrow and does not include all of the information in the paragraph.

11. Answer   B

Choice A is false. The passage states that she studied medical technology in college and learned of numerous incidents of radioactive contamination at the plant. Choice C is false. Most women in the 1970s were traditional homemakers. The last sentence states that women who moved out of the role of homemaker endured a lack of respect. Choice D is not discussed. Choice B reflects Silkwood's efforts to expose worker safety problems at the plant.

12. Answer   A

Choice B was not discussed in the passage. Choice C is false because the passage states that Kerr-McGee knowingly manufactured defective nuclear products. Choice D is incorrect because she was not paid for her efforts to expose Kerr-McGee's unethical practices. A whistle-blower is a person who exposes unethical practices.

13. Answer   C

Paragraph 3 states, "Her **dismissive** treatment by some fellow workers, her employers, and the media also suggested the <u>lack of respect</u> that women had long endured." The other choices do not fit the meaning of the word.

14. Answer   B

This statement is not provable, as in the phrase "suggested the lack of respect," which is the author's interpretation of what her treatment suggested.

15. Answer   A

The author has provided numerous facts about what Karen Silkwood did to challenge one of the most powerful energy corporations in the country.

16. Answer   D

The details of the passage are in chronological (time) order, beginning with her childhood and ending with her death in 1974.

17. Answer   C

The action of her car's being forced off the road caused her death. Therefore, it is a cause-and-effect relationship. If the first event merely came before the second event but did not cause it, then time order would be correct. But in this case, the first event caused the second event to happen.

18. Answer   A

Choice B is too broad and does not focus on the topic of the passage, Karen Silkwood. Choice C is a conclusion that may be drawn from reading the passage, but was not the author's primary purpose in writing the passage. Choice D is a conclusion about one of the details of the passage.

19. Answer   A

Choices B, C, and D are all details that cover only one part of the passage. Choice A is broad enough to include all the information in the passage.

20. Answer   B

The phrase "may be viewed" is the author's own opinion and it is not a provable statement. Facts must be provable.

21. Answer   D

Since the father is nearly totally absent from the home scene, the result is that the children are raised mainly by the mother.

22. Answer   C

Most of the supporting details in this passage show the effects of salarymen's lives. Because they spend long hours at work and are expected to socialize after work, they go to nightclubs and do not spend time at home with their families. Another result is that the children are mainly raised by the mother.

23. Answer   D

The author reports on the research done on salarymen and does not express a judgment either for or against them. The author presents both the negative and the positive aspects of being a salaryman. Therefore, the passage is unbiased.

24. Answer   D

Straightforward is objective. The author has presented facts about salarymen without making judgments. There is no emotional language in the passage.

25. Answer   B

Choice A discusses Japanese boys and does not refer to salarymen. Choices C and D do not support the idea that salarymen work long hours.

26. Answer   C

The reason why salarymen eat dinner only a few times a year with their families is that they typically spend many hours after work at expensive nightclubs.

27. Answer   C

The question asks which conclusion can NOT be drawn, so it is asking for a false statement. Choices A, B, and D are all true based upon the information in the passage. C is correct because it assumes information that is not discussed in the passage. It cannot be inferred from the passage that Japanese mothers do not work outside of their homes.

28. Answer   A

Choice B is a detail because the passage discusses more than just factories. Choice C is a detail but does not cover all the information in the passage. Choice D can be concluded, but it is not the main point the author is making in the passage.

29. Answer   B

The second half of the sentence adds to the first half more information about the same topic. It states two separate facts about the factory system. It also uses a transition, "and."

30. Answer   D

The details of the passage are the effects of industrialization. The main idea is that industrialization caused many problems in society. The author's intent was to show this cause-and-effect relationship, not merely to list the problems during industrialization.

31. Answer   A

The author uses emotional language to describe the "horrid conditions" in early factories, describing them as "miserable places." Therefore, the author is biased against the early factories. Nothing in the passage suggests choice B or C. Choice D is incorrect because the author uses emotional language.

32. Answer   C

Choice C, *believed*, is the only word which makes sense in "workers who suffered accidents were believed to be at fault . . ."

33. Answer   C

The question asks which conclusion can NOT be drawn from the passage, so it is asking for a false statement. Choices A, B, and D are all true conclusions that can be drawn based upon the information in the passage. The passage does not state or imply that industrialization caused a decline in agriculture. Therefore, C is the correct answer.

34. Answer   B

The author is clearly critical of conditions in early factories and living conditions for working families during early industrialization. None of the other words accurately describe the author's tone.

35. Answer   A

The phrase "This situation was guaranteed to produce conflict" is not provable, and "wretched conditions" expresses a judgment or opinion. Choices A, C, and D are all provable statements; therefore, they are facts.

36. Answer   C

The main idea of the passage is that early industrialization had many negative effects on society. In this passage, it was the author's intent to show the negative effects of industrialization: poor working conditions, child labor, and poor health. Choice A is briefly mentioned in the first paragraph but is not explained. Choice B is incorrect because most of the details in the passage are not being used to compare industrialized society to agricultural society. Choice D is too narrow and focuses only on one aspect of the passage.

Note: All answers to diagnostics can be found within each chapter, immediately following the diagnostic.

ANSWERS TO EXERCISES IN THE READING WORKBOOK *WITH* EXPLANATIONS

CHAPTER 1: CONCEPT SKILLS

1. The Main Idea

1. Answer   A

The paragraph explains the reasons youths join gangs, which "contradict popular thinking on this subject."

False Choices

    B   This detail is provided in the introductory paragraph and explains the basis of the findings expressed in the passage.
    C   This is a supporting detail given in the first paragraph.
    D   This definition of street gangs is a paraphrase of the information in sentences 1–3.

2. Answer   D

The details in paragraph 3 support the idea that urban poverty causes individuals to develop a "defiant individualist" personality type. The topic sentence states: "Those who were gang members shared a personality type called a "defiant individualist." The rest of the paragraph provides details to describe this personality type.

False Choices

    A   In paragraph 3, street gang members are not portrayed as victims.
    B   While the passage states that poverty contributes to the development of a distinct personality type, it does not imply that these individuals would be successful if they weren't poor.
    C   As one of the five traits of the "defiant individualist" personality, competitiveness is a supporting detail and cannot be the main idea.

3. Answer   C

The second paragraph builds on the idea expressed in the first paragraph—that the commonly held perceptions about the reasons individuals join street gangs is not true.

False Choices

    A   This is a supporting detail and cannot be the main idea.
    B   This is a generalization that is argued in the paragraph, but it is not the main idea.
    D   This statement is another supporting detail of the paragraph and not the main idea.

4. Answer   C

Each paragraph of the passage gives examples of the First Ladies' activities while their husbands were presidents. The first paragraph introduces the idea that there is more to the job of First Lady than being the hostess at White House dinners. The second paragraph describes the roles of Abigail Adams, Dolly Madison, Edith Galt Wilson, Eleanor Roosevelt, Lady Bird Johnson, Rosalyn Carter, Nancy Reagan, and Barbara Bush. The last paragraph focuses on Hillary Clinton.

False Choices

    A   While this statement may be true, it is not the main idea of the paragraph.
    B   The information in the paragraph does not support the idea that the role of the First Lady has become more important in the past 50 years.
    D   The role of the media in the First Ladies' lives is not the focus of the passage. The only reference to the media is in the first paragraph, which mentions that the media "chronicles every word she speaks and every hairstyle she adopts."

5. Answer   A

Paragraph 2 describes what each of eight different First Ladies contributed. Lady Bird Johnson, Rosalyn Carter, Nancy Reagan, and Barbara Bush picked an issue while Abigail Adams and Dolly Madison counseled their husbands. Edith Galt Wilson and Eleanor Roosevelt had more involvement in helping their husbands run the government.

False Choices

    B   This is a supporting detail in the paragraph, not the main idea of paragraph 2.
    C   This is a supporting detail in the paragraph, not the main idea of paragraph 2.
    D   Not all of the details in the paragraph support this idea.

6. Answer   D

This statement summarizes the last part of the first sentence of the paragraph and is supported by the details.

False Choices

A   The passage does not describe her as a "model" First Lady, but rather as a woman who held a leadership position.

B   This is a supporting detail and cannot be the implied idea.

C   No reference is made to Hillary Clinton's education or its impact on her activities.

7. Answer   B

The main idea of the passage is summarized in the last two sentences of the last paragraph.

False Choices

A   This is a supporting detail explained in the first sentence of the third paragraph, so it cannot be the main idea of the passage.

C   This is a generalization that is a misinterpretation of the information provided in the passage.

D   The only mention of television in the passage is the reference to a 1980s public service advertisement. The scenario is used as an attention-getting device in the introductory paragraph.

8. Answer   D

The statement best explains the idea of paragraph 4.

False Choices

A   This detail is not expressed in the paragraph. The paragraph states that adolescents who had a positive relationship with their parents would more likely do what their parents did. Therefore, in this positive relationship, if the parents didn't smoke, the adolescent was less likely to smoke.

B   This statement is too general for the passage.

C   This statement is the opposite of what is expressed in the passage.

9. Answer   A

This is expressed in the first sentence of the second paragraph and is supported by the details of the paragraph.

False Choices

B   This sentence is a supporting detail in the paragraph and cannot be the main idea.

C   The passage supports the idea that adolescents whose parents use drugs or alcohol will probably not copy their parents, unlike the statement that suggests that they "may or may not copy their parents."

D   This is an opinion that is not supported by the information in the paragraph.

10. Answer   C

The third paragraph does explain the three levels that are affected by observational learning.

False Choices

A   The passage says that at the level of the group, a person may be "captivated" by people who have

characteristics that are attractive to them. This is a supporting detail, not a main idea.

B   This statement is supplied as supporting evidence in the passage in the second sentence.

D   This statement is a supporting detail and not the main idea.

2. Supporting Details

1. Answer   B

As stated in paragraph 4, whether ESP is a valid, reliable phenomenon will depend on the results of studies scientifically designed to prove it; if they show there is nothing to it, then ESP will be considered pseudopsychology. These studies are still underway, so ESP has not been completely proved or disproved.

False Choices

A   To say that ESP is a pseudopsychology is to draw a conclusion not based on evidence from the passage. Pseudopsychology is "superstition or unsupported opinion pretending to be science." The passage states that experiments have not proved or disproved ESP, so ESP cannot yet be considered pseudopsychology.

C   In the passage, no relationship is made among astrology, palm reading, and ESP.

D   This statement is not mentioned anywhere in the passage.

2. Answer   D

The author defines pseudopsychology as "superstition" in sentence 5.

False Choices

A   This is not true. The author states that pseudopsychology "is not a branch of psychology."

B   No mention is made in the passage that pseudopsychology is a science.

C   Pseudopsychology is not a study, it is a superstition.

3. Answer   A

In paragraph 4, the author explains that if a person involved in an ESP experiment has an unconscious bias towards a particular color of card, he or she might select that color more often; this would affect the results of the experiment.

False Choices

B   ESP experiments must be set up properly to avoid bias and expectancy of effects, but whether or not these experiments are difficult to set up is not a supporting detail of the passage.

C   The passage does not state that ESP experiments have shown that telepathy is largely guesswork.

D   The passage does not state that telepathy experiments are a waste of time.

4.   Answer   B

According to paragraph 4, a "better experiment" would eliminate these two problems. Visible clues could be avoided by putting the receiver and sender in different rooms. Unconscious bias could be avoided by including a control condition in which the receiver is told to guess cards when the receiver is not sending.

False Choices

A   Eliminating guesswork is only one aspect of designing a better experiment.

C   Playing cards are traditionally used in these kinds of experiments. Since the method already exists, it would not contribute to a "better" experiment.

D   Measuring the percentage of times the receiver chooses the correct card has been a method used in telepathy experiments and is not a new concept; therefore, it would not make a "better" experiment.

5.   Answer   A

As quoted from the first paragraph in the passage, "the adult is only about the size of a house cat."

False Choices

B   According to the passage, they "look so much alike that even experts can have a difficult time of telling them apart."

C   The ranges of the two species overlap. (line 14)

D   According to lines 31–32, "they are separate species, despite the pronounced similarities in their body form and coloration.

6.   Answer   C

The female warns an intruder by "raising her tail, stamping her forefeet, raking the ground with her claws, or even doing a handstand." (lines 7–8)

False Choices

None of the three are mentioned in the passage. Lines 7–8 do not include A, hissing; B, running in circles; or C, swishing her tail.

7.   Answer   D

Biologists thought that all spotted skunks were the same species until 1960s studies of their sexual reproduction showed they were two species. (lines 19–21)

False Choices

A and B Migration patterns and range overlap were not involved in the discovery that the species were different.

C   The passage does not mention any study done with the skunks' potent musk sprays.

8.   Answer   C

In line 23, the passage describes the reproductive cycle of the western spotted skunk as including "delayed development."

False Choices

A   The western spotted skunk mates in the late summer and early fall. The blastocyst stays dormant in the female through the winter, and the young are born in May or June.

B   The reproductive cycles occur at different times. The eastern spotted skunk mates in late winter and gives birth between April and July. The western spotted skunk's reproductive cycle is explained in False Choice A.

D   The western spotted skunk's reproductive cycle is longer, not shorter.

9.   Answer   B

The eastern and western spotted skunks are interesting because they illustrate "some important concepts about biological species." (lines 3–4)

False Choices

A   This is one aspect of the difference between the two skunks, not the only reason that they are interesting.

C   The passage does not mention anything about these skunks becoming extinct.

D   The markings of these skunks are similar, but it's not the sole reason they are interesting.

10.   Answer   B

The most important discovery about the eastern and western spotted skunks is that they are different species. Until the 1960s, biologists thought that they were one species.

False Choices

A   The fact that their habitats overlapped was one of the pieces of information that made biologists think they were the same species.

C   The similarity in the appearance of the eastern and western spotted skunk contributed to the idea that the two were the same species.

D   Information about the western spotted skunk is given in the passage, not about how the eastern spotted skunk defends her young.

3. Author's Purpose

1.   Answer   C

The topic sentence of this paragraph indicates that examples of the practical uses of fungi will be given in the paragraph. In fact, four examples are provided.

False Choices

A   The paragraph is not limited to describing foods that are fungi. It also explains that fungi produce antibiotics.

B   The paragraph does not discuss how fungi are used to ripen cheeses. The paragraph's purpose is not to describe a process.

D   No arguments are presented in the paragraph.

2. Answer   B

The first sentence of the passage gives the purpose of the passage: "John Castle's lifestyle gives us a glimpse into how the super-rich live."

False Choices

A   The reader may find his lifestyle appealing, but the passage does not attempt to persuade the reader that Castle's lifestyle is to be envied.

C   The author does not criticize Castle for wasting his money. Instead, he tells us the kinds of things Castle spends money on.

D   There is no attempt to inspire the reader to become wealthy. The reader may be impressed with Castle's wealth by reading about his estate, his ranch, or his yacht.

3. Answer   D

The passage does convince teachers that they must report suspected cases of child abuse and neglect. The first paragraph defines child abuse. The second paragraph informs teachers that they should become familiar with their state's laws. It encourages teachers to file a report. In fact, teachers can be fined or imprisoned if they do not make the report. The concluding paragraph reinforces the point about reporting child abuse, applying the "reasonable person" standard.

False Choices

A   Child abuse is defined in the first paragraph, but the entire passage is not definition.

B   This is a supporting detail covered in the second paragraph. It notes that each state has its own requirements, so teachers should become familiar with those in their state.

C   The passage does not discuss indicators of child abuse.

4. Answer   A

The passage contrasts cultural differences in criticizing in public. Competitive cultures like the United States readily criticize, while collectivist cultures such as Japan find public criticism uncomfortable.

False Choices

B   The passage does not give instruction about how to criticize effectively.

C   As a result of reading the passage, the reader may see that there are vast cultural differences regarding criticism and therefore may gain respect for those differences; however, persuasion is not the purpose of the paragraph.

D   As a byproduct of the discussion of the cultural differences in public criticism, the passage explains what people from different cultures may feel when they interpret criticism through their own cultural filter.

5. Answer   D

The passage illustrates the pubic roles of eight First Ladies. It begins with Abigail Adams and ends with Hillary Rodham Clinton.

False Choices

A   The readers may infer contrasts among the First Ladies as they read the passage. Some of the First Ladies were more directly involved in their husbands' career while others chose a particular issue to work on.

B   This is not a process paragraph explaining how the job of the First Lady is done.

C   The First Ladies in this passage were selected for their contributions; however, no attempt is made to convince the reader that they were feminists. The word "feminist" is not even mentioned in the passage. True, these were strong, capable women; however, assuming they were feminists would be the reader's opinion.

6. Answer   D

The purpose of the passage is clearly stated in the first sentence: "President Truman's decision to order the atomic bombings on the Japanese cities of Hiroshima and Nagasaki has been the subject of intense historical debate."

False Choices

A   The passage does not describe the effects of the atomic bombs on the people in the two Japanese cities.

B   Because the passage argues both sides of the debate, the reasons for dropping the atomic bombs is given; however, the paragraph is not solely about causes.

C   Both sides of the debate are presented without an attempt to persuade the reader one way or the other.

7. Answer   B

This passage explains the problems of single parenthood as stated in the first sentence of the passage: "A single parent may experience a variety of problems." Meeting the child's emotional needs, providing proper supervision, financial difficulties, and unmet emotional and sexual needs are examples.

False Choices

A   The passage does not argue that single parenthood has disadvantages.

C   Although the problems may make children's lives challenging, the passage does not persuade the reader that the children are suffering.

D   The passage presents the problems for parents, some of which affect the children, but the focus of the passage is not on the effects of divorce on children.

8. Answer   A

The passage clearly classifies the ineffective, harmful types of quick diets people try. The purpose is stated in the last sentence of the first paragraph: "This attitude results in choosing quick-weight-loss diets that are not effective and may be harmful."

False Choices

  B   Certainly the information shared in the passage will persuade the reader that crash diets are harmful, but this is not the purpose.

  C   In telling the reader about the different types of crash diets, the passage describes each one as a means of support.

  D   At the end of the passage, the author suggests the proper way to lose weight in lines 18–19: lose weight slowly, eat properly and in moderation, and exercise.

9. Answer   C

The first sentence of this passage gives its purpose as contrast: "The dramatic difference between respective burial rites."

False Choices

  A   The passage does not attempt to give the details behind the Egyptians' belief in the afterlife. Their beliefs are reflected in their burial rites.

  B   The passage mentions that the pyramids were the core of the nobility's city of the dead as a supporting detail.

  D   The tombs of the pharaohs are briefly described in supporting details in the passage.

10. Answer   C

The passage gives the reasons individuals join gangs. This information is a result of research done by an anthropologist who studied nearly forty street gangs in New York, Los Angeles, and Boston.

False Choices

  A   The passage does not attempt to discourage youths from joining a gang.

  B   The belief that all gang members come from homes with no authority figure is disproved by the information presented in the second paragraph of the passage. The study showed that equal numbers of gang members came from intact families. No attempt at argument is made.

  D   The last paragraph defines the "defiant individualist" as the personality type gang members share. This description provides supporting detail for the main idea of the paragraph and is not the purpose of the passage.

CHAPTER 2: STRUCTURAL SKILLS

1. Patterns of Organization

1. Answer   D

The passage clearly states that it will provide suggestions for balancing work and school.

False Choices

  A   The passage does not summarize the problems of a working student.

  B   This passage is not organized around the reasons for attending school full-time rather than working and studying. The issue is not addressed at all.

  C   Getting along with supervisors and coworkers is not a topic of this passage.

2. Answer   B

The passage explains that slavery was based on three factors: debt, crime, and war and conquest.

False Choices

  A   One of the supporting examples is that the first people to be enslaved through warfare were women. This detail is a part of the war and conquest factor.

  C   Most of the discussion is based on pre-modern forms of slavery. There is no contrast between the two in the passage.

3. Answer   A

The passage gives an extended definition of "cyberliteracy." Extended definition passages use a variety of methods to explain a term, such as example, contrast, cause and effect, process, and so on.

False Choices

  B   Part of the passage contrasts online and written communication, but contrast is not the organizational pattern. Written communications, such as letters, give the writer a chance to think about what he or she wants to say. In contrast, electronic "discourse" is quick, more like oral communication.

  C   Critical thinking is discussed to help define cyberliteracy. Electronic literacy requires that we understand that communication in the online word is different; it is neither purely print nor purely oral.

  D   The passage does not tell how to become cyberliterate.

4. Answer   C

The passage offers examples of the forms of entertainment in the Roman Empire. The people enjoyed such things as chariot races and gladiator combats to the death. The spectacle of feeding humans to wild beasts was commonplace.

False Choices
- A   The passage is not organized around effects.
- B   One form of entertainment was the gladiatorial combats. This fact is used as one of the supporting examples.
- D   The passage does not attempt to analyze the Romans' preference for sadism and voyeurism in their entertainment.

5. Answer   C

The second paragraph explains that the Romans uninhibitedly enjoyed watching people being killed, either in gladiator combats or by beasts. These forms of entertainment were sadistic and voyeuristic.

False Choices
- A   In the second paragraph, the author makes the point that the Romans would have been "mystified" by the "anxieties people feel today about the make-believe violence in the movies and on television." However, that is a supporting point, not the pattern of organization of the paragraph.
- B   The paragraph gives examples of sadistic entertainment, but it does not define the term.
- D   The paragraph is not organized by describing Hollywood gladiator movies.

6. Answer   D

The topic sentence of the paragraph alerts the reader that the paragraph will describe a process: "Nonflowing bodies of water such as lakes become contaminated in stages."

False Choices
- A   The second sentence of the paragraph lists the types of chemical pollutants, but that is a supporting detail.
- B   The growth of algae is one of the stages of contamination. It is one part of the overall process explained in the paragraph.
- C   The paragraph does not give a definition of water pollution although it explains how nonflowing bodies of water become polluted.

7. Answer   B

The paragraph offers an explanation of panic disorder as an example of one type of anxiety disorder.

False Choices
- A   Agoraphobia is discussed toward the end of the paragraph, but it is not contrasted with panic attacks. The point made is that people who have panic attacks may become afraid to leave the house (agoraphobia).
- C   The paragraph does not discuss strategies recommended for dealing with panic attacks. The second paragraph explains how some people try to change their behavior to try to avoid future attacks.

- D   No causes of panic attacks are provided in the paragraph.

8. Answer   A

This passage gives examples of what people do to avoid or minimize their panic attacks by changing their behavior.

False Choices
- B   The second paragraph does not define panic disorder.
- C   No steps for treatment are covered in this paragraph.
- D   The paragraph describes ways people may go about changing their behavior to minimize the chance of having more attacks. However, the paragraph does not contrast them.

9. Answer   C

This passage provides an extended definition of plagiarism. The first paragraph gives the formal definition. Paragraph two provides an example. The third paragraph explains the possible effects of plagiarism and tells why it is a serious offense.

False Choices
- A   Analysis of a situation in which plagiarism occurs is not the organizational pattern of the passage. This is accomplished in paragraph two.
- B   The paragraph is not developed by listing.
- D   Paragraph two explains that you can reproduce parts of a paper you find on the Web without permission under copyright and fair use guidelines; however, this is a supporting detail in an example of plagiarism. The organizational pattern is not a description of the process of using information from the Web or any other process.

10. Answer   D

The third paragraph gives the reasons why plagiarism is a serious infraction. The topic sentence indicates this: "Plagiarism is a serious infraction in most settings." Plagiarism violates your obligation to yourself to be truthful, your obligation to society to produce accurate information, and your obligation to other students and researchers.

False Choices
- A   One effect of plagiarism on students is given in the paragraph as a supporting detail.
- B   The paragraph gives the reasonable criteria for ethical decision making. These are supporting details within the paragraph. Ethical decision making is not defined.
- C   The paragraph is not organized by contrast.

11. Answer   B

During the seventeenth and eighteenth centuries, women conducted the process of childbirth. This passage gives examples of their roles in that process.

False Choices
- A   The third paragraph offers a religious reason to explain pain in childbirth. This is a supporting detail in a discussion of the use of alcohol and no painkillers.
- C   The end of the fourth paragraph contrasts the convalescent period of women from well-to-do families and women from poorer families. This is a supporting detail.
- D   No dangers of childbirth are described in the passage.

12.   Answer   A

Midwives assisted in childbirth, not doctors. The paragraph describes midwives with respect to their ages, their value, and their skills.

False choices
- B   No attempt is made to argue the advantages of midwives over doctors. The paragraph makes the point that doctors did not assist in childbirth.
- C   Martha Ballard's skills are offered as a supporting detail in the paragraph to illustrate that midwives had a lot of experience.
- D   The paragraph does not explain how the midwife assists a delivery.

13.   Answer   C

The first sentence of the passage is the thesis, which indicates the contrast: "Deborah Tannen, sociologist and author, explains the differences in the listening behavior of men and women."

False Choices
- A   Illustration is used as support for the contrasts made.
- B   This point is only one of many supporting details in the discussion of contrasts between men and women.
- D   Tannen says that men communicate with men and women in the same way. A man's goal is to obtain respect and to show his knowledge, and he prefers to dominate a conversation. The author does not focus her discussion on how male listening behavior affects women.

14.   Answer   B

In the first paragraph, the author contrasts the different listening cues men and women use. Women use more listening cues and let the other person know they are paying attention; on the other hand, men use fewer listening cues, interrupt more, and often change the topic to one they know more about.

False Choices
- A   The paragraph does not give examples of how men do not listen to women; it contrasts their listening behaviors.

- C   The paragraph does not explain the listening process women use to get close to a person.
- D   No mention of male disrespect for female conversational patterns is made in the paragraph.

15.   Answer   D

The first paragraph provides background about the Columbine shootings; however, the rest of the passage analyzes Harris's and Klebold's friendship to understand their "horrific actions."

False Choices
- A   No attempt is made to provide the details of the shootings. The first paragraph merely mentions that a dozen students and one teacher died.
- B   The effects of these murders are not the primary organizational pattern. In the first paragraph, the author provides his opinion of the effect: "a school shooting of such immense proportions occurred which radically, if not permanently, altered public thinking and debate about student safety and security." (lines 1–3)
- C   In the second paragraph, the author explains that Harris and Klebold "plotted and planned, colluded and conspired." He adds that they amassed weapons, strategized, and made final preparations. These details of their preparations support the discussion of their efforts to feel important, but this process is not the organizational pattern of the passage.

16.   Answer   C

The paragraph is a description of the process the fireflies use to signal mates. Each species has a specific pattern of flashes that are meant to lead the male to the female. Most females stop flashing after they mate.

False Choices
- A   An explanation of these patterns supplies necessary supporting details in the overall description of the process.
- B   At the end of the paragraph, the author explains that in a few species, mated females will continue to flash and attract males of other species. Then she "grabs and eats him." This information is provided as supporting detail for the description of the process.
- D   The paragraph does explain that the different species of fireflies flash in different patterns and colors. However, these details help to explain the process.

17.   Answer   A

This passage explains the effects of some of the well-known quick-weight-loss diets, such as very-low-calorie diets, liquid-protein diets, and crash diets.

False Choices

    B   The passage does classify the types of diets, but the emphasis is on their effects.

    C   Paragraph 5 discusses the problems with prescription drugs. These are supporting details.

    D   No attempt is made to contrast any of the diets described. Each is discussed separately to establish its effects.

18. Answer   B

The third paragraph does, indeed, describe the effects of very-low-calorie diets. Such effects are metabolic imbalances, water and lean protein loss, and slowing of metabolism.

False Choices

    A   The paragraph explains the effects, not the process.

    C   A brief definition is provided in the first sentence of the paragraph, but the paragraph is not organized by definition.

    D   The reader could infer that very-low-calorie diets are harmful, but the passage does not argue against them.

19. Answer   B

The passage presents both sides of the argument regarding Truman's decision to use atomic bombs on Hiroshima and Nagasaki.

False Choices

    A   As part of the argument of Truman's defenders, reasons the bombings ended the war are given. (lines 9–10)

    C   Time order is not the organizational pattern of the passage.

    D   The passage is not organized around causes for dropping atomic bombs, but some of the reasons emerge within the arguments presented.

20. Answer   D

This paragraph is organized by supporting a generalization with examples. The topic sentence states that "fungi have a number of practical uses for humans."

False Choices

    A   The paragraph does not use process to organize its information.

    B   Fungi is not defined in the paragraph, and definition is not used as an organizational pattern.

    C   While the overall pattern is example, classification is used in the supporting details.

2. Relationships Within a Sentence

1. Answer   B

The dependent clause that begins the sentence sets up the cause, and the independent clause gives the effect. One group of people conquering another is the cause; the effect was the enslavement of some of the vanquished.

False Choices

    A   No contrast is established. Note the absence of words like "however," "on the other hand," and "in contrast."

    C   Process deals with steps or methods within a procedure and does not apply here.

    D   Words such as "in conclusion" or "finally" would be used in a summary, but they are not used in the sentence.

2. Answer   D

According to the passage, when one group conquered another, some of those conquered were enslaved. Women were the first group enslaved through warfare. The sentence lists the qualities for which women were valued as slaves.

False Choices

    A   The sentence does not summarize. Note that words such as "in conclusion," "in short," and "in summary" are not used.

    B   Addition is close to listing because every new item is an addition, but addition is not limited to listing. A list is a type of addition, so listing is more specific and a better choice.

    C   "Specifically" and "thus" are words used in sentences that clarify ideas.

3. Answer   D

The sentence expresses a cause-and-effect chain of events. The algae feed on inorganic pollutants (cause), which increases their growth (effect), and slime covers the water (effect).

False Choices

    A   Spatial order describes how something is arranged in space, which does not apply in this sentence.

    B   The sentence mentions the types of inorganic pollutants the algae eat; however, the pattern of the sentence is cause-and-effect.

    C   Addition is usually indicated by "also," "in addition," and "furthermore." None of these words are present in the sentence.

4. Answer   A

This sentence defines cyberliteracy. It contains the term "cyberliteracy" (class), "an electronic literacy" (differentia; that which differentiates it from other kinds of literacy).

False Choices

    B   With words like "combines" and "and," the sentence does have elements of addition, but the sentence uses the definition form.

    C   The effect of cyberliteracy is that it "changes how we read, speak, think, and interact with others." This effect is a part of the definition, which helps to clarify the term.

D   Words such as "in conclusion" and "finally" are clues that the sentence is a summary. This sentence does not summarize.

5. Answer   C

The sentence explains that men communicate with women the same way they do with other men. The sentence pattern is set up to be a comparison. Note the use of "the same way" as an indication that items are being compared.

False Choices

A   The phrases "for example" and "for instance" are used to indicate examples; in the sentence, information is compared rather than added.

B   The sentence does not show a cause-and-effect relationship. "If," "therefore," "as a result," and "so" are examples of words that are often used to express cause and effect.

D   Clarification involves an explanation of a point made, in this exercise, within a sentence. No clarification is expressed in the sentence.

6. Answer   A

The sentence begins with the transition "In addition," which alerts the reader that new information is being added. The sentence explains that midwives did other things "in addition" to assisting in childbirth, such as attending baptisms and burials of infants.

False Choices

B   Time is not an element of this sentence.

C   Listing is similar to addition; it is a type of addition. However, addition is the best choice because of the introductory phrase, which sets up the pattern for addition: "In addition to assisting childbirth."

D   The sentence does not summarize or draw a conclusion.

7. Answer   D

The prepositional phrase "After delivery," which begins the sentence, indicates time order. The rest of the sentence explains what happens after the mother delivers her child.

False Choices

A   There is no cause-and-effect relationship in the sentence. A banquet for the new mother was not an effect of her delivering her child.

B   The sentence does not provide a summary.

C   The relationship of ideas within this sentence is not addition.

8. Answer   B

The first part of the sentence makes the point that the boys' friendship gave them "what was otherwise missing from their lives." The rest of the sentence explains and clarifies what that means by providing more specific in-

formation—"they felt special, they gained a sense of belonging, they were united against the world."

False Choices

A   No comparisons are made in the sentence. Words that show comparison such as "in comparison," "similarly," or "in the same way" would not make sense if placed in the sentence.

C   The first part of the sentence does not contrast, or show a difference between, the second part of the sentence.

D   Time is not addressed in the sentence.

9. Answer   C

The sentence sets up a contrast between fireflies' flashing patterns. The first part of the sentence, which is an independent clause, explains that some fireflies flash more often than others or during different hours. The second part of the sentence is a dependent clause beginning with "while"; this word indicates a contrast. "Other species give fewer but longer flashes."

False Choices

A   A sentence of comparison shows similarities. This sentence shows differences.

B   No new information is added in this sentence.

D   Process deals with steps of methods within a procedure that does not apply.

10. Answer   C

Spatial order connects the ideas within this sentence. In the first part of the sentence, the reader is told that a causeway linked each pyramid to a temple. The second part of the sentence explains that a building was located "adjacent" to the pyramid.

False Choices

A   The sentence is not a simple list.

B   The locations of pyramids and accompanying buildings are described in the sentence, not time order.

D   The use of "and" within the sentence does suggest addition; however, descriptions such as "a processional causeway linked each pyramid to a temple" and "adjacent to the pyramid" clearly indicate spatial order.

3. Relationships Between Sentences

1. Answer   D

The first event ("inmates experience uncertainty and fear") causes the second event ("Therefore, they avoid contact with other prisoners and guards").

False Choices

A   The second sentence does not summarize the first.

B   There is no comparison of similarities between the two sentences.

C. Despite the fact that a process transition is used at the beginning of the first sentence ("First"), the author is showing a cause-and-effect relationship, not steps in a process.

2. Answer   C

The first sentence makes a point. The second sentence explains what the "partnership" means in more detail.

False Choices

A   There is no comparison of similarities between the first and second sentence.

B   The events in the first sentence do not cause the events in the second sentence to happen.

D   The second sentence does more than just restate the same idea—it explains the first idea more clearly with detail.

3. Answer   C

False Choices

A   Even though there is a difference in the amount of freight described in the first sentence and in the second sentence, the transition word "Later" indicates that the author is showing that as time went on, the amount of freight transported increased.

B   The second sentence does not provide an example of what is discussed in the first sentence.

D   Because of the dates and the transition word "Later," the author is trying to emphasize the progress of shipping over a period of time, rather than just giving additional information.

4. Answer   B

The first sentence describes what motivates people. The second sentence begins with the addition transition "moreover," indicating the author wishes to add more information to the point that was made in the first sentence.

False Choices

A   The second sentence does not provide an example of the first.

C   There is no cause-and-effect relationship between the ideas or events described in the two sentences.

D   The second sentence does not show a difference (contrast) between the ideas in the first.

5. Answer   A

The first sentence makes a general point about needs and how they will push you to reach a particular goal. The second sentence provides an example of one type of need: hunger.

False choices

B. The second sentence does not summarize the information in the first one.

C. There are no terms or words defined in either sentence.

D. The second sentence does not compare any similarities to the first.

6. Answer   B

The second sentence describes what will happen if the female skunk's warnings are not heeded. The effect is described in the second sentence: she will spray odor with considerable accuracy.

False Choices

A   The second sentence does not show a contrast (difference) to the information in the first sentence.

C   The second sentence is not an example of what the first sentence is describing; it shows the effect of the skunk's warnings when they are not heeded.

D   The two sentences do not show similarities.

7. Answer   D

The second sentence shows the similarity between the two species by describing their similar appearance. Notice the transition word "both."

False Choices

A   The second sentence does more than just add information; it shows how the two species are alike in color and markings.

B   The second sentence does not give an example of the first.

C   The second sentence does not summarize what is in the first.

8. Answer   D

The time clues in these sentences show that the author is presenting a sequence of events: during the winter months, the blastocysts remain dormant, then in spring they resume growth.

False Choices

A. The second sentence does more than add information; it presents the information in the order that it occurs.

B. The second sentence does not restate the first.

C. There are no terms defined in either sentence.

9. Answer   D

The first sentence states in the conclusion what Andrews and her colleagues found. The second sentence clarifies and specifies that conclusion by citing what adolescents who had a positive relationship with their mothers did in regard to cigarette use or nonuse.

False Choices

A. The second sentence does more than just add information; it provides a specific example of the conclusion stated in the first sentence.

B. The second sentence is neither a cause nor an effect of the ideas described in the first.

C. The first sentence is not a generalization. It is a specific finding of this study. The second sentence then goes on to clarify what the first one says.

10. Answer   A

The first sentence makes a general point. The second sentence explains what this means in more specific terms.

False Choices

B. Even though there is contrast in the second sentence, the question is asking for the relationship between the first and second sentences, not just within the second sentence. Remember that the relationship within one single sentence may not be the same as the relationship between two different sentences.

C. The second sentence does not show a cause or effect of the first one.

D. The second sentence does not summarize the information in the first one. The second sentence is much more detailed than the first.

CHAPTER 3: LANGUAGE SKILLS

1. Word Choice: Context Clues

NOTE: The explanatory answers will look a little different in this section. You will be provided with the definition of the underlined word from the question and, if needed, of the correct choice.

If you chose an incorrect option, you should look up the meaning of that word. Use this as an opportunity to develop your vocabulary and dictionary skills.

1. Answer   B

"Gravitate" means to be drawn to or attracted to something or someone. The sentence points out that future teachers who are not fond of any particular academic subject may be more attracted to teaching the lower grades. "Be attracted" was provided as a defnition.

2. Answer   C

"Dispel" means to cause to go away, to remove. The author of the passage attempts to remove several myths about teaching. "Remove" is a synonym.

3. Answer   D

"Incompetent" means without the skill or talent to do something; not qualified or suited for a purpose; not doing a good job; or having *inadequate* skills for the job.

4. Answer   B

"Prevalent" means widely or commonly accepted or practiced. Candidates use television as the most common method to reach voters. "Common" is a synonym.

5. Answer   A

"Manipulate" means to influence, manage, use, or *control* to one's advantage by artful or indirect means. Polit-

ical candidates attempt to control the images they want presented to the public through advertising and image building. "Control" is a synonym.

6. Answer   D

"Interplay" means a reciprocal (shared by both sides) action or reaction; interaction. Campaign coverage is an interaction between hard news and the human interest angle. "Interaction" is a synonym.

7. Answer   A

"Habitable" means fit to live in, *livable*. The passage discusses Africa's geography. The savannas (grassy plains) are the areas where people can live, as opposed to the jungle or desert. "Livable" is a synonym.

8. Answer   C

"Interspersed" means placed or mixed among other things; *scattered*. "Scattered" is a synonym.

9. Answer   B

"Humus" is a brown or black organic substance consisting of partially or wholly decayed vegetable or animal matter that provides nutrients for plants and increases the soil's ability to retain water. In the sentence, "or organic matter" follows the word "humus" and provides a context clue.

10. Answer   C

"Erosion" means the wearing away of material from the earth's surface by the action of water and wind. "Washing away" describes the effect of the torrential rains on soil.

2. Biased Language

1. Answer   D

The first item in the list of the passage's concluding sentence clearly states the author's bias for losing weight slowly.

False Choices

A   The author is biased against taking prescription drugs for weight loss because of evidence that they could cause heart damage.

B   The author is biased against the theory that a liquid-protein diet will control insulin levels and thus burn fat because no research supports this.

C   The author does not express an opinion on using prescription drugs, but he points out the fact that they can have harmful effects.

2. Answer   A

This paragraph describes the harmful effects of very-low-calorie diets, which can result in "serious" metabolic imbalances.

False Choices

B   The author believes in moderating food choices: "eat properly and in moderation."

    C   The passage mentions that obese and overweight individuals resort to harmful diets; however, the author does not show a bias towards obesity.

    D   The author expresses bias in the last sentence. Notice the judgment word "best."

3. Answer   D

The author believes that the plea-bargaining system "saves the state the time and money that would otherwise be spent on a trial." He is against spending money on trials.

False Choices

    A   The author does not show a bias against live television trial coverage. He says that most cases do not go to trial. "Highly publicized trials are dramatic, but rare."

    B   The author says that 90 percent of all cases are settled with plea bargaining. The defendant pleads guilty to a lesser crime. The author is not biased against this. He feels that it saves the state time and money and lets defendants plead guilty to a lesser charge.

    C   The author makes no comment about the verdict of the O. J. Simpson murder trial.

4. Answer   C

The author is in favor of plea bargaining. He feels that it saves the state time and money and lets defendants plead guilty to a lesser charge.

False Choices

    A   The author does not express a bias for or against television's portrayal of courts and trials. He comments that they are dramatic and not realistic.

    B   No bias is expressed towards police and detective shows on television. The author says that television's portrayal of courts and trials is as unrealistic as police and detective shows.

    D   The author is against trial by jury due to the expense.

5. Answer   B

The author expresses a bias for considering caffeine a drug, as stated in the last sentence of the introductory paragraph: "Nonetheless, it is a drug and should be recognized as one that can lead to health problems."

False Choices

    A   According to the author, eating chocolate and drinking coffee and cola cannot be considered drug abuse; however, the author is not in favor of ingesting these substances if they are sought out to produce a caffeine high.

    C   The author is biased against using caffeine to produce a "high."

    D   The author is stating an opinion, that caffeine should be considered a drug.

6. Answer   A

The author is biased against employers' asking unlawful questions during an interview.

False Choices

    B   The author does not express an opinion about answering direct questions. He says that if a person is confronted by unlawful questions, he or she should answer using the gentle method first. If that doesn't work, then the person should use a direct method of responding.

    C   The passage does not mention closed questions.

    D   It is legal for an employer to ask about whether the interviewee meets the legal age requirements of the job and whether he or she can provide proof of age. The author is not biased against legal questions.

7. Answer   C

The author is in favor of developing strategies to deal with unlawful questions.

False Choices

    A   The author states that it is not a good idea to immediately tell the interviewer that he or she is asking an unlawful question because the interviewer may not be aware of the legality of various questions.

    B   The author does not suggest that a person should answer an unlawful question to get a job. This is not addressed in the passage.

    D   The author does not suggest that a person turn an employer in.

8. Answer   D

In this passage, the author is biased against hate sites. The reader can infer this from the comments made in the passage. For example, he says "Never before has there been such an intensive way for depraved people to gather and reinforce their prejudices and hatred."

False Choices

    A   The author is not opposed to people's expressing opinions on the Internet. He is against people with prejudicial attitudes who speak and act out.

    B   The author does not discuss penalties for creators of hate sites in this passage.

    C   The author is using emotional language and clearly expresses opinion. This passage is very biased.

9. Answer   B

The author is in favor of unique experiences. He says that "predictability washes away spontaneity, changing the quality of our lives."

False Choices

    A   The author feels that packaged travel tours are standardized and do not produce unique, spontaneous experiences.

C The author is biased against *USA Today* news reporting because it gives "short, bland, unanalytic pieces" of information.

D McDonald's is used as an example of the standardization of everyday life, which the author is biased against.

10. Answer   B

The author is biased against the standardization of everyday life. It causes predictability in life, which he feels changes the quality of our lives for the worse.

False Choices

A The author says that shopping malls are another example of the standardization of our lives, which he is biased against; however, he does not express a bias against shopping in general.

C The author is not against hamburgers; however, he does not like the "robotlike assembly of food" offered by McDonald's.

D According to the author, "efficiency brings dependability." It also lowers prices. However, the author feels that it comes at a cost, which "washes away spontaneity."

3. Author's Tone

1. Answer   C

The tone of the passage is critical. The author criticizes the way our lives are being McDonaldized—made standard and predictable. For example, he states, "Predictability washes away spontaneity, changing the quality of our lives."

False Choices

A Nothing in the passage is humorous.

B In a way, the tone suggests pessimism. The author seems resigned to the fact that our social destiny is to be packaged. However, the overriding tone of the passage is critical.

D The passage does not offer a sense of remembrance, of looking back to another time.

2. Answer   A

This passage provides information by explaining how to balance work and school.

False Choices

B The author does not give the names of respected sources or significant statistics. Instead the tone is familiar and helpful.

C Cautionary means to warn or beware and may even imply that the reader should change an action or behavior. Although the passage gives suggestions, they are not presented as a warning.

D Sarcastic implies a cruel or mocking tone. The writer gives the information in a helpful way.

3. Answer   B

For the most part, the passage explains the mating habits of the different species of fireflies in an objective tone. The information is scientific and neutral with the excep-

tion of the subjective description of a species of firefly referred to as a "femme fatale."

False Choices

A The passage may be interesting, but it is not funny.

C The author is not negative or critical in his description of the material.

D No techniques are used to establish an argumentative tone.

4. Answer   A

The passage presents the practical uses of fungi and is written in a neutral tone.

False Choices

B Respectful is an emotional, subjective treatment and does not apply.

C The author does not use excited, active language in the description.

D The reader may be bored with the topic, but the tone is not boring. It is filled with relevant and interesting details, especially for someone who is interested in the topic.

5. Answer   A

Cautionary means to warn or beware and may even imply that the reader should change an action or behavior. The passage explains what can happen to a student or a researcher if he or she plagiarizes. It explains why plagiarism is such a serious offense.

False Choices

B Defiance is an attitude that shows lack of fear or respect. No defiant language is used.

C The term "annoyed" means to show mild anger, which does not apply to this passage.

D The subject described in the passage does not evoke sadness.

6. Answer   C

In this passage, the author presents one side of an argument in a neutral way. He does not agree or disagree with the arguments made by Truman's critics.

False Choices

A The author does not use a complaining tone.

B The tone of the passage is not passionate but consistent with an objective presentation of information.

D No attempt is made to be humorous.

7. Answer   B

"Tragic" accurately describes the tone of the passage, which graphically describes the events of the fatal shootings. Notice the emotional language in the first sentence.

False Choices

A While the event caused sadness to those in Littleton, Colorado, it also touched hearts across the United States, but the passage does not use subjective words to create a sad tone.

C   The author does not use excited, active language.
D   There is nothing flattering about the description of Harris and Klebold or their crimes.

8. Answer   D

The writers of The Declaration of Independence knew they were composing an important document. This declaration established the original thirteen colonies as free and independent states no longer under the rule of Great Britain. They chose formal language to emphasize the importance and seriousness of the document.

False Choices

A   Reverent implies worshipful and does not apply to the passage.
B   Instead of looking back and remembering, the words in the passage look ahead to the "Acts and Things which Independent States may of right do."
C   The Declaration of Independence is a strong statement announcing the dissolution of all political connections between the colonies and England. Its words are stated with conviction.

9. Answer   C

This excerpt from President Bush's speech on September 11, 2001, was intended to inspire the people of the United States—to assure them that the terrorists have failed, that their acts "shatter steel but they cannot dent the steel of American resolve."

False Choices

A   The passage is not objective or impartial. Bush's language is strong and forceful.
B   Bush's language could also be described as passionate and emotional, yet the message was intended to unite the people of this country.
D   Parts of the passage were described graphically; however, overall, the tone goes beyond this.

10. Answer   A

The author describes the Tiwi custom of "covering up" the elderly women. The passage is filled with graphic, descriptive details and is written in a narrative style.

False Choices

B   The term "annoyed" means to show mild anger, which does not apply to this passage.
C   The passage does not use argumentative language.
D   The idea of "covering up" evokes an emotional response in the reader, but the tone of the passage is quieter.

CHAPTER 4: REASONING SKILLS

1. Fact and Opinion

1. Answer   C

The sentence is a generalization, as indicated by "even more spectacularly." This point is supported in the passage by the factual information in the sentences that follow it.

False Choices: Each of the other options is a statement that can be verified.

A and B can be verified by checking shipping records in 1816, 1817, 1840, and 1841.
D can be verified by checking prices of coffee in Cincinnati and in New Orleans in the years 1816 and 1818.

2. Answer   C

This statement is an opinion that speculates why Mendel chose to study garden peas. The word "probably" does not indicate that the point was verified.

False Choices: Each of the other options is a statement that can be verified.

A, B, and D can be researched and verified by reading about Gregor Mendel's life and discoveries.

3. Answer   B

The statement expresses the opinion of the author in his assumption that people are ignorant of African geography and environment. In addition, he assumes that people have misconceptions about African culture and history. The statement is the thesis of the passage, and the author supports his opinion with factual information.

4. Answer   A

This is a fact that can be verified by researching mosquitoes and tsetse flies as transmitters of diseases to humans.

5. Answer   B

This is an opinion that is not supported by fact. "Many Americans" is a generalization.

6. Answer   A

The sentence offers a statistic that can be checked by researching the number of votes that are submitted by mail in California.

7. Answer   B

This sentence sets up a cause-and-effect relationship that speculates what would happen if everyone voted electronically. The words "if," "may be," and "could" show that the sentence expresses an opinion.

8. Answer   B

A speculative cause-and-effect relationship is established in this sentence, indicating that an opinion is being given. No data is offered to support this claim.

9. Answer   A

This statement is a fact that can be verified by going to the Federal Election Commission website and locating the National Mail Voter Registration Form.

10. Answer   A

It is a fact that can be verified by checking to see whether these men made this argument when presenting their case to the Supreme Court.

2. Inferences and Conclusions

1. Answer   D

The conclusion that women from different social classes experienced different post-childbirth treatment is supported by details in the last paragraph. Regarding choice A, there is no mention in the passage as to whether or not midwives had children of their own. As for letter B, we know that skilled midwives received certain considerations, such as housing, but there is no indication as to their salaries. Letter C is false since we do not know why doctors did not typically deliver babies at that time. We only know that they did not.

2. Answer   C

The word "skilled," which means good at one's job, suggests that there weren't many midwives that were skilled or had years of experience delivering babies.

False Choices
    A   The abilities of doctors are not discussed. The passage explains that most women were assisted by midwives, not doctors.
    B   The use of medication was not considered a skill. The prevailing belief at that time was that the pain women experienced in childbirth was "God's punishment for Eve's sin of eating the forbidden fruit in the Garden of Eden." Therefore, women were offered alcohol to ease childbirth pain.
    D   Midwives did not provide religious guidance—with the exception of advising women to pray during labor. This was simply a reinforcement of the prevailing religious beliefs of the time.

3. Answer   B

This statement can be inferred from the information presented in paragraph 3 about how people learn from paying attention to others' behavior. The last sentence of that paragraph says, "you are more likely to be captivated by models who have certain attractive characteristics." Children who like their parents and enjoy a good relationship with them are more likely to pay attention to them, thus picking up their bad habits.

False Choices
    A   According to the passage, not all adolescents model their parents' behavior. The modeling behavior is attributed to whether or not adolescents have a positive or negative relationship with their parents.
    C   The passage does not make a judgment about whether or not parents who use alcohol set a poor example for their children. Andrews is more interested in the parent-child relationship and its effect on modeling parents' drug or alcohol use.
    D   The research shared in this passage does not conclude that all adolescents are willing to experiment with drugs and alcohol. Andrews wanted to know which adolescents would be most influenced by their parents' use of drugs or alcohol. Adolescents with positive relationships with their parents would most likely imitate parents' behavior.

4. Answer   D

The reading stresses that, "Men, research shows, play up their expertise, emphasize it, and use it to dominate the conversation. Women play down their expertise." Women also "seek to build rapport and establish a closer relationship," and so are more likely to discuss personal and relationship issues.

False Choices
    A   The passage states that men and women are socialized to listen differently; there is no mention that men are "naturally" more aggressive.
    B   Tannen discusses the differences in listening styles of men and women and supplies the reasons for this; however, she does not say that men and women do not communicate "well."
    C   There is no mention of this in the text. Men and women are equally likely to listen and discuss as they are socialized to do.

5. Answer   D

The quote is implying that society teaches men and women how to listen differently. Thus, people learn how to listen and converse based on what they learn from environmental social cues.

False Choices
    A   This says exactly the opposite of what the quote is implying.
    B   The passage does not suggest that people can or should seek professional help to change their listening styles.
    C   The passage does not say that men disrespect women. In fact, they listen to and converse with women in the same way they do men.

6. Answer   A

Many of the supports in this passage make this point. The entire second paragraph delves into Harris and Klebold's friendship and activities. The author explains that the two boys were viewed as outcasts, "geeks and nerds." Because they were excluded from the mainstream culture of the school, they bonded with other "outcasts" to form the "Trench Coat Mafia." Their image was one of power and dominance. The author goes on to explain how for more than a year, the two planned to kill teachers and students at their school and one day carried out their plan.

False Choices
    B   Not all students who are outcasts will commit acts of violence. This is a generalization that cannot be supported from the information in the passage.

C   Just because Harris and Kelbold succeeded at mass murder at their high school does not necessarily mean that this could happen at any high school. The event did bring the issue of safety to the forefront of concerns; however, the generalization that all schools are not safe is not supported in the passage.

D   This is an illogical conclusion.

7. Answer   B

This need to show that they were important is supported in lines 15–17: "Harris and Klebold desperately wanted to feel important; and in the preparations they made to murder their classmates, the two shooters got their wish."

False Choices

A   There is no mention of whether or not military school would have helped them.

C   While their anger may have been understandable, it was not reasonable, especially given the extreme way they expressed it. Rather, their rage was intimately connected to their relationship with each other.

D   Since they committed suicide, they did not seem to have a goal of "winning." Rather, they wanted to be seen as important.

8. Answer   C

The reading clarifies that "What some workers don't know (and what some of us forget) is that "delete" does not mean *delete*. Our computer keeps a hidden diary, even of what we've erased. With a few clicks, the cybersleuth, like magic ink, makes our "deleted" information visible, exposing our hidden diary for anyone to read." Furthermore, "With specialized software, cybersleuths can examine everything employees read online, everything they write, and every web site they visit." This would include e-mails.

False Choices

A   This statement contradicts paragraph one, which says that bosses know that workers conduct some personal business at work and that some interpersonal slacking even helps build work relationships. Bosses "wink as we make a date or nod as we arrange to have our car worked on."

B   Paragraph one clarifies that bosses only care about workers who abuse the phone privilege. "It's the abuse that bothers bosses, and it's not surprising that they fire anyone who talks on the phone all day for personal reasons." That implies that bosses only notice phone calls when they go too far, but they don't in general know how much time employees spend on the phone.

D   The passage implies the opposite since Xerox employees were fired for downloading pornography.

9. Answer   B

The reading states that "researchers reported that mitochondrial DNA from the Ice Man closely matched that of modern central and northern Europeans," implying that mitochondrial DNA has not changed much over the last 5,000 years.

False Choices

A   While his tools indicate he may have been hunting, we have no idea whether it was a snowstorm, an animal, or even an enemy that killed him.

C   The statement is not supported by the passage.

D   This statement is not supported by the passage.

10. Answer   A

According to the passage, "Every report of success in isolating ancient DNA has been met with skepticism and further analyses to make sure the DNA traces were not contaminated with DNA from bacteria, fungi, or other organisms." The passage further states that "DNA is unlikely to remain intact, except when organisms fossilize in extremely cold or dry places." Therefore, DNA from a fossil discovered in a wet, humid rainforest would be less trustworthy than DNA discovered in a hot, dry desert.

False Choices

B   The passage tells us that the "Ice Man" is ancient but does not state that he is the oldest human ever discovered. This statement is a false fact.

C   We don't know what caused the glacier to melt; it was August, so it may have been melting simply because it was summer.

D   While paragraph one reports that scientists have isolated such DNA, it does not say that such DNA is never contaminated.

This section provides you with 20 items because of the difficulty of the type of question. Ten explanatory answers have been provided. Use the next ten questions to practice thinking through the test independently.

Think it through, use the explanatory answers as your models, and explain your own reasons for the choices you made. Compare your thinking to the definition of this skill at the beginning of the section in the workbook. *Thinking* about your thinking is an important tool. Therefore, only brief explanations of the remaining 10 questions have been provided.

11. Answer   A

The second and third paragraphs explain the importance of this "free" coverage, implying that without it, candidates do not receive enough media coverage to get their messages across to the public and therefore do not get elected.

12. Answer   C

The other answers reach too far in their logic or are not supported by the text.

13. Answer   C

The third paragraph states that "some individuals seek out caffeine for its own sake in over-the-counter products and in illegal substances to produce a caffeine 'high.'" The other answers are either contradicted by or not supported by the text.

14. Answer   A

The passage states that "Never before has there been such an intensive way for deprived people to gather to reinforce their prejudices and hatred." The other answers either reach too far in their logic or are not supported by the text.

15. Answer   B

This is implied in the last two sentences of the reading. The other answers are either contradicted by or not supported by the text.

16. Answer   D

Since scare tactics are counterproductive, the best programs probably do not use them. The other answers are not supported by the text.

17. Answer   A

The last paragraph discusses how Drudge "paved the way for communication power to be transferred from media giants to anyone with a modem."

18. Answer   B

The first paragraph shows that Drudge posted a story that was planted by someone's political enemy. Therefore, he did not confirm the story with the source.

19. Answer   C

This one requires that you read the question carefully. You are looking for the FALSE answer. The only one that is clearly false is C since the first sentence of the paragraph states the opposite indirectly.

20. Answer   A

The other answers either reach too far in their logic or are contradicted by the text.

3. Assessing Support for Reasoning and Argument

1. Answer   B

The passage is filled with emotional support to show that the factories were dangerous places. For example, factories are described as "miserable places" with "dangerous machines." Safety standards were "practically nonexistent." There was "little job security."

2. Answer   B

The author describes early factories in the following paragraph in detail.

3. Answer   C

This option provides specific information to support the author's claim. It gives the number of hours per day and per week and the number of days per week that the women worked in textile mills.

False Choices

A   This is a broad statement that adds little to the sentence in the question.

B   The statement is a generalization and is irrelevant.

D   This detail is a broad statement and does not support the sentence.

4. Answer   B

The statement is adequately supported by details in the passage. For example, the second paragraph provides an illustration of that point by citing a sleep deprivation study done using young adult volunteers.

5. Answer   A

Many objective supporting details are given to explain the three areas affected by sleep deprivation: attention, mood, and performance. For example, paragraph four explains that going without sleep changes the normal circadian rhythms of the body. Throughout the passage, results of studies were provided.

6. Answer   D

This detail has concrete data that is verifiable, so it is the best statement of support.

False Choices

A   This is a broad generalization that does not support the sentence.

B   This may be a true statement, but no specific information is offered.

C   The statement is not verified with specifics.

7. Answer   B

Most of the details provided in the passage are emotional. The author speculates on the effects of genetic manipulation. For example, the author suggests that inserting genetic materials in athletes could help them increase their ability, such as beating the two hour marathon record by a half hour. In paragraph three, the author speculates about adding the gene for growth hormone but not being able to regulate it.

8. Answer   A

The statement is not supported by evidence.

9. Answer   B

The author's claim is not adequately supported. No scientific data is offered to prove that athletes will be able to run faster. It is speculation.

he
l

…s an example of a type of material, red
… t when injected, has specific risks: blood
…al infection, and congestive heart failure.

…oices
This does not address health risks; it simply
states that the effects of injecting a material are
unknown.

B   In this sentence, "may" suggests a possibility but
    does not provide factual evidence for the au-
    thor's claim.
D   This sentence offers a speculation of what could
    happen by injecting artificial genes to help in-
    crease a sprinter's muscles. It does not support
    the sentence with concrete evidence.